Power, Race, and Higher Education

TEACHING RACE AND ETHNICITY

Volume 5

Series Editor

Patricia Leavy
USA

International Editorial Board

Theodorea Regina Berry, *Mercer University, USA*
Owen Crankshaw, *University of Cape Town, South Africa*
Payi Linda Ford, *Charles Darwin University, Australia*
Patricia Hill Collins, *University of Maryland, USA*
Virinder Kalra, *University of Manchester, UK*
Marvin Lynn, *Indiana University, USA*
Nuria Rosich, *Barcelona University (Emerita), Spain*
Beverley Anne Yamamoto, *Osaka University, Japan*

Scope

The *Teaching Race and Ethnicity series* publishes monographs, anthologies and reference books that deal centrally with race and/or ethnicity. The books are intended to be used in undergraduate and graduate classes across the disciplines. The series aims to promote social justice with an emphasis on multicultural, indigenous, intersectionality and critical race perspectives.

Please email queries to the series editor at pleavy7@aol.com

Power, Race, and Higher Education

A Cross-Cultural Parallel Narrative

Foreword by Laurel Richardson

Kakali Bhattacharya
Kansas State University, Manhattan, Kansas, USA

and

Norman K. Gillen
Del Mar College, Corpus Christi, Texas, USA

SENSE PUBLISHERS
ROTTERDAM/BOSTON/TAIPEI

A C.I.P. record for this book is available from the Library of Congress.

ISBN: 978-94-6300-733-7 (paperback)
ISBN: 978-94-6300-734-4 (hardback)
ISBN: 978-94-6300-735-1 (e-book)

Published by: Sense Publishers,
P.O. Box 21858,
3001 AW Rotterdam,
The Netherlands
https://www.sensepublishers.com/

All chapters in this book have undergone peer review.

Printed on acid-free paper

ADVANCE PRAISE FOR
POWER, RACE, AND HIGHER EDUCATION

"Riveting, courageous, innovative and brave! This spell-binding book not only holds your attention, it holds you to account as you read a beautifully integrated narrative that weaves theory, research, artistry and practice into an utterly compelling positioning of our power relations within society and the academy. PhD supervisors and candidates should use this book as a springboard for pursuing deeply reflexive and risky research that will surely be personally transformative and critical, all within a creative lenses.

Bhattacharya and Gillen have officially raised the bar on PhD research practices. Never before have I read an account that brings together the parallel narratives of a PhD supervisor working with a PhD candidate. A complex research study steeped in Chicano feminism and cross-cultural theories of engagement, pushes against privilege in ways that is often uncomfortable yet arguably essential. Choosing a structure of parallel narratives that employ script-like theatrical elements, Bhattacharya and Gillen masterfully craft a woven story that gradually reveals an awakening of male White privilege. Historically, the academy demands that we hold our research to a high standard of reflexivity, where we not only document and research the lives of others, but also interrogate our positionality and ourselves within our research. Bhattacharya models this high standard with increasing intentionality as Gillen progresses through his PhD. Practicing compassion in those moments when Gillen wonders if he can go on, Bhattacharya reframes her mentorship and encourages his next steps. To Gillen's credit he accepted his supervisor's call to self-reflexivity ever more deeply over time until his own awakening of positionality emerged. This book is a gem! PhD supervisors and their students often share research interests, and perhaps other professional interests, but seldom if ever take the immensely courageous step of examining their concurrent positions through rigorous theoretical practices *and* vigorous critically creative practices in a full length manuscript. This work is at once rigorous and vigorous. It is the best of what we all aspire to be in our PhD supervisor – student relationships and within our qualitative research communities. It is an inspiration to me and I am certain it will be an inspiration to others. May we all be so committed to our artistry, pedagogy and scholarship that we risk revealing our deep

engagement as a process of personal interrogation considered through a compassionate spirit."
– Rita Irwin, Ph.D., Author of *A Circle of Empowerment: Women, Education, and Leadership*, Professor of Art Education in the Department of Curriculum and Pedagogy, and Associate Dean of Teacher Education, at the University of British Columbia in Vancouver, British Columbia, Canada

"This book is filled with ghosts, of both the haunting and foreshadowing kind. The ghosts are former teachers, family members, mentors and fellow travellers. But there are also colonial ghosts, post-multicultural ghosts, and borderland motherghost Gloria Anzaldúa, who sounds a call to action throughout these pages.

Bhattacharya – a self-identified Brown woman – and Gillen – a self-identified white man – come together not only in intercultural, narrative, and pedagogical ways, but in political and personal ones too. Spanning the fields of race, ethnicity, multiculturalism, power, qualitative methods, and arts-based research, this book pulses with heartful and insightful thoughts for those interested in critical race and intercultural scholarship. It also, wonderfully, offers just plain powerful and ready-to-go teaching exercises that can be used by readers to start our own journeys of intercultural learning and teaching in all our classrooms. Buy it now!"
– Anne Harris, Ph.D., Author of *Creativity and Education*, Faculty of Education, Monash University, Melbourne, Australia

"This is a great book. Bhattacharya and Gillen jointly retell their introspective struggles with their professional and personal identities in this compelling confessional tale. *Power, Race, and Higher Education* intimately explores the sensitive and emotionally charged interpersonal dynamics between a dissertation supervisor of color and her White male doctoral student researching a Chicana's life story. Through vulnerable personal narratives and ethnodramatic scenes, the co-authors reveal their respective journeys in academia with their sometimes challenging, yet always supportive, working relationship. Told in honest and straightforward language, this engaging book has much to say about scholarly responsibility, White privilege, and our necessary reconciliation toward equity and a deep awareness of self."
– Johnny Saldaña, Author of *Ethnotheatre: Research From Page to Stage*, Professor Emeritus, Arizona State University

"I love this book! Writing with intellectual humility and great insight, Kakali Bhattacharya and Kent Gillen use story, self-reflection, ethnodrama, and other forms of dialogue to explore some of the most urgent questions facing twenty-first-century educators: How do we build commonalities without ignoring or sidestepping privilege, complicity, and other forms of desconocimientos (willed ignorance)? How do we assist students from a variety of backgrounds to self-reflect on the ways these backgrounds have shaped them? How do we work with students whose worldviews and life experiences are starkly different from our own? In short, how do we effect transformation? *Power, Race, and Higher Education* offers intertwined personal narratives, pedagogical suggestions, and deep reflection that perform vital bridging work for educators, students, nepantleras, threshold people, and other social-justice actors."
— **AnaLouise Keating, Ph.D., Author of *Transformation Now: Toward a Post-Oppositional Politics of Change*, Professor & Doctoral Program Director, Department of Multicultural Women's & Gender Studies, Texas Woman's University**

"In melding inquiry with creativity and critical consciousness, Drs. Bhattacharya and Gillen share how their evolving professor-student relationship developed into an innovative example of qualitative research. In *Power, Race, and Higher Education*, the authors demonstrate what is possible when academics, educators, and researchers confront their biases and interrogate the histories and perspectives that shape their identities. Bhattacharya and Gillen narrate their experiences of conducting research and share how critical self-reflection can enhance the presentation of stories of underrepresented communities. To their credit, they do not shy away from difficult and complex questions related to race, power, privilege, and representation. In confronting their personal life experiences, readers are able to read first hand the messiness and nuance one must embrace when designing research studies and delineating one's research purpose, methods and epistemological framework. It is a book that will inform scholarly conversations with both undergraduate and graduate students, and influence future qualitative researchers."
— **Enrique Alemán, Jr., Ph.D., Executive Producer and co-writer of *Stolen Education, A Documentary Film*, Professor & Chair, Educational Leadership & Policy Studies, University of Texas at San Antonio**

"This book could not be more timely. In today's cultural climate, in which the festering wounds of oppression are breaking violently open, Bhattacharya and Gillen invite all of us to interrogate our positions of difference. Through critical exploration of personal narratives, the authors demonstrate the complexities of addressing racism and colonization. There is nothing 'easy' about this work, which is well overdue. Yet they approach it with compassion and mindfulness. I will be using this book in my own courses as a model to delve into deeper conversations about the impact of power and privilege in society."
– **Jessica Smartt-Guillon, Ph.D., Author of** *Writing Ethnography*, **Assistant Professor of Sociology, Texas Women's University**

"*Power, Race, and Higher Education* is highly recommended for upper-division and graduate classes as well as senior administrators in universities and colleges because of its erudite exploration of how students and their professors 'do' power in academic settings. The book very skillfully peels off, layer-by-layer several things, including opaque films of socialization and 'taken-for-granted' narratives of everyday living, that obfuscate the nature, existence, and inevitability of power exchanges between professors and their students. The authors (one a white, male student and the other a brown, female professor) adroitly reveal their respective 'stand-points' of power and privilege, as well as their powerlessness and under-privilege. In so doing, the reader is drawn into the authors' respective spaces of power, and made to participate, as it were, in their interrogation and deconstruction of the systemic artifacts that have shaped the outcomes of their interactions with each other. The book's strategy of acknowledging the 'anatomy of power' but focusing, even ethno-dramatizing the 'physiology of power' and how it is 'done' between a white, male student with ascribed-status privileges and a brown, female professor with achieved-status privileges makes it even more engaging and illuminating. *Power, Race, and Higher Education* is indeed a *primus inter pares.*"
– **Bilaye Benibo, Ph.D., Distinguished Faculty and Professor of Sociology, Texas A&M University, Corpus Christi**

"Amazing in its brilliance, the book attempts to humanize the perplexing themes of contemporary cross-cultural existence of our time. The authors take us on a scholarly journey riddled with self-doubt, with joyful exuberances and utter dubiety in leading lives that intersect multiple identities, chaotic flows of real and imaginative elucidations of being human in an enigmatic and globalized world, work and life in a structured academic construct. We traverse the broad areas of academic imagination through lenses of resistance and adaptation, negotiation and celebration, and ultimately, that of survival and overcoming. Fantastically rewarding for students and scholars who want to immerse themselves in the very nature of inquiry that effectively leads to empathy and understanding of human nature. I can't wait to adopt this book for my graduate Cultural Studies course."

– **Anantha S. Babbili, Ph.D.,** *Former Provost and VPAA***, Professor of Communication, Media Studies and Global Leadership Texas A&M University-Corpus Christi**

Dedicated to Caroline Sherritt

May we always see through the fog and ask fearless questions.
May we admit our ignorance.
May we have grace and forgiveness for each other when
we make mistakes.
May we make friends with our shadows.
May we come together in our shared humanity.

TABLE OF CONTENTS

FOREWORD

It is not common for professors and their students to transparently discuss the process of mentoring, negotiating ideas while conducting dissertation research, and working through differences where difficult conversations of race, privileges, whiteness, and systemic oppression rise to the surface. More importantly, it is rare that one would get an insider's perspective of what it could look like while there are deep value-based differences between a professor and her student and yet there are possibilities for caretaking and nurturing.

That is what Bhattacharya and Gillen do in this book, where they explore the ways in which power works in higher education and society as a whole and how they benefit, oppress, and suffer from various systemic networks of power structures. Bhattacharya identifies as a Brown woman, transnational academic of South Asian heritage. Gillen identifies as a White man, who mostly lived in Texas all his life. Bhattacharya has institutional privilege by being a faculty member. Gillen has the privilege of being a White man in U.S. They are committed to doing anti-racist and anti-oppressionist work, but in the process of mentoring and being mentored they discover how much they have to unpack their positionality, attend to deeply repressed wounds, and uninterrogated privileges that have shaped how they negotiate their roles within and outside academia.

This is a must-have book for anyone interested in changing the culture of unrecognized privilege and whiteness. If you want to open up classroom conversation about race, gender, and privilege, then here is the book that will do that – and more. This book helps students learn how whiteness and maleness translate into power and privileges in everyday interaction. And, it does this in a way that neither shames nor guilt-trips. Practical help is given to have the daunting conversations about culture, race, and gender in the classroom. If you want to build bridges over race, culture, and gender in your classroom, then this book will give you a secure footing.

I will never know the privileges of being a White man or the challenges of being a Brown transcultural woman, but I have had the privilege and challenge of immersing myself in this stunningly original co-authored book. As I was reading, I found myself interrogating my own privileges as a White middle-class American woman. The book's invitation to recognize one's unearned power and privilege really works and I highly recommend this book for graduate and undergraduate classes in any courses where the professor wants to help students recognize how their unrecognized privileges give them power in their daily lives – and wants them to find strategies for leveling the playing field.

Bhattacharya and Gillen share their parallel stories of unpacking systemic challenges, whiteness, and privileges. Highly original in scope, organization, and writing style, this book exemplifies what it teaches: ways of recognizing systemic privilege and strategies for dismantling it. This book is breathtaking in its honesty, integrity, and openness. Bhattacharya and Gillen have modeled the difficulties in recognizing systemic privilege, the challenges of facing it, and strategies for changing it.

My eyes and heart have been opened by this groundbreaking book on how teaching/learning about race, power and privilege can be accomplished. The conversations that Americans need to have about race, power and privilege are in this book – and the pedagogy for taking care of all engaged in the conversations. This book is a gift to any academic who wants a pedagogy that can construct bridges between cultures, genders, and race. I highly recommend this book.

Laurel Richardson

Distinguished Emeritus Professor and Academy Professor, Sociology, The Ohio State University, Cooley Book Award Winner, Lifetime Qualitative Researcher Award Winner, and author of Seven Minutes from Home: An American Daughter's Story

PREFACE

The Ghosts in Our Writing Spaces

While there are two named authors in this book, there are others who have informed, invaded our thoughts, memories, and dreams of the past and the future, and stayed present in our writing. Some of these ghosts are what we understand to be the literal meaning of ghosts. They are those people who are no longer in this world, but once was. We share a relationship with them in spirit, even when their material form is not with us. Then there are people with whom we have journeyed in our lives. Parts of them are parts of the book. And then there are beings, ideas, and inspirations in our imagination, dreams, and fantasies that are integrated in this book. We have actively imagined conversations that never happened, as if we were "dreaming while awake" (Anzaldúa, 2015, p. 5), moving between fictionalized narratives, ethnodramas, realist stories, and desired narratives. We have used these narratives to make sense of the stories that unfolded for us, within us, and with each other.

Most importantly, we dealt with the ugliest part of our collective human history – White supremacy and its effects, not just in theory, but in material lived realities. And in doing so, we got into the messy territory of who is a friend or foe, who can we trust, and who do we look towards for inspiration. To that end, we revisited our histories of growing up, how we understood what it meant to be racialized. Unknown to both of us, our histories became perfect mirrors. Kent understood a racialized narrative at an early age, that taught him who he is in relation to Black and Brown folks. Kakali remained puzzled after immigrating to Canada when she was being treated with disdain, anger, and hatred as she did not know anything about discrimination at an early age growing up in a protected, privileged life in India. The ghosts of those memories shape our writing.

Caroline, who has passed away, but was a mentor and colleague to Kakali, and a mentor to Kent, has served as a mirror. Her presence is pervasive throughout the text. Some of the narratives with Caroline are realist with evidence from email records or direct conversations. But there are other narratives where Caroline's presence becomes a call for looking at our pain, shadows, dialoguing with parts of ourselves that remained long buried, and attending to the wounds that became visible.

Kent is a White man. Kakali is a Brown woman. Kakali supervised Kent's dissertation while he was a doctoral student. Kent worked with Angie, a Chicana woman, for his dissertation. This certainly is eyebrow-raising action in the world of academia, and especially within the context of anti-oppressionist work. This, then, makes us ask who can do what work? What is the role of someone who is interrogating his privileges? What bridges can be built if at all? We certainly agree that cultural insiders would and should narrate their stories, center themselves, and write themselves into existence in ways that no cultural outsider ever could. Therefore, Kent's journey then becomes less about "telling the story" of some downtrodden Brown woman, and more about the understanding of his privileges, Whiteness, and ways in which he has benefitted from a White supremacist system, by reflecting on stories that Angie was willing to share, out of her sheer generosity. Certainly, one could imagine that the stories Angie might share with a cultural insider would be different than what she has shared with Kent.

We also carry the ghosts of fear, hatred, bigotry, and marginalization with us that divide us, make us want to stay in our own lanes when the thought of bridge building becomes a daunting task. This is when we have leaned on Gloria Anzaldúa's work, who has passed away. Anzaldúa (2015) reminds us about our axes of differences but also about our shared humanity. Ghosts, as commonly understood, are shadowy creatures, perhaps figments of our imagination, who appear at night in spooky spaces like a graveyard or in old buildings or dark alleys. However, Anzaldúa's presence in this writing is neither spooky nor fear-inducing. Instead, we worked hard to avoid putting a superficial framing of "let's just all get along despite our differences" in our writing. We chose to dig deep into the differences and look directly at the wounds generated by those differences.

What we did was jolt our consciousness into waking up to the realities of our differences in our past and present and in the possibilities of our future. How could a woman of a Chicana background learn to dream that the world is her oyster when she is worried that her brothers, father, and uncles could very likely be in prison on any given day? How could a Brown woman in academia negotiate showing up fearlessly with courage and integrity and not worry about the consequences of retaliation, because she did not stay in her lane and know her place? Could the Brown woman only expect to implore those in the dominant group to hopefully become benevolent dictators aligned with her causes if she promises to stay in her lane? What would be the work of a critical White introverted ally, who, for the most part, is reluctant to deal with the social world, but has committed himself to continuously interrogating his privileges? This is difficult work and bears the certainty that we will mess up. And when we do, our individual and collective wounds would surface, our histories would collide, our ancestors and those who came before us would become part of how we make sense of things. We would need forgiveness from each other. We would need to just keep trying, because bridge building work is messy without any immediate gratification.

Our willingness to challenge our belief systems, interrogate our privileges, and look at the messiness of our stories created a series of ongoing narratives of falling apart and coming together. It was as if we were breaking apart previously held belief systems, looking at them closely, experiencing our fragmentations, feeling the isolation, and being willing to remain open to "putting our fragmented pieces together in a new way" (Anzaldúa, 2015, p. 20).

We have not answered all of our questions. But we are making our way through the fog. Talking about race is difficult and brings up different types of pain for everyone. We cannot engage in oppression Olympics where we situate one person's pain as superior to another's. Nor can we dismiss the centuries-old systemic pain inflicted on minoritized populations, while benefitting mostly White folks. We need to hold both of these truths in the same space and perhaps begin to ask ourselves what might be the path forward towards healing. If we make friends with our shadowy wounds, we can then see how natural and self-preserving it has been for us to build up walls, create divisions between us, and how over centuries of doing so, we have isolated ourselves from each other. In this book we have taken our first steps to think of what lies beyond the wounds. We have deeply excavated our wounds, stayed with our pain, and dialogued honestly with each other when we hit divisive walls. At the very least we came to the following realizations.

We cannot deny the suffering of our fellow human beings when we benefit from the very same conditions that produce the suffering. Yet, we cannot deny the anger we feel inside when we experience suffering as individuals and as a collective. How do we then move beyond that which divides us to discover that which connects us in our shared humanity? Perhaps it is hypocritical to ask a question that even we cannot fully answer. But at least, we made an attempt in this book, with the help of every idea, every person, every inspiration, every emotional, mental, and intellectual breakdown that inspired and haunted us.

ACKNOWLEDGEMENTS

KAKALI'S ACKNOWLEDGEMENTS

There are several people who continuously fed our spirit, nurtured our well being, stimulated us intellectually, and pushed us out of our comfort zones, who need to be credited. First, I want to thank my mother, Sumita Bhattacharyya, who appears in the text and has approved my narration of her role. She has taught me to be open, direct, and honest, where people can trust that there are no hidden agendas behind my words beyond what is expressed. This has made me travel lightly in the world and accept the consequences of all my actions.

My partner Paul Maxfield and my most amazing furry companion, my miniature poodle, Gigi-Bhattacharya-Maxfield-the-first, have offered me unconditional love and support no matter what project I have taken on. Paul would take care of the house, meals, and even my spirit. Gigi would offer cuddles, become the best armrest one could expect, and allow me to love on her as I navigated the stress of handling demanding tasks. In fact even right now Gigi has her butt up against me as I write this. Paul has had the unenviable position of listening to every shitty first draft of writing that was intended for various parts of this book and offered strong critiques, lovingly – always lovingly.

My soul sister Rose Knippa kept me honest and in integrity throughout the process of writing this book. Bidisha Ray loved me ever since I was a little girl and continues to do so no matter what I do or how I do it. Kristen Kahler, who became a friend with whom I could talk with for hours after I moved to a new town called Manhattan, Kansas, listened to my stories with an open heart.

My contemplative practices family kept me uplifted every year with retreats, conferences, and general connection. I have met the most open-hearted people in this group and they inspire me everyday how to not put up walls even when it feels safe to do so while navigating social structures of oppression.

Several academic scholar friends helped my thinking along the way. Violet Jones asked me to decolonize my mind and methodologies when we were graduate students. Heather Adams has supported me in every idea I have had, no matter how premature those ideas were. AnaLouise Keating has offered to the world her thoughts on post-oppositionality, which has pushed how I have thought about oppression and liberation and my deep gratitude to her for bringing forth unpublished works of Gloria Anzaldúa whose influence is paramount in this text. I remain grateful to Dr. Jude Preissle who asked Kent a difficult question, which prompted this book in the form of an answer. My mentors from University of Georgia, Kathleen deMarrais and Kathy Roulston continue to support me and help me proliferate my work to this day, decades after graduation. They exemplify the kind of mentoring that I aspire to enact in my relationships with my students.

Many thanks to Patricia Leavy and Sense Publishers for seeing the value in this work even when we were in the early stages of conceptualization and supporting us in our journey patiently, as we worked towards completion. Gratitude to Shalen Lowell for helping us get to the finish line.

Finally, deepest gratitude to Caroline Sherritt, who is no longer in this world, but I seem to continue to have a relationship with her anyway. Without her, I would have not met Kent, and this book would have not been written.

KENT'S ACKNOWLEDGEMENTS

As in the case with my co-author, many of those who have exerted significant influence over my career have been among those who immigrated to this country years ago in order to work toward successful careers in various American institutes of higher education. I would like to use this opportunity to acknowledge two of them. The first, Dr. Alex Lotas, was instrumental in, to use his very own words, "getting my hooks into you" and seeing that despite early setbacks, I would eventually obtain important personal and professional goals. Though I have neither seen him nor spoken with him in 20 years, I can still feel those hooks. He will not be forgotten. Nor will Dr. Vanessa Jackson, who was equally influential. Any success I have achieved thus far would not have been possible without her encouragement during earlier years. I salute both of you.

Further acknowledgments should also go to Dr. Enrique Solis, who assisted me in preparation for the interviews that I would eventually carry out with the research-participant Angie; Dr. Kamiar Kouzekanani, who before Dr. Bhattacharya's arrival on the scene, offered as much helpful advice as anyone else in my early forays into dissertation-proposal writing; and Dr. Caroline Sherritt, the one major supporting player in this saga who was always there, for and with me, both before and after this story played out. In a certain sense, she is still there.

Additional gratitude to Mrs. Juanita Gillen Sloan, former business teacher and the late mother of a very contrary boy who wishes she was still here.

Finally, of course, there is Angie, whose narrative functions throughout this work as that of a third presence. Though the book contains parallel remembrances of the two authors, it is my witnessing of Angie's story that results in generating most compelling insights. Without her, none of what follows would have mattered.

MEETING DIFFERENCES

This is a text of parallel narratives. I, Kakali, write from the perspective of a Brown-skinned woman. Although I was born in India, I have lived in Canada and in the U.S. much longer than I have lived in India. Kent writes from the perspective of a White man born and raised in the U.S., who has spent most of his life in South Texas. As an educator of color, I mentor students and teach them about ethnicity, race, multiculturalism, within the context of designing and conducting qualitative research projects for doctoral dissertations. Kent writes from the perspective of being at the receiving end of such mentoring where he had to interrogate his privileges as a White man while he was conducting his dissertation case study of the educational experiences of Angie, a Chicana woman, in Corpus Christi, Texas, during the 1950s and 1960s. We do not claim that our voices are completely distinct or separate from each other's as we understand how entangled we are in our relational existence. Yet at the same time, we do not claim that we are somehow representing Angie's voice in truthful accuracy here. What we can claim though, is that by engaging with Angie's story, we opened up this complicated space, where we had to negotiate some rough terrains about teaching and learning about race and power in higher education from our situated perspectives that culminated in this book.

The book is broadly divided into six chapters with Kakali introducing each chapter contextually with her experiences and Kent concluding with his perspectives. We explore the issue of how cross-cultural studies can be done, if at all, and if cross-cultural studies are really studies of the Other or if they are critical catalysts for situating self in relation to Other, understanding one's position and unearned privileges in one's cultural context. We focus on the challenges of mentoring by a woman of color of a White man who recognizes for the first time in his life social structures that benefit him without having to earn such benefits.

Highlighting tension-filled dialogues while creating an ethnodrama in Kent's dissertation, we reflect closely on the implications of the ethnodrama where the researcher is a character and a disembodied narrator. Finally, we present a set of pedagogical practices relevant for undergraduate and graduate instruction based on our experiences of mentoring and being mentored. In this opening chapter we discuss the differences in understanding un/earned privileges with examples and associated struggles.

KAKALI'S NARRATIVE

I recall that day vividly, as if it were a scene from an action movie. The setting is Canada, 1987. I am sitting in the back of my stepdad's brown Oldsmobile. My mother is sitting up front with my stepdad, who is taking us on a drive on the highway. Destination unplanned. I am 14 years old and have just arrived, now living with Mom and her new husband in Mississauga, Ontario – a place right out of the storybooks about foreign countries I used to read while still living in India. These past two months, while donning sweaters every morning and walking through the snow, marveling at the tall, sloping rooftops on houses – it has all made me feel as if I was living a storybook life, the kind my friends back in India never experienced. I even take pictures to enclose with my letters to them.

On this particular day as we travel down the highway, my nose presses against the cold back-seat window and my eyes watch the pine trees zip by. Snow pushes up against either side of the highway, where they fill deep ditches. Cars and trucks of every make and model pass by in both directions; I have never seen so many different types before. In Canada, I sometimes wonder if I have travelled into the future.

Then, a red pick-up pulls up on our left side. But unlike the other cars flying by us, they slow down. Inside the truck are three White men who appear to be in their early twenties. They focus upon us now, as if excited or surprised at discovering our sudden presence on the highway – and then they begin to laugh. Although my stepdad is determined to ignore them, I cannot look away from these men. Perhaps sensing an attentive audience now, one of them rolls down his window and looks directly at me. Shortly, another begins making strange noises like an animal. And then the others join in. They grunt and cavort for my amusement, sticking their necks out the window and making faces. They make fists with their hands and move them under their armpits. They bounce up and down in their seats, screaming "hoop, hoop, hoop," laughing hysterically. Their actions remind me of excited little monkeys.

Now, the truck inches closer to our vehicle, and I feel that if I roll down my window and reach out, I can just touch them. My stepdad struggles to maintain control of the car as he swerves to the side of the road, bringing us dangerously near those snow-covered ditches. The more we swerve, the more these men and their truck threaten to force us off the side of the road altogether.

I am puzzled by this sudden intrusion into our otherwise idyllic drive. Why do these men appear so amused? And what motivates them to drive their truck closer and closer? Another inch nearer, and we will surely wind up in the ditch. Finally, however, they ease the truck back into their own lane. They now stretch their hands out the window with their middle fingers upraised from within curled fists. This is a gesture I have never encountered. Then, another finger sprouts up from the driver's window, pointing to the sky, while all of them continue their chorus of "hoop, hoop." Then they drive away.

I wonder what to make of those middle fingers pointing to the sky. Is this a religious gesture? Were they pointing toward God and expressing how happy they are since Christmas is just two months away and they want to spread their joy? Or is there some other festival at this time of year about which I have no knowledge? God knows in India we have a festival for every damn thing and we were always celebrating something or other. I cannot help asking out loud, "What does that mean, that middle finger pointing up?"

My stepdad's voice is stern. "Nothing for you to know or be concerned about." And that being that, we turn around and head home in silence.

***

Cut to the year 2004. A city in the Deep South of the United States. I sit in a coffee shop, talking to Yamini, a participant in my dissertation project. I am exploring how women who are international students from India negotiate their experiences while in their first year of graduate studies. This study is motivated by reflections on my first year in Canada, where what stood out to me then has now become routine. The participants' experiences may reveal how they perceive and understand their gendered and racial experiences in a new culture. I have decided to use conversations in place of traditional semi-structured, in-depth interviews.

"So how was your day?" I sip my coffee as I wait for Yamini's answer.

Yamini's facial expression changes. She frowns, her eyes look up to the ceiling. Then, she sighs and slumps down in her seat. "Something happened today that was not good."

"Oh?"

"Well, I went out for a jog this morning."

"Okay."

"I was wearing a western jogging outfit. I got it from Old Navy. And I was jogging on one side of the road by Five Points. You know where they are doing all the construction and there is a deep ditch on the side of the road? Along there."

I know that area well. If people jogging are not attentive, they could fall into the ditch and hurt themselves badly. "Then what happened?"

"Well, this hot red pick-up truck was driving by. It slowed down and started driving right beside me. And then it came so close to me that I thought I would fall into the ditch. I just don't understand." Yamini's eyes well up as if she is holding back tears.

"What is it that you don't understand?" I am not sure I want to hear the answer. Whatever it is, it is making her tear up and I can feel a growing knot in my stomach instantly.

"There was about an inch left between me and the ditch. That's how badly these White guys wanted to run me over. Then they gave me the finger and called me a sand nigger and told me to die." Tears roll down Yamini's cheeks.

Sand nigger? Racism is now distinguishing between shades of light and dark brown? I shake my head and reach over to offer Yamini a hug.

Yamini reaches out to me and we hug. Sobbing heavily in my arms, she struggles to find the words. "Why was I so offensive to them? I wasn't doing anything Indian. Jogging is western, right?"

The painful innocence of that question is at once palpable and heartbreaking. Yamini has been in the U.S. for three months. She recognizes the possibility that White Americans may cause her harm if she behaves in ways that are perceived as "too Indian." She believes she would be protected from such harm if she engages in western activities – like jogging. And she would thus not stand out as an outsider and invite danger.

Yamini sees me as her elder sister, even though our initial meeting was to discuss her role as a participant in my dissertation. Over the past few months we have become close and she looks upon me as a cultural elder, and we have developed a kinship relation. I feel now as if I am supposed to share some wisdom, some way to make her pain go away, some way to help her dismiss this event from her memory – or tell her that this was a one-time isolated incident that is rare, and in saying this I might erase what seems like a traumatic event imprinted on her psyche.

In the end, however, I cannot help Yamini. All I can think of is the loss of my own innocence when I first arrived in Canada, when I did not understand why a group of White men wanted to run us off the road, into a *similar* ditch, while imitating the sounds of monkeys and making obscene gestures. And now, a near-identical incident happens, this time to someone else, someone I care about. That past event, the one my stepdad refused to discuss, remained repressed within me. But I am compelled now to face the ugliness of that event and the pain it caused me when I began to realize what it all meant. I must seek to understand that the presence of some – those like Yamani and like me – could be so offensive as to animate certain White Americans to cause us serious physical and emotional harm. And once I acknowledge the existence of such hatred and ugliness, I must then summon the courage to attend to a deep, 15-year-old wound – one that I must resolve to heal. Such a commitment is not an easy task.

***

Return now to the year 1987. I am enrolled in a Canadian high school. Tonight is parent-teacher night. Mom visits Mrs. Higgins, my 12th grade English teacher, a White woman in her 50s who has lived in Southern Ontario all her life. My mother is a woman in her late 30s, who has recently migrated to Canada from India. She was a science educator in high school in India, and she has been able to secure a similar position here.

Mom walks into Mrs. Higgins' classroom, dressed in a long dark brown skirt, close-toed brown shoes, and a bright flowery blouse. Her dark black hair, messy at the end of the day, rests on her shoulder. Mrs. Higgins is sitting at her desk. She is wearing a crisp, clean White blouse and a knee-length grey pencil skirt with black pumps. Her golden hair barely touches her shoulder.

My mom knocks and peeks her head through the open classroom door, and Mrs. Higgins waves her in. "Come in, Sumita. Have a seat please."

"Thank you, Mrs. Higgins. How are you?" Mom has learned to ask this *how are you* question as a form of initial greeting. She is still struggling with the notion that people do not want to know how you are really, but rather this is a way of saying hello. There were times when she tried to respond to this "how are you" question with how she really was. She started saying she was busy, stressed, trying to manage a crazy day, and before she had finished her first sentence, the questioner had already walked away and turned the corner. So now she throws out the question generously to see how people respond so that she can learn the best way for her to respond to others. Often she mirrors others' response.

"I am fine, Sumita. Thank you for asking. And you?"

"Yeah, fine too."

"So let's talk about Kakali. She is a really bright girl."

5

"Okay. So how come she is not getting 80s in her assignment? Is there something we can do to help her?" My mother is nothing if not direct. We need to receive at least 80 percentage points out of 100 as a final grade for university entry without having to take extra qualification tests to ensure that we are at competency level to handle our academic tasks in English.

"Well…let me see how I can explain this to you, Sumita. English is not your first language, is it?"

"No, it is not. But my daughter went to an English medium school in India. She learned English the same time she learned her mother tongue. So she has no problem with reading, writing, or understanding English."

"Oh, that's very good, Sumita! You were good to put her in a school like that. How nice of you! See, the thing is that your daughter does not speak English as her first language. Tell me something. Do you folks speak English at home?"

"No! Why would we?"

"I think that could help your daughter do better in the class. More exposure to English. I just think that this is still different and new to her."

"Is my daughter getting the lowest score in your class, Mrs. Higgins?" Mom starts a line of inquiry, which immediately makes Mrs. Higgins forehead curve into wavy frown lines.

"Um, no, she is not. There are students who are doing much worse than her. Kakali is a bright, foreign student in my class. She has such a nice multicultural perspective." Mrs. Higgins smiles and nods her head up and down repeatedly after she finishes her sentence.

"Mrs. Higgins, is my daughter the only person in your class whose first language is not English?" Mom continues her line of inquiry.

"Well, if I think about it now, well, yes, it is."

"I see. Then all these other students must speak English at home, correct?" My mother should have been an investigative criminal lawyer.

"Yes, I suppose so."

"So how come English-speaking students are not doing better than my daughter in your class? Should it not mean that speaking English at home is not a determining factor for performing well in your class?" My mother goes in for the kill.

Mrs. Higgins realizes what just happened. She is trapped in her own argument. She doesn't like it. Her face hardens. Her eyes stop smiling. Her lips get stiff. She locks her eyes onto those of my mom.

"Listen, Sumita. I will be honest here. I don't think your daughter can do well in English the same way native speakers can. It's just not possible. This is not her language. She can try. But I don't think it would happen. It would be good for her to take some qualifying tests before being admitted to the university."

My mom stands up, reaches her right hand out to Mrs. Higgins, shakes it, and says, "Thank you for your honesty," and walks away.

For the next few months, I put all my efforts into improving my English grade. I study around the clock, I speak English at home, and I write letters to my friends in India in English. I even start to dream in English. I read widely, deeply. On my final report card, my grades in all subjects show an A, with a numerical score of 90 or more points. For English, I have a 79 – one point shy of the 80 I needed to avoid taking the qualifying English test for university entrance.

I don't know which is worse – that I was not seen as a good, civilized, colonized subject, or that I was made to earn that spot again even though I had already earned my good, colonized subject-position from my education in India long before Mrs. Higgins came into the picture. It was not until years later that I understood the messiness of wanting the colonizer's approval as a good, colonized subject so that I could navigate the Master's house better than the other colonized subjects, who might not be as good a subject as I could be.

***

I arrived in Canada from India in the late 1980s when I was 14 years old. My mom had divorced my father and married an Indian gentleman in Canada, which was the reason for my migration. Years before, while still in India, I had been in a boarding school whose superintendent, Mrs. Rosario, was an Anglo-British woman. I guess when the British left India, some Anglo folks chose to make India their home. Mrs. Rosario's family was one of them. The boarding school operated like a convent so that the boarders would be seen as top students in the main school, which contained both day-scholars (who commuted to the school) and those who boarded there. I was placed there as a result of a custody settlement between my parents upon their divorce. This institution was known as an *English medium* school, which implied all our classes were taught in English. Excluding our native-language classes, we were assessed in English. On Sundays, Mrs. Rosario took us to church and taught us religious hymns to sing; moreover, we celebrated Christmas, even though none of the boarders were Christian. Our entertainment in the boarding school consisted of listening to an almost-broken radio during limited listening hours.

Mrs. Rosario tried to teach us how to be western. She would insist that we have breakfast at 6:30 am on weekdays and 7:00 am on weekends, when we were allowed to have Indian breakfasts. But on weekdays, we had to have milk and cereal with a banana. This, Mrs. Rosario would tell us, is what civilized people eat for breakfast. Mrs. Rosario lamented that none of the cooks knew how to prepare other meals that her family enjoyed, like porridge or pancakes. Sometimes at night, before I fell asleep, I fantasized about sitting with golden-haired, White ladies of Mrs. Rosario's family, eating porridge and pancakes – and how they would marvel at the way I would use a knife and fork, or the way I would gently take the White napkin from my lap and wipe the corners of my lips – and I would beam with pride over my adaptation of good western table manners.

Needless to say, I was incredibly naïve about the world, differences, or anything else. At that point in my life, all I cared about was how to have fun with my friends. Concepts of race, gender, class, sexuality or any other axes of difference were unfamiliar to me.

Yet, I was extremely privileged on multiple counts. My father's income placed me in the upper middle-class, which allowed me to enroll in an expensive boarding school. I was born into a Hindu family, the predominant religion in India. While India embraces religious eclecticism, I never had to worry whether my religious views and needs would be preserved by the dominant group. In fact, I did not worry about religion on any level. That is what privilege does. It renders oppression invisible to those who benefit from it. I was also born into the priestly class, which falls into the caste system of India. My last name automatically identified me as a Brahmin, meaning that I have collected enough good deeds in my previous lives to land on the top of the caste hierarchy. At that time, discrimination against people based on their caste was illegal in India, but there were plenty of discriminatory practices against people of other castes (which continue today) that were also out of my awareness then.

Overall, during my first 14 years of life in India, not only was I unaware of my privileges, I did not even realize that people have different privileges from my own. In other words, I recognized no privileges whatsoever, in any form. I assumed we all had equal opportunities for the manifestation of our aspirations. I assumed that if I failed to achieve something, then it was because I did not try hard or I lacked the aptitude. And I assumed this to be true of everyone, regardless of his or her class or caste. But after crossing oceans to live in Canada, my privileges, my assumptions were all washed away, leaving me in a completely unfamiliar space.

***

Early 2001, an institution of higher learning in the American Deep South. For the first time, I am standing in front of students as a teacher. Well, I am not really a teacher. Just a teaching assistant. Instructor of record. I am a graduate student, recently moved from Canada to pursue and achieve a master's degree, afterward remaining in the U.S. to enroll in the doctoral program here.

My first course is titled *Multicultural Perspectives for Women in the U.S.* I feel strange standing here, looking at the students. Me, a Brown woman from India, visibly different in looks and accent. They, mostly women from the South, from affluent backgrounds, White, blondes, some brunettes, visibly different in looks and accent from me. I am about to teach them their country's history, atrocities committed by their ancestors, which continues in the present with the help of networked social systems of oppression against those who look like me or whose skin tone is even darker than mine. Why would they care for what I have to say? I wonder how long it would take for them to dismiss me as the *angry minority* teacher. What if they just stand up and walk away from the class?

I decide that I need this job, so I should not rock the boat too much or let the students know my stand on things – although my perspectives are difficult to hide, given the reading list I have put together. One of the first readings I have assigned is Peggy McIntosh's essay (1989), *White Privilege: Unpacking the Invisible Knapsack.* I have asked everyone to come up with at least 10 unearned privileges in their lives and ways they might unlearn or extend those privileges. I have offered an example from my own perspective. My unearned privileges include those I enjoy as an able-bodied person, privileges that are inaccessible to those who are not. I use disability as an example because I consider race too sensitive a topic for us to address right away without establishing trust and rapport. Nonetheless, I worry that the students might complain about me. We do occasionally discuss race, but only when students bring up race-based topics or ideas. In this way, I feel I might create as safe a space as I can before focusing more on social-justice issues connected to ethnicity, class, and/or gender.

Fast forward to a decade later. I am now teaching at a research institution in another part of the U.S., working with predominantly White students. In my class, students are asked to perform their subjectivities in some artistic manner, connecting intersected narratives from their subject positions to their desired topic of inquiry. Usually this activity allows students to develop

9

awareness of the personal beliefs, values, and assumptions that inform their research agendas. After all, research interests do not generate in a vacuum; instead, they grow out of a contextual narrative.

One of my students, Gail, a White woman in her late 20s, talks to the class about her interest in women of color in science, based on her career interest as a science educator. Sonja, a Chicana student, also in her late 20s, responds by asking Gail, "Have you considered intersectionality in your work?" Sonja has a strong theoretical foundation as a result of several previous classes, and she now generally speaks using theoretical tenets. This class, however, is Gail's first ever in her graduate career, and has publicly confessed about her lack of prior exposure to theory. Gail looks visibly embarrassed as she struggles to answer Sonja's question.

"Well, I know some of them could be poor, but really I just want to know how to help women of color in science."

Sonja prepares to respond, and I anticipate that she may offer a strong theoretical argument. I worry about how unsettled Gail would feel in front of her peers if she is being interrogated about her theoretical knowledge, something she has already confessed as her weakness. So I interrupt the dialogue by announcing to the entire class, "We will discuss theory in another class. So let's table that discussion for now." Then I turn to Gail and say, "Gail, intersectionality is a complex issue and we have to explore your relationship with intersectionality meaningfully before being able to answer the question thoughtfully. So let's have that conversation when we discuss theory later in the class."

After class, Sonja and Gail both approach me, but separately. I speak with each one in private. In my conversation with Gail, she reveals that she neither appreciated Sonja's question nor my interruption. She feels she was ganged up on, and our actions made her feel like a victim of reverse racism.

I let those words hang in the air. *Reverse racism.* I could almost see the words floating in big block bubble letters, like those on the cover of Gail's binder, but without the purple color or the glitter. Suddenly the words grow larger, darker, almost smoky, making it difficult for me to breathe. I gulp. My entire body stings. My tongue threatens to become wild. A restless spirit inside me wants to jump out and really go into a diatribe about how inane and fictional the notion of reverse racism is and what it might possibly indicate when a White woman is being asked to defend her work academically, that she would fall back into the role of victim.

Somehow though, I silence what my restless spirit nudges me to say. Instead, I ask Gail to consider the possibility of defending her work academically, as that would be an expectation no matter what theoretical home she finds herself in, and to consider what could potentially be some opposing arguments, to make her work stronger and to demonstrate that she has read widely and deeply. Gail nods at my suggestions, packs up her bags, and exits the classroom. I do not ask what Gail's thoughts were as a result of the conversation because I could sense being emotionally drained, with limited capacity to address anything else with the kind of open-hearted compassion required for bridge-building work.

In my private conversation with Sonja, she reveals to me her frustration at the ways in which she has been silenced in her other classes and how that pattern has followed her throughout her education. She shares a hallway conversation she had with Gail trying to explain her position, and how it did not go well, leading to more tensions between the two. My heart breaks for Sonja, and I try to tell her that I understand her position and that I have been much more subtle, rather than overt, in my own resistance. I tell her that this strategy has worked well for me in academia. She nods respectfully. I silence Sonja and myself.

Inwardly, I debate my decision to engage students in discussing their unearned privileges in future classes – because with each week, the tension between Sonja and Gail becomes more transparent and palpable. If there are any racial issues raised by the readings assigned or the videos we watch, Sonja and Gail take opposite positions. I question whether making space to discuss this tension would further divide the class and damage the learning experiences of the students. The truth is, I do not think I have the necessary courage or the tenacity to entertain the volatility of conversations centered on unearned privileges and their consequences. Perhaps such a session would derail the class. I question whether it is my role to yank someone from their position if they are unwilling to do so themselves. Maybe I would cause visible factions in the class. Maybe the students would incorrectly perceive me as someone who hates White people. I fear the class might then become more explicitly divisive, where it would become clear who agrees with me and who does not. Can I really take the time out of teaching the course's content to deal with something far more fundamental and necessary in order for the students to engage the content with more authenticity and intellectual honesty? I feel paralyzed.

***

In higher education I carry this shuttling between being a good colonized subject on the one hand, while on the other, rejecting the position of being a colonized subject. I think of how I am still in the Master's house (Lorde, 1984a), even in my resistant critical work. I interpret perhaps some of that resistance as knocking down the walls of a room in the Master's house. I have been in this house since birth, so I do not know what it could be like on the outside. I try to read in my native language. I keep up with literature, music, and poems in Bangla. But I know my generation and the next that came after me no longer value native language-learning as much as I do, entirely for the purpose of economic survival, since knowing English makes one more employable than knowing one's native Indian language, even in India. And I cannot help but think of the loss one experiences when one loses language. And yet I do not know where I would want to be, or if there ever could be a pure decolonized space, away from the Master's house.

Project colonization is so pervasive that I am using English to critique the dominance of English and its asymmetrical power structure. I am attempting to show the Master that I am just as good as he is – while at the same time trying to locate another space. As an educator, I try to bring my Otherness into the classroom because I am already Othered before I even speak. I cannot identify being Indian the way someone in India would. I cannot identify being a Canadian fully. And I cannot identify being fully American either. I think of myself as this nomadic world traveler, who Gloria Anzaldúa (2009) calls a *nepantlera*, one who travels through multiple worlds without the need to belong in any. They are threshold theorists, moving in and out of many worlds while living on the borders. Our conflicting desires in these messy spaces leave us vulnerable to become brutally honest with ourselves, in terms of imagining what freedom might look like, with our mind, bodies, and spirit in action. For me, there seems to be this deep call for accepting the fact that I author myself through dominant and resistant discourses simultaneously; and perhaps that might not change – as long as I am in the Master's house as a self-aware subject. So I look to Gloria Anzaldúa's (1987/1999) magic when she says:

On that day I say, "Yes all you people wound us when you reject us. Rejection strips us of self-worth; our vulnerability exposes us to shame. It is our innate identity you find wanting. We are ashamed that we need your good opinion, that we need your acceptance. We can no longer camouflage our needs, can no longer let defenses and fences sprout around us. We can no longer withdraw. To rage and look upon you with contempt is to rage and be contemptuous of ourselves. We can no longer blame you, nor disown the White parts, the male parts, the pathological parts, the queer parts, these vulnerable parts. Here we are weaponless with open arms, with only our magic. Let's try it our way, the *mestiza* way, the Chicana way, the woman way." (Anzaldúa, 1987/1999, p. 110)

This need to move in-between worlds, in-between emotions, in-between struggles and accomplishments lands me in precarious positions as a mentor to people in a dominant group. How do I teach people who enjoy enormous amounts of privilege, that most of them are unearned, and that their posturing, their way of knowing the world and living their lives is all a result of the invisibility of those privileges (McIntosh, 1989)? How do I motivate White folks to empathize with people who are oppressed on a daily basis? How do I interrogate their position, and become a critical ally, especially when teaching with this Brown body while occupying a predominantly White space?

KENT'S NARRATIVE

It is neither a clear nor hazy day. As my dead mother drives me to school in her convertible, she turns toward me and smiles, but only faintly. She says nothing; she simply exists. In a short while, she pulls off the road and into a large parking lot, and I notice a huge stadium looming up before us. I realize we have arrived at school, and I then remember why. Dr. Bhattacharya's class is due to begin soon, and I know I must be there.

The classroom is situated somewhere the other side of the stadium. I decide to walk through the structure in order to get there. Once inside, however, I see the place is absolutely packed with people, waiting expectantly for something to happen. There are fewer environments I detest more than crowded ones, so I decide to traverse the outer circumference of the building, using a deserted concrete walkway. It may take longer to reach class, but at least this way I can avoid the commotion.

Then at this point, I realize this is all a dream. None of it is real. Yet I desire the dream to continue because I am curious what will be discussed in class. I reason that if I can experience a tactile situation, I will remain asleep and the dream will not be over. I therefore decide to reach out to my right and touch the gray, painted concrete wall that lines the walkway. And as I do, I can feel the cold, unyielding texture.

Then, the dream ends, and I reluctantly open my eyes. Sadly, I now conclude there will be no class. As consciousness overpowers my relaxed senses, I wonder what will be missed. And then I am reminded that I have

13

finished all classes. There is now only a dissertation to complete. But not even that remains because yesterday, I gave up – and an important objective I began pursuing over four years ago is now lost. Dead and nonexistent. Perhaps in mulling over a lost goal, I should return to sleep and forget the challenges I have failed to confront. Challenges just like the one below:

From: Bhattacharya, Kakali <Kakali.Bhattacharya@tamucc.edu>
To: Kent Gillen <kent.gillen@gmail.com>
Date: Fri, Oct 22, 2010 at 8:55 AM
Subject: Some thoughts

Kent,

There is something that has been bothering me deeply from the onset of this project. It is your refusal to identify the privileges that you carry with you as a White man. [You must] identify unearned privileges that people have as part of the subject position(s) they occupy in our social structure. White male ranks at the top of the list. Yet nowhere in your dissertation that I have read so far have you unpacked your privileges in relation to the participant's. I am not sure if you didn't understand that you needed to do this or if I have been unclear or if you are simply resisting this to dismiss this idea as irrelevant to your work. However, if you do not identify the privileges with which you carry yourself and construct knowledge about this world, you are situating yourself as ahistorical, value-neutral, acultural, in the context of the participants' experiences. Therefore, you would automatically fall into the trap of the colonizing White gaze that describes the exotic other…

This isn't an issue of identity politics, which you have argued in your dissertation. It is an issue of identifying that you too, as White man, carry with you values, assumptions, beliefs, epistemologies, and privileges that shape the way you see and process the world…If you do not unpack that in your dissertation, you are leaving [out] a key part out of your dissertation and as such it would be incomplete. If you resist identifying and acknowledging any of this, then you [are] claiming that your subject position has no influence on how you have constructed knowledge or understanding in this research…

KB

As I drift back to sleep now, I feel the pressure of the deadline that approaches. I am visited now by a specter, the ghost of a new knowledge that fails to fully materialize. Yet rather than confront the intrusive, mysterious White mass, I turn away. And in doing so, I avoid all admissions of privilege and persist in a stasis of denial, the result of which looms more ominous with each passing day and threatens the survival of all that I have heretofore accomplished. And with each protracted delay in confronting these hard truths, I realize the sudden stroke of the executioner's axe swings nearer.

All the while, the spirit remains unseen, elusive, and impenetrable. On all occasions where I sense its presence, I succumb to an obsessive desire – the irrational yet tempting urge to dig a deep, dark hole and hide away from all responsibility, all new enlightenment. Countless times, I have been offered the keys to unlock the secrets that others wish me to discover. Such tokens often take the form of advice from those who would endorse my release into the outside world...

You must identify the privileges that you carry with you as a White man.

... But it is I who must insert these tokens, open all locks, and claim my own freedom. To do so, however, I must pen my reluctant signature at the bottom of a confession, the content of which I am not allowed to read because no one has set forth the conditions. The lines written in this contract are, I am told, my responsibility alone...

What baggage do you carry with yourself?

It is I who must author my own confession. Yet I have failed to oblige the warders. I have just received a communiqué from one of them. She states that she would have me prostrate myself before the community and admit to all of which I am oblivious, ignorant, unaware...

Unpack your position and the privileges with which you process the world.

These verses, repeated often, have become a hellish litany – a series of demands, requested no doubt with the best of intentions. But like the prisoner who has spent nearly a lifetime accommodating his own loss of freedom, I have refused her gift of release.

Think beyond the drama, beyond hiding behind the curtain.

The chants are ceaseless now. The drama has become a long nightmare with no end in sight. Why? – Because I refuse to awaken. Because I know the unseen specter that lurks on the other side of that curtain beckons me forth to confront a new knowledge that has eluded me since childhood.

***

My schooling gave me no training in seeing myself as an oppressor, as an unfairly advantaged person, or as a participant in a damaged culture. (Peggy McIntosh, 1990, "White Privilege: Unpacking the Invisible Knapsack")

***

Figure 1. Kent, the dissertation researcher, at age four

In northeastern Texas during 1960, I attended an elementary school located just a few blocks from home. My mother had deemed the streets safe enough for me to walk through alone every morning. Mom was unaware, however, that on some days, I was accompanied to school by an African-American woman, a maid for one of the neighborhood families. She was the mother of children approximately my age, so I guess she felt maternal and protective toward me, an 8-year-old kid, walking by himself. Soon, those walks alongside her became a morning ritual. She was friendly, and I found her presence comforting. As we ambled side by side, I would tell her about the second grade or what I did at home; and she would listen, always making a kind observation here or there as any good mother would.

One morning, after arriving at school, I was accused by one of my schoolmates of having been seen walking with a "n_____ woman." I told him, "So what?" I saw nothing wrong with that. To me, she was just like anyone else. But my school chum judged that answer insufficient; further, he informed me it was forbidden to go around with a Black woman as if she were my equal, as if she were as good as those of my color. Soon, word got around class, and I was chastised on and off throughout the day by every kid in the second grade. It was humiliating.

The next morning, when I encountered the woman halfway to school, I told her I could not walk with her anymore. I cannot recall if I told her the reason, or whether I hesitated to give her a reason, or if I assumed she would automatically accept such a decision, as if it were a command to a recruit from a superior. If I did not volunteer a rationale as to my shunning her presence, she must certainly have asked – because what I do remember is this. I told her what the kids at school had told me. At first, she insisted it was all nonsense, that what they had said meant nothing, nothing at all. But I had to keep her away from me, so as not to be seen with her. Indeed, I did not want to *risk* being seen with her. The criticism from my peers at school had been enough to persuade me that they must be right, and that she was wrong, that it was *not* all nonsense. So I did what I had to do. I insulted her – not once, but repeatedly. I just stood there and unleashed every kind of epithet I knew. After a minute of this abuse, her quiet protestations ceased and she finally gave up and walked on. I could sense by her posture that she was dejected, perhaps even devastated, but also angered by the things I had said. She continued on, while I remained standing there, watching her figure recede down the street, further and further distancing herself from me, until I thought it was "safe."

And then I continued to school. I felt only anger and shame – at myself, at her, at everyone else I knew. I felt confused, as if at war with myself. I had said those things to her because I had been made to feel that I had to do it. I had chosen to obey the instructions of my friends. I had succumbed to peer pressure. Their desires had taken priority. After all, they *must* have known better – I *did* have no business being seen on the streets with her. And in acquiescing to their ideas of what was wrong and what was right, I had rejected a good-hearted woman based solely upon her skin color. Indeed, I had told her this in so many words, expressions that boiled up from the irrational. Yet, a part of me argued, the kids at school had to be right. They seemed so confident in their convictions. So in order to get along with them, I felt obliged to go along with their prejudices. Anyway, how could I enjoy school without any friends? I certainly did not want to be labeled the classroom outcast. I wanted to fit in. *That* was how one survived. Without friends, I reasoned, I was nothing.

Thus, as a young White boy, raised and schooled in Texas (see Figure 1), I was indoctrinated into what McIntosh (1989) referred to as "a damaged culture," the tragic product of a dysfunctional, collectivist mindset: "Stay away from them," I was warned. "They're not our kind. Don't go near them. Don't even talk to them. They don't belong in the same neighborhood as us. Don't even touch them. You never know what will rub off. Otherwise, you'll wind up looking like them. Being like them." The message was clear – that those who looked like me were superior to those who did not.

In this small, quiet college town of Denton, where my mother was a graduate business student and teaching intern, I was enrolled in her university's lab elementary school. It consisted of an all-White student body, taught by an all-White faculty. One morning, our second-grade teacher took the class on an excursion – a "field trip" – to the local jail. We were herded upstairs to the holding cells where the inmates were locked up. Every prisoner in there was young, Black, and male. It was a subtle way of reinforcing the same lesson we were taught everywhere else. "They" were to be kept separate from "us" – and it was part of the White police force's implicit duty to see this was done. Separateness, therefore, appeared in the guise of a legal mandate.

When we asked the jailer what the prisoners were fed, he replied that their menu consisted of bread and water – pretty much the same diet we gave our pets. Nothing sweet or enjoyable – just bland, as if they deserved nothing nutritious or tasty. We were told the prisoners were kept there because they were "bad." We did not ask or wonder why they were bad. We, as White children, understood the point of our visit – "they" were not like "us." They were doing penance for having been born the wrong skin color. It did not matter what they had done or *not* done, or what they had been accused of doing. Simply, it was their not being White that had earned them their imprisonment.

From within their cells, they regarded us with disinterest. We could only imagine what was going through their minds. Probably, they felt embarrassed. Not a word was spoken, either by them or us. I remember the tension, and I also recall the immense relief when we were finally told that we would now return to school...End of lesson.

After school was dismissed that afternoon, I sprinted across the college's practice field and through the smoke-filled confines of the expansive Student Union building, where a beat jazz combo (piano, stand-up bass, and drums) entertained a hundred or so college students as they sat at tables conversing and indulging in their snacks and late-afternoon colas. Once I arrived inside the business building, I located my mother (see Figure 2) in the first-floor office she shared with another teacher. I told her about school, beginning of course with the field trip to the town jail. She listened, but she said little in response. From her muted reaction, I drew the inference that this was indeed the way of the world – that Whites were meant to run the affairs of our existence and those who were people of color were destined for a lifetime of bread and water and incarceration. There was no need to question why. Simply, that was the way things were designed. It was therefore assumed by many of us privileged White kids that this was "their" destiny. We were to remain on the outside; *they* were doomed to a life on the inside – hidden away, made invisible to the rest of us.

Figure 2. Kent's mother

On one occasion, during summer vacation from school, my mother and I took a trip to West Texas to visit friends she had known from earlier days in college. We spent much of the time on two-lane rural highways, listening to eclectic Top 40 AM radio stations that played everything from country and rockabilly to rhythm and blues. At one point, Sam Cooke was introduced by a disc jockey, and the interior of our new Ford Galaxie was filled with the sounds of "Having a Party." Sam Cooke, I knew, was one of my mom's favorite performers. Every time his mellow voice was transmitted through the small speaker of our car's radio or the larger, more elaborate high-fidelity system back home, she sang endless praise of him, his voice, his music, his talent. As far as my mother was concerned, he was aces – much more so than Elvis, whom she regarded as nothing more than a hip-swiveling, young pretty-boy.

I knew that Sam Cooke was Black. Why did my mother celebrate African-Americans as entertainers and reject them in any other role? I never commented on this, and I would not allow myself to dwell on the apparent discrepancy between what I had been taught about those who were not of my color and my mother's worshipful attitude toward Sam Cooke, a non-White signer. It just didn't do to contradict Mom. I was just grateful she was enjoying herself.

My mother suffered from mood swings that were surprisingly quick. I would be taught, for example, not to use certain words during conversation, and I was careful to follow her instructions. Then on other occasions, because of apparent frustrations or events I knew nothing about, she would let rip with an obscene interjection. She was by no means a physically abusive parent – though I did receive the sudden slap on the bottom when the situation warranted it. Five years earlier, when we were living further south, in Corpus Christi, she had been widowed at age 26, when my father (see Figure 3) contracted polio and was confined to an iron lung the final months of 1955, passing away the following January. Years later, I learned from my great-aunt that after my dad died, my mother was convinced she could not go on living. Her family had to constantly remind her that she *must* stay alive – because she had something important to live *for*. That something was me. Had it not been for that, according to her aunt, my mother would have taken her own life. As far as she was concerned, my father had been the source of everything worth living.

For my own part, the loss of Dad took a different toll. I was only 3. Before his death, older relatives had discussed with me the likelihood that my father would go away permanently. I recall dismissing the notion as silly. I could not envision it. Yet, when death finally came, I was so traumatized by his

Figure 3. Kent at age two with dad

disappearance that memories of the first three years of my life vanished. Wiped away like a freshly cleaned slate. I am told I was actually present at his funeral. I was reported to have been standing beside his open grave as his body was interred. Yet I can never remember being there.

After Dad's death, my mother decided to go back to work to earn money while a baby-sitter looked after me. Years before, she had been a substitute typing teacher in one of the only two high schools in Corpus Christi, where my parents had initially decided to settle. While pregnant with me, she had been the private secretary to a hard-working Baptist merchant, who was building one of the largest food-store chains in the Southwest. But after I was born, she had quit, devoting herself entirely to raising me.

Now that Dad had passed on, Mom decided to combine her past two jobs – teacher and secretary – into one. Her goal was to move north to Denton, where she had first met my dad, and earn a master's degree in business education. In the fall of 1957, she was accepted into the business department's secretarial-training program, where she took graduate classes in addition to teaching shorthand, typing, and business mathematics. Our years there included the earliest events I am able to recall. And though it is often observed that we remember only the good things that occurred in the past, I have little trouble recalling the bad. Such memories relate to the kind of instances that most others might never reveal. Yet, for me, it no longer makes a difference...

Figure 4. Angie in first grade

During the summer of 1957 when my mother was packing our belongings for the move up north, there lived a 6-year-old girl in a small town just outside of Corpus Christi. She was entertaining a group of neighborhood kids in her back yard. Like me, she had also lost her father early on and had only her mother to depend on. Unlike me, however, she was part of a large family, consisting of a 7-year-old brother and two older sisters. Their mother earned money as a housekeeper, cleaning and cooking for the more well-to-do households in town while the girl's grandmother watched over the kids.

The girl's name was Angie (Figure 4). She was a Latina-American who spoke only Spanish. What little English she knew were phrases she picked up from listening to popular songs on the radio. She was to start school in less than a month and would be attending first grade in a district controlled and run by an Anglo administration and faculty. Ironically, in neighboring Corpus Christi, where I had spent my earliest years, bilingual education had been successfully implemented during the 1940s (Buzbee, 1942); but in the small outlying town in which Angie lived, the powerbrokers had continued delivering an education that was taught exclusively in English by an all-White staff.

In preparation for her initial schooling experience, Angie's sisters taught her as much of the new language as they could. She hosted backyard Kool-Aid parties for her neighborhood friends, where one of their favorite activities involved play-acting to music that contained English lyrics. Angie and her guests would take turns singing "silly" novelty tunes, with words that were easy to remember, from songs like "Along Came Jones" by the Coasters or the Everly Brothers' "Wake Up, Little Susie." The rope-and-board swing that was suspended from a tree branch behind the family's house would serve as the "stage" from which each child would perform. It was a pre-teen Amateur Hour, nothing more. But it was also an effective linguistic tool. By the time school started, Angie had mastered enough rudimentary English to correctly interpret a teacher's instructions to other Latino classmates who were still Spanish-only speakers. These efforts, in fact, would be Angie's first act of teaching – which in itself is part-interpreting – in a lifetime in which she would be rewarded a successful career as a tenured professor at an institution of higher learning.

However, such a future was difficult to imagine back then. Angie's mother had set a goal for her youngest daughter – to work in an office, preferably air-conditioned – an objective totally unrelated to the kind of unskilled labor she performed daily for the various high-income Anglo swells who ruled the town. In 1957, the population of Angie's community consisted mostly of Whites; perhaps one-fourth to one-third were of Hispanic descent. There were very few African-American families; indeed, Angie would encounter no more than one or two Black students during her stay in elementary school, grades one through six.

The same year that my second-grade class in Denton was experiencing the tension of a rare encounter with the Other in the town jail, Angie's neighborhood was the scene of nightly visits by the White constabulary, which ceased upon various Hispanic men with frequent regularity. It was not unusual to hear her sisters discuss which of their friends might have been snatched up by the law during the previous evening. Angie often feared the same fate might await her older brother.

There were times when Angie found school uncomfortable. Once, during a first-grade session when the White teacher asked everyone in class to stand up and tell the class what they had for breakfast, Angie, a self-described "church girl," felt compelled to invent a small lie in order to save herself from embarrassment. Perhaps this instance can be best illustrated in dialogue form.

Imagine you are an audience member in a theatre, anticipating a play that is set over 50 years ago. The playbill you were issued in the lobby informs you that the first scenes are set in a 1950s coastal village in South Texas. As the curtain rises, you observe the following:

A typical classroom of around 20 first-grade students: boys with crew cuts, done up in Butch wax; the girls wearing dresses of varying colors and patterns, most of them clad in White socks. A young woman, MISS CARTER, is perched on a stool, center and down stage, facing slightly away from the audience and directly toward students who are in chairs upstage. We join the scene as MISS CARTER has already begun speaking...

MISS CARTER: ...and I think it might be a good idea if we go in order by the first letter of your first names. All the way from the letter A to the letter Z. Well, Angie, I guess that means you will be the first. Would you like to please stand and tell us what *you* had for breakfast this morning?

ANGIE *(hesitantly and looking down)*:
Uh, I had oatmeal.
Long pause.

MISS CARTER: Okay. Anything else?

ANGIE *(still looking down)*:
No, Miss Carter. Just oatmeal.
(Shorter pause)

MISS CARTER: I see. Well...uh, did you have it with sugar? Butter?

ANGIE:	No, Miss Carter. Just oatmeal.
	(Muffled laughter from one or two students)
MISS CARTER:	Oh. Well…what did you have to drink with it?
ANGIE:	Oh, I can't remember. Milk, I think.
	(Laughter from the children. Angie tenses, tightens her fists)
MISS CARTER:	I see. Well…
	(Lights fade to dark on classroom stage.)

Instead of revealing the truth – that she had actually eaten a taquito – she reported that her morning meal had consisted of oatmeal, a plain food that suggested no cultural overtones. "Why not tell a lie?" she reasoned inwardly. "It's what they want to hear, isn't it? So that's what I'll tell them." Angie's schoolroom perjury was testimony to how quickly she learned to negotiate the cultural divide that was (and is) a part of growing up in the borderlands of South Texas.

***

In Denton, Texas, where my mother and I lived during the late 1950s and early '60s, there was virtually no Hispanic presence in the classroom or anywhere else. The university's lab school was a totally homogenized environment. We of the privileged White faction were an exclusive but large community, and we felt nothing would ever change that. While attending the third grade, I joined a Cub Scout pack that was all-White. Our den-mother was White. We met in her house each Wednesday afternoon after school for milk and cookies, dressed in our dark blue uniforms and bright yellow neck-scarves. We proudly displayed our accomplishments in the form of animal-badges, along with rows of silver and gold arrows that lined our chests like a medal collection. We started a campfire by rubbing two sticks together. For that feat, we were awarded another arrow for our moms to sew on. We taught ourselves to cook our own breakfast. For that, we were awarded another arrow. Joining the Cub Scouts was just another way for me to fit in, to dress up as they did every Wednesday for school. Besides, I thought the uniforms looked splendid.

One afternoon, our troop hiked along a creek bed and plundered what was once the hunting ground of Native-American tribes, digging up old arrowheads – savage reminders of the "bloodthirsty scavengers" of the past who had often pillaged and massacred innocent, peaceful White communities by the hundreds. How did we know this? Our culture, with its cowboys-and-Indians mystique, had told us so. It was a faux history lesson that was played out time and time again in Saturday-afternoon matinees at the downtown movie theatre – or on TV-western serials, where in each episode the wild treachery of the tomahawk-wielding red heathen was conquered and tamed by the brave, "pale-faced" cavalry soldiers who also wore dark blue uniforms and sported bright yellow neck-scarves. We were the good guys who had conquered and tamed a nation of sub-human hostiles.

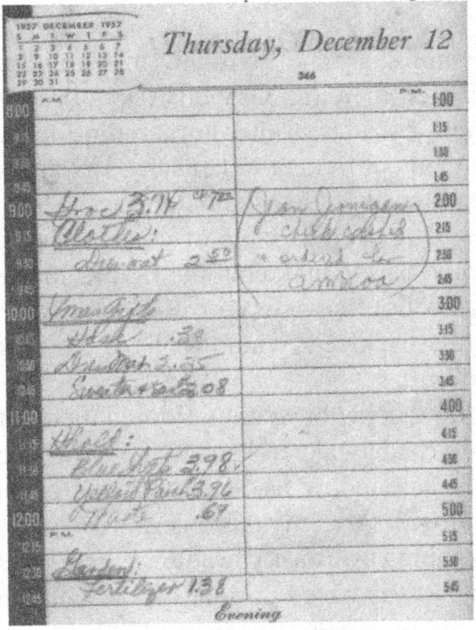

Figure 5. 1957 appointment book, used by Kent's mother for listing items, prices

While being indoctrinated into White privilege, I was not aware that my mother's stressful behavior was the result of her inability to sustain us financially. Even writing down her purchases in a small notebook did not keep her meager budget balanced (see Figure 5). Thus, she would be forced to borrow money from her parents, who owned and worked 125 acres of cotton just outside an agricultural community located 30 miles east of Dallas and about an hour's drive from where we lived. My grandparents gladly parted with whatever money they could in order to make certain their oldest daughter and grandson were reasonably solvent. As a teaching intern in a small-town college, my mother was often urged to attend as many

25

out-of-town conventions for business educators as she could afford. She must have enjoyed going to these functions because there were many times when I was left with my grandparents, due to one convention or another.

My grandparents swore by the Pentecostal faith, a belief that included a suspicion of all things Catholic, including Presidential candidates. In 1960, Granddad and Grandma would refuse to vote a straight Democratic ticket for the first time in their lives, all because John F. Kennedy was a "papist." And Catholics were just one of many segments they despised. But while I stayed with them, they took good care of me and kept me well-fed and well-indoctrinated.

One summer evening around twilight, my grandparents and I were returning from a church meeting. Granddad was driving us in his Pontiac the usual way home – by a street that bordered a rural shanty-town of dirt roads lined with unpainted, rickety old shacks. It was the segregated other-side-of-the-tracks existence of East Texas Americana. As we skirted the edge of this desolate area, I noticed a group of young black men, some of them carrying sticks. I could barely make out the figures in the dying light of that summer's evening. Feeling the safety of distance and four wheels beneath me, I rolled down the back-seat window of the car and began screaming, "Hey, you n_____s!"

My granddad, yelling at me to shut up, floored the Pontiac in the direction of the farm-to-market road to take us back to the farm. I kept looking through our speeding car's rear window as Shanty-town's occupants ran after us. When we arrived home safe, my bare legs received a painful lashing, administered by Grandma with a flyswatter. I then sat through my second sermon of the night; it was based on that oft-quoted Biblical verse: "Thou shalt not do a dumb thing like that ever again!" And I swore I never would.

***

Throughout her pre-school years in the South Texas community where she was brought up, Angie never intermingled with White children or Anglo families. Her first up-close exposure to the son of one of the parents her mother worked for was in class during her very first day of school. That was the moment she realized she would be learning beside the children of those who employed her mother to clean their houses.

Angie resented the White authority that compelled her to assimilate by telling lies, as she had done when asked what she ate for breakfast. She objected to the necessity of committing such an act in order to survive in a community ruled by a people different from hers. And if a condition exists where it is not advisable to be true to others (or even to oneself)…well, if this is not a subtle form of colonization, then what is?

If they could do this to her, make her invent lies for teachers and strangers with lighter skin than hers, she was determined that those who represented authority in her small town would never see her cry. No matter how hurt, no matter how embarrassed she felt in front of others, no matter how ridiculed or degraded – no one would ever bear witness to the shedding of her tears. A six-year-old *Mexicana* could weep alone; but never in front of others. And certainly not in the presence of the White teachers and children in her school.

One day, Angie's class was practicing reading skills. Her teacher had instructed that if they ever encountered an unfamiliar word, they were to sound it out, syllable by syllable, and eventually they would be able to figure out just what the word was. Learning by phonetics. One by one, each student was asked to read aloud from her/his class reader:

SCENE TWO: *Miss Carter's first grade class, Spring 1958.*

MISS CARTER: Now children, open your books and turn to page 14…Angie, would you please read aloud while the rest of us follow along?

ANGIE *(slowly)*: "Dick and Spot will meet Jane at the beach. Run, Dick, run. It is getting dark. Dick and Spot will go to…to…to…"

MISS CARTER *(interrupting)*:
Say aloud each syllable of the word, Angie.

ANGIE: To. Get. Her.
(Laughter from the class)

MISS CARTER *(who, in spite of herself, cannot stop laughing either)*:
No, no, no, it's "together."
BLACKOUT of stage right as the children's laughter abruptly stops. ANGIE emerges quickly from the blackness, appearing to be on the verge of tears. But she is determined to hold them back. Her voice trembles but only at the beginning of her next speech.

ANGIE *(addressing herself)*:
Never let them see you cry… Then, I will go *home* and cry. Or on the way home, I will cry. But they are not going to see me cry.
She walks offstage, as the lights fade …

27

For Angie, the risk of making herself appear foolish in school was just one of many hardships. The house she lived in had no running water and thus in order for her and other family members to obey the call of nature, they had to attend to such needs in an out-house located behind their residence. Occasionally, her friends would invite her into *their* homes; and Angie would be overcome with envy and resentment that *they* lived in a house with hot and cold running water, not to mention two parents at home, while she had none of these things. She found it difficult to accept that those items her friends took for granted were also the ones that seemed a luxury to her.

However, Angie's mother was able to maintain enough credit to buy clothes for her family from a national mail-order vendor, who shipped them from out of state. She no longer wished to shop in any of the stores of her town because the White owners frequently watched and trailed her to make certain she did not exit with anything unpaid for. Although the money she made as a housekeeper was a paltry sum, she managed to save enough to buy a set of encyclopedias for the children to augment their learning at school. Thus, whenever she assisted them with their homework and her son or one of her daughters asked, "What is this?" or "What does that mean?" she would simply tell them, "Well, let's look it up in one of those books, *mija*. That's why we got them."

As a youngster, Angie thought of her contemporaries as belonging in one of two categories. Hispanic boys were either "wild boys" or "passive boys." And when girls were referenced, they were cataloged as either "wild girls" or "church girls." Angie was a church girl. The Catholic religion provided her with a solid spiritual foundation. It was the Church that facilitated Angie's self-discovery later on in her teens. It also gave her the opportunity to interact with many girls her own age. Her best friend, however, was one she did not meet at church, but at the place that provided her much discomfort – school.

SCENE THREE: *Elementary School playground, fall of 1957.*

A small section of playground divided in two by a high fence. On the one side is a young first-grade Latina with short dark straight hair and a pink dress she has worn many times since the previous Easter. She is crying and sniffling. ANGIE enters from the right and approaches the crying girl.

ANGIE:	What's wrong?
GIRL:	*(Starts to cry louder)*
ANGIE:	Can I help?

GIRL:	¡Vayase!¹
ANGIE *(In Spanish)*:	Please, not till you tell me what upsets you?
GIRL:	*(Crying has turned into annoying sniffling)*
ANGIE:	Well, all right… *(She turns to leave)*
GIRL *(in Spanish)*:	They say they cannot understand me?
ANGIE *(in English)*:	*Who* says they say they cannot understand you?
GIRL *(in Spanish)*:	Them. *(Pointing in a direction where other children are playing.)*
	From here, all dialogue is spoken in Spanish.
GIRL:	Anything I say, they laugh at me. They call me names. "Wetback." "Chuca." One boy said in Spanish, "Why don't you go back where you came from?" *(Pause, then continues)* I think that is what he said. I could barely understand him.
ANGIE:	Forget it. That is gringo-talk. Gringo-talk from coconuts who think they are better than others and all because their families swam the Rio Bravo before the others. Do not let it bother you. *(Pause)* You should hear my older sisters when they sass back to the *pochos*. And like typical coconuts, they understand none of it… Oh, and some of the things they say to the *gringo* boys. *(Laughs suddenly)* It is good that the gringos cannot understand a word they say to them – otherwise *(and here, she makes a motion with her finger as if slitting her throat.)*
GIRL *(Laughing too)*:	I would like to have been there.
ANGIE *(after a pause)*:	I am called Angie.
GIRL:	I am called Linda. *(Pause)* But my mother now calls me Florecita, after the girl in *Los Gavilanes*…
ANGIE:	Ah, the sombrero movie. My uncle took us to see that one at the drive-in last summer. I *adore* Pedro Infante.
LINDA:	What is a "drive-in?"
ANGIE:	A huge outdoor parking lot where people stop their cars at night and look at movies.

29

LINDA:	They show movies here from Mexico?
ANGIE:	Not here; but in the city. I heard our mother once say, "Herd enough of us into one place, and they cannot but help to find new ways to take our money."
LINDA:	I think I would like to go to a drive-in... ANGIE *(in English)*: Tough luck, Linda. You'll need a car first. And driving lessons... *(And then, in Spanish)* Now repeat the words I have just spoken... *(In English, slowly)* Tough luck, Linda.
LINDA *(also in English)*:	Tough luck, Linda.
ANGIE:	You need a car.
LINDA:	You need a car...

Angie and Linda soon discovered they lived just down the street from one another. And though they did not share the same classes, they maintained their friendship. With Angie's help and Linda's own diligence, she overcame the linguistic divide of a borderlands existence – learning and speaking English at school during the day, then switching back to Spanish when she came home. If there was one overriding characteristic shared among nearly all of Angie's Latino classmates, it was this constant navigation, back and forth between two languages, two cultures. Years later, Angie would look upon her multi-lingual experience as something to be not simply acknowledged, but celebrated.

Angie's marginalization at school and in town was not one of her own choosing. Mine was. Sometime during the third grade, I noticed I was more comfortable when isolated from others. As the son of a widowed mother, I felt different. Like Angie, I knew of no one among my contemporaries who did not have both a mother and a father at home. Even with the few I considered friends, I felt distanced. Slowly, I withdrew from everyone at school or at the church we attended. Unlike Angie, religion was never a heavy consideration in my life. I desired neither to suffer from hurt nor to inflict suffering on others. In so doing, I became my own best friend and my own worst enemy.

Angie could depend on Linda, her family, and many others from church; I relied on my mother and no one else, but I found I preferred it that way (see Figure 6). During the summer between the second and third grades, I often walked alone from our house, located just off campus, all the way down to where the freeway from Dallas intersected with our street. I then proceeded north along the frontage road for a mile or so to an underpass beneath the

Figure 6. Kent at age of 5, Christmas alone

highway. There, I sat beneath the bridge and held conversations with an imaginary friend who rode an imaginary bicycle. Thus, at the age of 8, I was creating dialogues in my own head with another boy who did not even exist. I found it less stressful than having a real person to talk to or someone who might respond with words I had not thought up or with a verbal comeback I had not anticipated. It felt safer than actually coping with someone who might suddenly become angry should I say or do the wrong things. I not only avoided confrontation; I hid from it. So instead of having conversations with others, I made them up with an invisible boy. In other words, I was conducting dialogues with myself.

It always seemed an easy model to copy, this business of dialoging. One entity talked, the other listened. There was no overlap. And no instance where one person asked the other to repeat himself. It was a little boy's dream – completely unreal. Years later, I would find that I was most attracted to readings in dialogue form, whether they appeared in the plays of Shakespeare in high school or an Oriana Fallaci interview with a political figure in one of my mother's magazines.

***

From the time of my childhood in Denton, a life of distant observation was all I ever desired. Over the years since, I have socialized with others on occasion, watching sports on TV with a small group of acquaintances or participating in bowling leagues and so forth. Yet, the friendships never last long. No real bonds are felt. Part of the reason is internal – if I begin to feel close to anyone, I back away. The possibility of commitment to anything or anyone still causes me considerable discomfort. It always has. I could explore this condition, probe it, rationalize it, intellectualize it – but to what avail?

However, I discovered in my early 40s that I could commit myself to the idea of education. Before she passed away in 1980, my mother had predicted repeatedly that I would become a teacher. I resisted the notion. Me? A teacher? Yet here I am, over 30 years later, almost 20 of which I have spent as an adjunct instructor of college English. Teaching is something I do well. I enjoy it increasingly with each passing semester, and I feel as though I will never burn out, as many others do. It is the only productive endeavor in which I have been involved. I consider teaching *my* reason for living.

The profession of education was also the locus at which the life of Angie and my own intersected. At the time, I had just moved into a faculty office almost directly across the hall from hers. We hardly spoke to one another during that time. For years, we knew each other only in passing. Until I began our series of audio-recorded dialogues in the spring of 2009, we never carried on any meaningful conversation. Until then, education was the only thing we shared in common. The fact that we could tick off the same cultural reference points was of little consequence; we could do that with almost anyone of our generation. We were both born in the same geographical region. Angie was schooled there; I was too, beginning in 1964 (grades 7–12) when my mother was offered a teaching position at the college where Angie and I currently hold classes. Yet apart from those commonalities, we are different in every imaginable way.

In reflecting on Angie's childhood experiences in relation to my own, I am struck by the differences in the directions our lives took. In high school, Angie became an activist and a supporter of causes for which she still feels a passionate commitment. She took an interest in the widening multicultural environment that South Texas has evolved into since the 1960s and today she continues to transform the lives of many college students, regardless of their gender or ethnicity. She is a soft-spoken crusader for new, innovative cultural-affairs curricula, yet she remains under the publicity radar. Angie, unlike me, *was* committed.

What will follow in subsequent sections of this story will include an interweaving of the following components: (1) excerpts from interviews that I, the researcher, conducted with Angie; (2) reflective pieces by the researcher and his graduate-school mentor on the subject of cross-cultural research in general and on the intersections between the researcher and the researched that resulted from this collaboration; and (3) excerpts from a two-act ethnodrama that seeks to interpret the data from my interviews with Angie through the consciousness of me, the researcher and the play's author.

NOTE

[1]   Go away!

CHAPTER 2

BREAKING TENSIONS, BUILDING BRIDGES

The White anthropologist claimed that Indians are unsophisticated, that their minds are too primitive, that they cannot think in the "highest" mode of consciousness, rationality. These anthropologists split the world of imagination from the world of the spirit from the world of the soul from waking conscious reality, defining external reality as the official reality. The alarm goes off, you get up and go to your job. You cross the street. You buy groceries. You pay the bills. This reality is privileged over the others. But there is another world, and it crops up when we least expect it...when we're sitting and go in and out of different states of consciousness.

(Anzaldúa, 2009, pp. 105–106)

KAKALI'S NARRATIVE

August 2012. A strange parcel arrives in my mailbox at work one day – a small, brown package decoratively wrapped in a royal-blue satin ribbon. Checking the return address, I gasp when I see the name of the sender – *Caroline Sherritt*. I clutch the brown box in my hand, run to my office, and slam the door. I jump on the flimsy teal-blue futon couch in my office, curl into a fetal position, and start to cry. I keep one hand over my mouth so as not to be overheard, the other hand still holding the box.

Caroline Sherritt passed away two weeks ago, when she lost her battle with colon cancer. Caroline, a White woman in her 60s, was a full professor, a colleague, a mentor, a friend, blunt to a fault, with a loving heart, and open to interrogating privileges when someone would point out her blind spots. Caroline and I would have long, deep conversations about life, culture, our predispositions and prejudices, students we had in common, and our futile efforts to save people, especially men who seem to be lost.

How did this package arrive *now*, a half month after she has passed away? Caroline had spent her last few days in unbearable pain. She had lost an incredible amount of weight and seemed to be disappearing right in front of our eyes. The doctors had given her two weeks to live and told her to make peace with her life and say her goodbyes. At the time I was beginning

35

the school year as an Associate Professor at Texas A & M-Corpus Christi, Caroline had seemed relatively healthy, optimistic, and was preparing to teach her Fall Semester classes online. But after she was given the final timeline, she decided to spend her last few days in Florida with her son. She often invited me to visit her. I promised I would; but I never did. And now I hold this package, unable to understand how she managed to wrap and send it during her illness.

I think of my mother's cancer, which was diagnosed at the same time as Caroline's. I think of how easily I avoid calling or visiting my mother, because I dread hearing bad news or facing the thought of her absence in the world. I feel guilty now for not visiting Caroline – or my mother – because I prioritized work. I cannot separate myself from the overwhelming feelings of pain, shame, regret, loss, grief, and deep sadness running through me. I am reluctant to open this package, fearing it would only serve to linger my relationship with Caroline a bit longer. However, as I rise now from my office couch, I slowly unwrap it.

Inside, I find a Christmas greeting card wishing me a good holiday season. I also discover a small cube-shaped White box. I open it to reveal what seems to be the prettiest bird I have ever seen, designed out of mosaic gem colored stain glass. It might make a nice Christmas tree ornament. But instead, I decide to mount the bird on my car's rear-view mirror so that I can see it every day, not just during Christmas. I envision Caroline purchasing this present somewhere on her travels, thoughtfully packaging it for me before her illness incapacitated her. And now that she has passed away, I realize it must have been her son who forwarded the gift to me.

It was Caroline who had introduced me to Kent in 2009. She first told me about Kent in a conversation that went something like this:

Scenography: *I am sitting on my office couch, working on some emails on my laptop. My feet are stretched out on the ottoman in front of me. The door to my office is slightly ajar. Mellow classical piano music plays faintly in the background. The only other place to sit in the office is my chair facing the desk against the wall.*
                     CAROLINE approaches the doorway to my office.
CAROLINE: Got a minute?
KAKALI: Um, yeah, sure.
                     She pulls up the chair and sits down.
CAROLINE: I have this student. I don't know what to do with him.

KAKALI: Why? Is he giving you trouble?
CAROLINE: Not trouble, just a headache.
            KAKALI laughs.
CAROLINE: Well, his name is Kent. He is an intellectual, a really strong thinker, but he just thinks weird things and I cannot get him to focus on a dissertation topic.
KAKALI: Okay.
CAROLINE: I think you should work with him. Get him in your class. You two can talk your weird language. Students seem to come out of your class and talk in tongues.
            KAKALI bursts out laughing.
CAROLINE: (*smiles*) It's like you have your own groupies. Talk some sense into Kent. His research topic changes every day. The other day his bus was late or didn't pick him up, and now he wants to study the Corpus Christi bus system. He is all over the place.
            KAKALI laughs.
CAROLINE: And he's a film buff. He keeps sending me stuff on all sorts of old films. They are lovely and some I use in my classes too. But I just don't know how to get him to commit to a topic. So I am handing him over to you.
KAKALI: Okie-dokie. I'll email him and set up a meeting. Thank you… I think.
            CAROLINE gets up and leaves the office as if she was in a hurry or as if there was no other purpose to be in that space.

***

After my conversation with Caroline, I see that my advanced data analysis class has a student enrolled, named Kent Gillen for the Spring 2009 semester. From 2009 onwards, Kent takes all the qualitative classes that I offer at that institution. Kent performs brilliantly in all my classes. However, a year later, as we are moving toward the end of the dissertation process a week before his scheduled defense, I notice that while Kent has written an ethnodrama of a Chicana educator experiencing de/segregated schooling in the 1950s and 1960s in South Texas, he is not interrogating his White male privileges. Both Caroline and I have asked him repeatedly for the past year and a half to consider his positionality in relation to his research, but I have not seen any change in his work to suggest that he has done this. I have sent him an email asking him to unpack his privileges, and today we meet to discuss the content of my email (first introduced in Kent's narrative, Chapter One).

Kent,

There is something that has been bothering me deeply from the onset of this project. It is your refusal to identify the privileges that you carry with you as a White man. [You must] identify unearned privileges that people have as part of the subject position(s) they occupy in our social structure. White male ranks at the top of the list. Yet nowhere in your dissertation that I have read so far have you unpacked your privileges in relation to the participant's. I am not sure if you didn't understand that you needed to do this or if I have been unclear or if you are simply resisting this to dismiss this idea as irrelevant to your work. However, if you do not identify the privileges with which you carry yourself and construct knowledge about this world, you are situating yourself as ahistorical, value-neutral, acultural, in the context of the participants' experiences. Therefore, you would automatically fall into the trap of the colonizing White gaze that describes the exotic other...

This isn't an issue of identity politics, which you have argued in your dissertation. It is an issue of identifying that you too, as White man, carry with you values, assumptions, beliefs, epistemologies, and privileges that shape the way you see and process the world...If you do not unpack that in your dissertation, you are leaving [out] a key part out of your dissertation and as such it would be incomplete. If you resist identifying and acknowledging any of this, then you [are] claiming that your subject position has no influence on how you have constructed knowledge or understanding in this research.

KB

I realize the task ahead of me. I am a faculty of color mentoring a student who has White male privileges. I am also younger than my student and as such have not lived in the research site he has occupied most of his life. And we have to grapple, together, with just what it means for a White man to write about the life of a Chicana educator and why he has chosen to have an omnipotent narrator-voice, instead of unpacking his relationship with the study. Through all this, one question continues to linger in my mind about his entry point to this study, especially since he has been discussing Chicana feminism in his work. During his proposal meeting which occurred months earlier, the committee had asked him to fully flesh out his justification for using Chicana feminism in his work. I have not seen that justification in his current version of the dissertation draft.

While there are some perspectives that privilege the notion that only cultural insiders can engage in research relationships with participants that are similar to them, there are other schools of thoughts that advocate for ethical cross-cultural research. However, this work of bridge building across culture is not easy and one can argue that such bridge building is necessary for promoting a concept of empathy, shared humanity, extending privileges, and creating spaces for healing. I have not heard Kent speak of any of this, nor do I think such ideas are subtly or subversively embedded in his work. What I fear is that his writing has not reflected the kind of thoughtful, critical interrogation needed to understand his position.

On one hand, Kent is an extremely socially-conscious, progressive-minded individual. He understands social inequity better than most of my students. He would engage me in political conversations and situate himself as a progressive socialist. We would talk about what it means for people like us to live in a "red state" like Texas, a setting for extremely social, political, and religious conservativism. Truth be told, I have enjoyed having these conversations with Kent, in a locale where such conversations are not always welcomed. Kent is also able to theorize social inequities by mapping lived experiences into a broader sociopolitical discourse in ways that have made his peers envious of his skills in class. They respect him for the wisdom and depth he brings to his work. He is conscious about how he treats people and lives his life with as much ethical integrity as he can. He is self-aware and reflexive and open to learning things that are unfamiliar to him. He reads everything I assign him to read and finds additional readings. Sometimes he comes to meetings having read everything I might have published on some subject and cite my writing back to me to discuss his thoughts around certain ideas. I have never had to push him, as he has always been intrinsically motivated to write. If anything, I have had a hard time keeping up with his pace to give him detailed feedback in a timely manner. In so many ways, whatever might make Kent "weird" is what I appreciate the most about Kent, and I consider him to be an exemplary student and generally look forward to our discussions.

However, like any of us, Kent still has some work to do, regardless of how progressive and open-minded he is. He, like most scholars, is sometimes afflicted with complacency – the kind of dismissive attitude that may occur to us because of the blind spots in our own thinking, those that are difficult to discern, or those that are rendered virtually invisible. Thus, we need others to assist us in recognizing the presence of those blind spots. Today is one of those days when I, inhabiting the body of a woman, a minority educator, will have to emphasize how power and oppression work to benefit White men, like Kent, for the simple reason that he belongs to a privileged group, regardless of whether he is aware of those benefits or has ever asked for them. I am uncertain how this conversation will proceed, but I hope that as long as I keep my integrity intact, we should be able to build bridges. Further, I am hoping Kent's ultimate motive to do this work is *not* just to complete his dissertation. Instead, I am hoping he will be interested in extending his work further, considering additional implications and building more on that accomplishment in the future.

Kent knocks on my door, walks into my office, and slumps down in the chair across from my desk. Initially, as a teacher, I had devised an open-office arrangement, where the students and I would sit at the same side, decentering power, to discuss their work. Over the years, however, I found it necessary to use my desk as a barrier between the students and me, as my decentering efforts resulted in boundary-crossing in ways I found uncomfortable. Such decentering, I discovered, was perceived as an excuse by some students not to extend the same respect to me as they did to my White counterparts. This lack of respect would include a neglect to address me by my professional designation, while referring to my White colleagues by theirs. Sometimes students would call me *hun, darlin', sweety,* and *dear.* Other times, they would dismiss my professional expertise, as if the ideas I shared were just casual opinions, not generated from years of professional engagement in my discipline. Unfortunately, such dismissiveness occurred much more frequently from White students than from students of traditionally underrepresented backgrounds. Reflecting on such experiences, I realized my obligation to readjust the tone for my interaction with students and how I situate myself, my body, literally, in relation to the students who visit my office – and thus to establish and maintain some boundaries.

"Hi, Kent. How's it going?"

"Well, you tell me. What did you think of the draft?" Kent seems anxious to me.

"We have a lot to talk about today. Let's start with Chicana feminism."

"Okay." I think Kent might have sighed a little.

"Tell me. What is your entry point to Chicana feminism in your work? We wanted you to flesh this out at the proposal meeting. I am interested in hearing your thoughts." I am hoping that Kent would have some answer, or some things to share about how he might have been thinking about this topic.

"Entry point? What's that?" Kent is genuinely surprised.

"Entry point, as in how are you entering this conversation about Chicana feminism, when you're not Chicana or a woman. What is the bridge building work that you're doing here?" I am expecting that this explanation should clear things up.

"Entry point? I don't know really about an entry point, other than the fact that I entered the library and got the books I needed on Chicana feminism and read them."

My eyes widen. I slam my hand on my desk and say, "That's exactly it! That is the only entry point that you have at the moment! This is highly problematic because essentially you're saying that as long as you study some books, that somehow you can write about someone else's life, without interrogating your role as the narrator of such stories." I surprise myself with what came out of my mouth. I did say that out loud, didn't I?

"Okay. So what should I do?"

"Start at the basics. Read Peggy McIntosh's work, "White Privilege, Unpacking the Invisible Knapsack." You should be able to find it online. Then think of how you benefit from some of those invisible privileges."

"What about the writing I've done so far?"

"I can't really comment on any of it unless it is layered with your positionality. Right now, that piece is alarmingly absent." I try not to sound dismissive, but it might be too late.

"Okay, I'll go to the library and get the article then." Kent sounds dejected as he gets up to leave the office.

After he is gone, I begin to think of how troubling a position I am in – where I have to teach someone who enjoys privileges that he benefits from a social structure that is intentionally designed with *his* needs in mind, rendering people like me invisible or irrelevant, unless there is an interest convergence. And because he did not ask for any of it, and because he is a progressive-minded thinker, he cannot be held responsible for what he seems to benefit from without his advocacy for such benefits. And then, on the other hand, I am in a position of some power and authority in relation to Kent as his dissertation advisor, the gatekeeper that can either make or break his academic success. I am in this position to bring some awareness of how one can belong to a dominant social group and be complicit in the social structure of oppression that benefits him, even if he is personally a decent, ethical, socially conscious person. In other words, as an able-bodied person, I benefit from easy access to wherever I want to go, how I want to use the bathroom, etc., without ever asking for this privilege. Yet, someone with a disability in a wheelchair, say an army veteran, would not enjoy the same benefits that I do, even though I am not personally oppressing people with disabilities. We both live in a society where there are systems of inequities from which we benefit or suffer differently. What I am doing to Kent is shocking his sense of complacency to show him that there is work that needs to be done, and we all have to be part of that work. And then I have to be a gatekeeper to ensure that he has done some of that work or at least attempted to do *some* of that work. I am extremely uncomfortable and unsettled in this position, and yet I am compelled to disrupt the consciousness with which the current work is presented to me, where Whiteness is rendered as normal, acultural, ahistorical, value-neutral, and bestowed with authority to tell the story of others without interrogating its own historicity. If my relationship with power and authority were to be expressed as a Facebook relationship status, I would have to select, "It's complicated."

***

There are ghosts in our writing. Kent and I have often talked about how grateful we are to Caroline for introducing us, one of the primary reasons why this book is dedicated to her. But as we write our narratives, we carry with us ghostly whispers from stories that are in our consciousness. I have written about my interactions with Caroline elsewhere (Bhattacharya & Varbelow, 2014), illustrating how we have both challenged each other in our positions when it comes to race and power in higher education, but always with love, with generosity of spirit, and with an intent to engage in bridge-building work. We have always recognized that we are all works-in-progress and there is more work to be done by all of us, regardless of how ethical and progressive we might be. For example, if Caroline approached me with some question about India, assuming I can speak about and for *all* of India and its people, I have challenged her assumption and told her that she would be better off using Google or any of our library's databases to find the answers. Caroline, in her generous nature, understood the implications of my suggestion and admitted, "I guess I wouldn't be able to answer every single question about America either if someone asked me something similar." On the other hand, when I resisted teaching a course titled *Multicultural Analysis for Educational Leaders* because I thought I was being tokenized as a faculty of color, Caroline called bullshit on that. Literally. She screamed the word. "Bullshit!" She then reminded me that I have prior experience teaching similar courses in graduate school, that my research agenda is focused on cultural issues and power, that I am imminently qualified, and that our students need to hear from an expert and not someone who is tokenized, but someone who would challenge provincial and ethnocentric thinking.

Sometimes I carry on conversations with Caroline in my head. She has become my inner bullshit-detecting, critical White ally. I consider us both to be works-in-progress regardless of where our consciousness exists. Caroline has passed away, yet this does not prevent a continued relationship with her. Here is how a conversation with Caroline occurs:

CAROLINE: What are we talking about today?

KAKALI: Am I being too naïve about my inclusion and have a blind spot towards my tokenism?

CAROLINE: Oh, that "token" thing again? Are we going to keep talking about this?

KAKALI: Yes, we will, forever and forever. So there.

CAROLINE: Sheesh. Okay, fine. Rest in peace is a bullshit saying then.

KAKALI: Your fault for being in my head.

CAROLINE: Okay, let's hear it then. What's going on with your token self?

KAKALI: Well, I wonder if my inclusion in these predominantly White spaces makes me complacent and blind to my tokenism?

CAROLINE: Bullshit!

KAKALI: Uh-huh! I thought you'd say that. I think that sometimes it is easy to feel complacent when you get to be in spaces where people like you are usually absent. There is a sense that you have made it. But then it is just being a token in a broader White supremacist system and that does nothing to challenge the oppression created by the system.

CAROLINE: Bullshit!

KAKALI: Are there any other words that you might care to use? Or just this one?

CAROLINE: I am calling bullshit on this. First, the fact that you're asking this question already makes you not complacent in the system. Second, let me ask you a question. Do you go with the flow and just think I have made it and try to achieve personal success, or do you think your job is more than personal success?

KAKALI: My job is much more than my personal success.

CAROLINE: What does your job entail?

KAKALI: I think I am unapologetic about the perspectives I bring from my sensibilities arising from my consciousness, my socio-cultural location, and my body being in these predominantly White spaces.

CAROLINE: Yes, you are. And you need to keep pushing those perspectives forward in your work, in your teaching, in committee work, in your writing. That is the only way you can use your presence in this system to challenge your feelings of tokenism.

KAKALI: Bullshit! Okay, not bullshit. Just joking. I had to say it too, come on. That makes sense. Thank you.

CAROLINE: Yes, yes, I am very wise nowadays. Time for my coffee with Maya Angelou. Talk to you later.

For any kind of bridge-building work to occur, I have to situate myself within the academic spaces in which I work and what influences my thinking. I identify as a scholar who is informed by de/colonized epistemologies and transnational theories. It is important to unpack what these terms mean and how they shape my worldview so that my engagement with Kent, the tensions in that engagement, and my struggle with the complicated intersections where I find myself in academia could be further elaborated. Some of what I write next is a demonstration of the scholarly works I am curating for the reader to further explore and cite in their own academic journeys. And some of what I am writing is a demonstration of how several scholars who came before me made powerful arguments that stay with me when I engage in de/colonizing epistemologies and transnationalism.

De/colonizing epistemologies represent certain ways of knowing intersected by colonizing ways of knowing and the ways in which such ways of knowledge-making are disrupted by decolonizing sensibilities. Colonizing ways of knowing represents an invasion into native/indigenous ways of knowledge-making, rendering such a process primitive, uncivilized, while co-opting and stealing existing knowledge-making structures and rebranding them into something that is perceived to be superior or civilized. Additionally, colonizing ways of knowledge-making also attempt to invade or erase indigenous/native ways of knowing as irrelevant and impose a western sensibility where a power hierarchy is established, where knowledge-making is legitimized through benchmarks established by western scholars. I write de/colonizing with a slash in the word because I do not think there is a pure space where the effects of colonizing knowledge-making are absent. Even the mere mention of the term *decolonizing* marks an already existing relationship with colonizing discourses.

Linda Tuhiwai Smith's (1999) work opened me up to a process of de/colonizing my mind and my methodologies. Smith (1999) demonstrates how knowledge-making is privileged in academia, given the journals where scholarly work has been published, the language it has been published in, and cultural locations from where the work has been generated. Thus, Smith (1999) shows how knowledge-making from White researchers is considered legitimate, scholarly, and worthy, while rendering knowledge-making that occurs in the margin to be pedestrian and unworthy of academic attention. She argues:

> Academic knowledges are organized around the idea of disciplines and fields of knowledge. These are deeply implicated in each other and share genealogical foundations in various classical and Enlightenment philosophies. Most of the 'traditional' disciplines are grounded in cultural worldviews which are either antagonistic to other belief systems or have no methodology for dealing with other knowledge systems. Underpinning all of what is taught in universities is the belief in the concept of science as the all-embracing method for gaining an understanding of the world. (Smith, 1999, p. 65)

In other words, Smith's argument challenges current academic systems of knowledge for being unresponsive to belief systems that are traditionally marginalized and silenced. Consequently, when knowledge is produced from those previously ignored cultural spaces, they are considered "less adequate, less 'universal' and less 'scientific' – in other words, inferior" (Harrison, 1997, p. 6). So what does this mean then when I work with Kent, where I am well trained to succeed in academia, given my English language training, my educational upbringing in mostly Western countries, my exemplary graduate school preparation? Have I been complicit of the very same oppressive forces that I critique? Do I sound like a total hypocrite when I extend a criticism to the very system that educated and employed me? What exactly is my role as a "Third World" woman in Western academia? Have I been produced as a co-opted product of higher education and only now am I trying to resist it?

Mohanty (1991) reminds me to open up the category of the "Third World" woman as more than a singular, monolithic subject, thereby creating a colonized Other. She reminds me the complicated ways in which I am situated in academia and that there is no easy settling, defining my position just like there is no easy settling or defining how oppression works. What I do begin to think of is the energy-draining exercise in which we engaged when we continue to run up against an oppressor/oppressed binary relationship. Somehow it seems like a trap to me, almost like a distraction, because as long as we are engaged in this binary, we are engaged in thinking in opposition to the oppressor or oppressive discourses, instead of imagining what might lie beyond this binary, beyond this relationship.

But I cannot deny the realities, the material truths of lived experiences as a "Third World" scholar situated in Western academia, yet rendered in/visible by colonizing discourses. How would de/colonizing epistemologies function for people whose histories, cultures, and traditions have not been written or written from anglo-andro perspectives? Mutua and Swadener (2004) write:

> For most scholars of color and their allies we are the 'colonized,' feeling the consequences of the Eurocentric, scientifically driven epistemologies in which issues of power and voice are drowned by the powerful 'majority' players, reflecting the master's ideology. For us, *there is no postcolonial,* as we love our daily realities in suffocating spaces forbidding our perspectives, our creativity, and our wisdom. (p. ix)

Mutua and Swadener's situatedness illustrates the complexities of being an academic and attempting to "voice" de/colonizing perspectives while strategically negotiating their own colonizing positions. Echoing the complexity of a de/colonizing scholar in western academia, Smith (1999) examines the role of the native researcher:

> Currently, the role of 'native' intellectual has been reformulated not in relation to nationalist or liberatory discourses but in relation to the 'post-colonial' move across the boundaries of indigenous and metropolitan, institution and community, politics and scholarship. Their place in the academy is still highly problematic. Gayatri Spivak, who writes as a post-colonial Asian/Indian intellectual working in the

United States, argues that Third World intellectuals have to position themselves strategically as intellectuals within the academy, within the Third World or indigenous world and within the Western world in which many intellectuals actually work. (p. 71)

Smith and Spivak's argument about strategic positioning along multiple groups of audiences further complicates how one can remain vigilant about the contradictions of being a "native" researcher. The term "native researcher" is contradictory because membership in the native community is troubled by being a researcher in a non-native community and the membership in Western academia is met with many types of gatekeeping and negotiations through which production of knowledge is mitigated. Thus, interrogating who is listening, who is speaking, and what gets said and heard become critical points of analysis to construct de/colonizing epistemologies. Spivak elaborates:

> For me, the question 'Who should speak' is less crucial than 'Who will listen?' 'I will speak for myself as a Third World person' is an important position for political mobilization today. But the real demand is that, when I speak from that position, I should be listened to seriously, not with that kind of benevolent imperialism. (Spivak, 1990, p. 59)

I sit with these words. I do not want benevolent imperialism. I do not want anyone to save me. I want to dialogue. I want to build bridges. I want to work with allies. I do not want to live in Us-versus-Them spaces. I want to believe that together, as a human race, we have a shared humanity that is powerful and we can hold space for that shared humanity as well as our sociocultural differences simultaneously. We do not have to engage in a new contest of Oppression Olympics. We do not have to minimize anyone's pain and suffering, but we cannot ignore systemic forms of oppression either that create collective pain and suffering for our fellow human beings. We can hold all these contradictory ideas simultaneously in one space.

With Kent, somewhere in our relationship, we both have an unsaid understanding that we are allies – that I always have his best interest and he always will hear me seriously, not benevolently, but with care and concern. And as an educator, I am also responsible for pushing him out of his comfort zone, where things feel bad, heavy, dense, and have him work through those emotions to come to a place of understanding. I cannot, in any possible way, make discussion about oppression and privileges comfortable. Nor should I be expected to. This is difficult and painful work for all of us. It is not palatable. It is extremely unpleasant, yet a conversation emerging from these unpleasant spaces is necessary as our world becomes more diverse. In my current scenario, I am trying to motivate Kent to interrogate the oppressive discourses that benefit his daily existence and understand how the oppressed structures play out in the life of his participant simultaneously. What work should he have to do to understand the lived experiences of a Chicana educator who went through the desegregation movement in South Texas in 1950s and 1960s, when he has White skin and is a man? What is his connection? What is his entry point? What can he really hear? What would he be able to understand? What would the participant freely share? And would the participant have to explain her oppression to him, so that he could understand her life, so that she is positioned as a teacher even during the study? This responsibility to continuously educate one's oppressor about one's oppression is also a trapping as Audre Lorde states:

> Women of today are still being called upon to stretch across the gap of male ignorance, and to educate men as to our existence and our needs. This is an old and primary tool of the all oppressors to keep the oppressed occupied with the master's concerns. Now we hear that is the task of the black and third world women to educate White women, in the face of tremendous resistance, as to our existence, our differences, our relative roles in our joint survival. This is a diversion of energies and a tragic repetition of racist patriarchal thought. (Lorde, 1984b, p. 100)

Granted, Lorde's argument is from 1984, but the core concern of the argument is still valid. If one truly wants to understand how oppression functions, one could do the work themselves, instead of expecting someone who is oppressed to teach (justify?) their lived experiences. In other words, if I were to genuinely be interested in how we discriminate against people in wheelchairs, I could find out that information on my own, and make it my responsibility to educate myself, instead of putting that burden on someone who is in a wheelchair to convince/teach me of her suffering. Better yet, if I become friends with someone who is confined to a wheelchair, I would be able to witness the suffering first-hand and choose how I would want to be a critical ally, given that I enjoy certain privileges that my friend does not. I resonate with Lorde's argument that expectations placed on women and women of color to educate men and colonizers respectively, which are inherently oppressive acts that contradict the goals and intentions of "understanding" the position of the "Other." Understanding the differences between people is not just the Other's responsibility but a shared responsibility which requires genuine effort, curiosity, care, concern, and ethics on everyone's part, and not just on the part of the 'Others' to bring their own writing into existence in transparent terms so that "everyone" can get what s/he is saying.

Yet as part of being a minority in higher education, I am painfully aware of the perceptions I could create if I were to become completely vocal and transparent about my resistance to oppressive structures. The label "angry minority" would be applied to me immediately, and the content of my argument would be dismissed readily. As an educator of color, therefore, I convince myself to look for strategic ways in which I can cultivate conditions for people belonging to the master class to interrogate their privileges, understand their complicity in an oppressive system, and work towards disrupting social structures of power. Contingent on how I engage in such disruptive acts, if I can escape the label of "angry minority", then I can be an exception, the token who made it, because I did not make people in power feel uncomfortable or unsettled. And because I belong to an ethnic minority group, where its members are associated with the discourse of a model minority (as in not like the other minority groups) thereby situating one minority group against another, there is a danger in becoming settled in one's tokenized place, without questioning how such tokenized space continues to replicate an oppressive structure. Mitsuye Yamada writes about the complicated complacency of being a token:

> An Asian American woman thriving under the smug illusion that I was *not* the stereotypic image of the Asian woman because I had a career teaching English in a community college. I did not think anything assertive was necessary to make my point…it was so much my expected role that it ultimately rendered me invisible…contrary to what I thought, I had actually been contributing to my own stereotyping… When the Asian American woman is lulled into believing that people perceive her being different from other Asian women (the submissive, subservient, ready-to-please, east-to-get-along-with Asian woman), she is kept comfortable with the state of things. (Yamada, 2002, pp. 36–37)

Yamada's narrative highlights how her need to depart from "Asian" stereotypes and identify herself as atypical only perpetuates the colonial understanding of the "Other." In other words, by stating herself as "atypical" Yamada maintains "Asian" stereotypes from which she attempts to depart. Moreover, with the assurance of being 'atypical' comes a false sense of comfort, as if she is different from her people in some way, as if she is better, but this move still co-opts Yamada to concede to her situation instead of seeing how she is being racialized and how she is participating in her own racialization. Thus, by putting a critical eye on her own invisibility engendered by her own internalization of Asian stereotypes, Yamada demonstrates that colonization of the mind can be a powerful way to perpetuate suffering.

Colonization of the mind can also come from how we understand multiculturalism and diversity in our schools and communities. On one hand, folks are weary of being sensitive to what *might* be offensive if they are not being politically correct. On the other hand, language becomes a marker for someone's way of thinking and relating to differences in thought, language, culture, race, nationality, religion, sexuality, ability, etc. For example, as an educator and a scholar working with de/colonizing epistemologies, I am reminded of the ways in which notions of cultural diversity are taken up in academia, to increase *tolerance* (I tolerate my zits, but tolerating people seems not the best way to bring them into the fold), only to further create boundaries between that which is considered *ethnic* versus that which is considered *normal* (read: White). Minh-ha (1989) explains that the commodification of multiculturalism is in fact an act of erasure and separation. She states how efforts of increasing diversity function:

> They work toward your erasure while urging you to keep your way of life and ethnic values *within the borders of your homelands*. This is called the policy of "separate development" in apartheid language. Tactics have changed since the colonial times and indigenous cultures are no longer (overtly) destroyed (preserve the form and remove the content, or vice-versa). You may keep the traditional law and tribal customs among yourselves, as long as you and your own kind are careful not to step beyond the assigned limits. (Minh-ha, 1989, p. 80)

Minh-ha's conceptualization and expansion of "separate development" is not something unique to South Africa, but extends beyond its boundaries. In the U.S. and in other countries, gentrification continues along the lines of race, class, caste, tribes, etc. Spaces are often defined for people based on how they are hierarchically organized in their society. The term "wrong-side-of-the-tracks" is a poignant reminder of such space creation leading to issues of access. In other words, if one lived in the wrong-side-of-the-tracks in some U.S. town, then one was to expect poor access to education, healthcare, and other resources necessary for growth and progress. These borders then become instruments of oppression and co-optation. They provide the illusion of liberation (people are no longer owned as slaves) and yet they are still under the control of the oppressor group, carefully regulated and manipulated.

Kent and I are both intertwined in several systems of oppression based on our race and class privileges. We work towards anti-oppression agendas. We have work to do on ourselves as we move through an ever-morphing networked structure of oppression. And in our roles as mentors and mentees some of our fears, insecurities, shadows, and blind spots have come into collision with each other. We now have the task of understanding our entanglements and how we choose to work with them.

***

As I write this chapter, I think of all the states of consciousness with which I have engaged to explain the complicated nature of being a transnational woman, a faculty member in higher education in the U.S., I have evoked a relationship with a mentor who is no longer in this world, but her spirit continues to inform me, allows me to dialogue with a sense of vigilance that informs the way I shuttle between being a minority in academia and a change agent, between being a person in a position of power and a member of a minority group whose educating efforts are wrapped up in successfully training those who have privileges to interrogate such privileges. Yet such engagement comes from a state of consciousness that dares to imagine some utopia, some possibility outside of the master's house, and a deep sense of belief in the inherent goodness of people in general that can be activated if the right conditions can be cultivated. Then, those who benefit from an oppressive structure would no longer want to remain silent and would understand that our liberation and oppression are wrapped up, entangled with each other's existence. And the only way we can really disrupt a networked social structure of oppression is if we build bridges between where we are and where we would want to be. The reality I want to privilege is the one that comes out of a shuttling between different states of consciousness where I move in and out of the current condition of existence and one that I can imagine where equity and dignity of existence are not ideas that generate from the margin, but becomes a valued reality for all ethical beings.

KENT'S NARRATIVE

> Privilege or the idea of 'being privileged' is a touchy subject for White men. Some acknowledge and embrace it. More tend to resist it. (Kochman, 2011, p. 4)

I was one of those who resisted the idea that I, as a White person, benefitted from *unmerited privilege*. I was part of that group of Anglo-Americans who claimed the only advantages they held in life were those they worked for and maintained – and therefore such privileges *were* merited and justified. As for the concept of "*unearned* privilege," I would not entertain the notion. Who among us would concede their likelihood of success correlated positively with their lightness of skin?

Naturally, I encountered the idea of privilege in journals, books, and scholarly literature while researching cross-cultural endeavors, but I interpreted the issue as in relation to societies or groups suffering from the maladies of economic injustice and colonialism as practiced by White *Europeans*. Yet, this was decades, even centuries ago. Was I, as an Anglo-American in the 21st century, complicit with the practice of contemporary variations of systemic injustice? Absurd, I thought. As a progressive, I felt secure in my own "enlightenment," based upon my alignment with most liberal ideals. In other words, I practiced denial through interpreting the idea of *economic* inequity as that which was implemented by Whites who were reluctant to extend opportunities to people of color based upon misguided reactionary tenets or their individual or collective greed.

I recognized that there *was* (and still is) inequality. Further, I have always sympathized with political movements designed to lessen or eradicate such injustice. Yet despite being a socialist at heart, I feel ill-equipped to defend that perspective in political discussions with colleagues, mostly higher-ups, like department chairs or college deans, based upon a motivation that is two-fold: (1) to avoid confrontation and (2) to retain my own job – an unfortunate reality in my position as an untenured instructor. How smug we can be – the "culturally enlightened" – that we can endorse a more equitable society in all situations except those that may jeopardize our own economic security.

The reluctance of Whites to actively challenge an unjust social system is, I now believe, symptomatic of what Wildman and Davis (1995) have described as a situation where Anglo-Americans resist examining the world "through a filter of racial awareness, even though Whites, of course, are a race" (p. 897). They further insist that adopting a dismissive attitude toward racial issues "is a privilege, a societal advantage. The term racism/White supremacy emphasizes the link between the privilege held by Whites to ignore their own race and discriminatory racism" (p. 897).

While working toward my master's degree, I had read Gloria Anzaldúa's (1990) description of "people who practice Racism" as synonymous with "everyone who is White in the U.S." (p. ix). At first glance, I interpreted the remark as metaphorical. I felt she could not *really* mean what she was saying. Instead, I dismissed her opinion as an example of hyperbole to put forth a larger point. (What that "larger point" was, I could not say.) Refusal to reflect on her statement was a way of excusing a woman whose writing talent I respected more than most. I intended *not* to abandon reading her just because she had published an idea with which I dissented. Nevertheless, I could not resist suspecting that if she *was* serious and if she *really* believed all Anglo-Americans were racists, then Gloria Anzaldúa was prejudiced, a White-hater, and (yes) a racist herself. Was this an unreasonable conclusion to draw? At the time, I did not think so. Categorizing an entire ethnic faction as prejudiced was, to me, as senseless as pigeon-holing all Blacks as "shiftless" and "lazy," all Hispanics as "bandits" and "freeloaders," all Irish as drunks, etc.

Therefore, this was as far as I would allow reflection to go. My thinking remained at shallow depth. I refused to consider Anzaldúa's meaning as literal – that she *had* intended exactly what she communicated, word for word. As far as my own complicity as oppressor, this was a notion I dismissed. To me, the colonizer was not me; he was some other White guy, decked out in a pointed hood and robe, concocting strange ideas on how to kick up a ruckus on an aimless Saturday night with the rest of the gang. *They* have no problem with unmerited advantage. White supremacists, by definition, celebrate White privilege. There exists no reason for *them* to experience shame or guilt.

If it is reasonable to assume that an overwhelming number of White liberals claim self-enlightenment on the issue of race, then why do they abstain from reflecting on their own culpability in the continuation of an inequitable socio-political environment? What is at the core of their refusal to demystify its perpetuation? I recently asked my undergraduate writing class[1] to respond to Peggy McIntosh's (1990) article, "White Privilege: Unpacking the Invisible Knapsack," in which she listed 50 examples of "privileges" accorded to Anglos by virtue of their status as the majority population. One White student's response to McIntosh is recorded below:

I can contest that... [i]f a person chooses to go through life following only White customs they will not get very far. You will be passed up

53

professionally many times because you are not bilingual. Societies'
goals are not to make the White person feel more comfortable. The
goal is to make the Spanish person happy. You cannot call any business
number without having to go through the options and say that you do
not wish to listen in Spanish. You cannot buy an item from the store
without there being Spanish on it. Letters are sent out in both English
and Spanish. A colored person is more likely to get help from the
government. They are also more likely to qualify for scholarships and
job opportunities because schools and employers are looking for more
diverse populations...

If there was "White Privilege" when this article was written, I most
certainly do not believe it still exists. Although I may come off as
sounding racist, I am not. I believe that all people should be treated
equally. No matter how or where they are born, no matter what they are
given in life, and what they have gone through. If I do sound racist I do
not particularly care, because this is America and I can say what I feel
and what I believe to be true.

Another White student in her mid-20's, married to a Latino and employed
with the military, had a similar take on the issue of White privilege:

...I found it infuriating. I don't think this is relevant in this day in age
[sic]. I can't help but think cultural identity issues are petty and unworthy
of this much writing and attention...Many people are quick to call you
out for the slightest insinuation of discrimination and those who are
discriminating are deemed ignorant and arrogant. In my opinion, some
use their perceived disadvantages as a crutch, an excuse for mediocrity.
We are all better off if we ignore our differences and choose to see
ourselves as equal. Move on! So what you're different? Quit fighting
something that you cannot change.

Perhaps it is of some interest that the first student has refuted McIntosh
with examples that are usually sub-categorized under the heading of "reverse
racism." However, in the case of the second student, inequality is an error
of misperception because apparently the best remedy to the "unworthy"
matter of cultural identity is to "move on" and to "quit fighting" and admit to
ourselves that we are all "equal." Such a reaction, however, presupposes that
years of unjust treatment can be neatly swept under the carpet. All we have
to do is forget about it.

Here, the issue of White privilege has prompted the unleashing of an arsenal of self-defensive verbiage, fired off with more than the usual bombast. And yes, perhaps I am being somewhat unfair in citing the work of two students in a class geared for writers with comparatively little composition experience. Technically, they are both very competent writers. Yet, rather than engage with the content of McIntosh's article, both writers opted to react to the surface issues of privilege and advantage in a society that has taught us (mistakenly) that everyone is "equal."

But how can I blame the students when this was once the way I viewed racial issues? I was in *their* corner. I reacted in much the same manner – that everyone participates on a level playing-field. Never mind that the playing field has been structured and systematized by the White majority, thus facilitating further marginalization (Fish, 2000). I too dismissed sentiments such as McIntosh's on the grounds of "reverse racism." It would be several years before I acknowledged observations such as those expressed by Yamato (1990):

> With the best of intentions, the best of educations, and the greatest generosity of heart, Whites, operating on the misinformation fed to them from day one, will behave in ways that are racist, will perpetuate racism by being "nice"…You can just "nice" somebody to death with naiveté and lack of awareness of privilege. (p. 21)

How did I come to experience a transformation regarding the awareness of my own privilege? My attempts to chart that journey are difficult because in doing so, I must confront facets of my racial identity and intercultural experiences – episodes such as those related in the previous chapter, some of which I am shameful to admit. However, I realize no one is asking me to experience shame or guilt. Instead, it is wished that I acknowledge "awareness of privilege" and then decide what courses of action to take in order to lessen it. How did such awareness come about? To begin answering that, I would have to go back several years…

***

Spring 2009. Corpus Christi, Texas. I spend a Saturday morning viewing microfilmed archives of our local newspaper, the *Corpus Christi Caller*, at the city library. The issues I target cover the 1950s and '60s. I have in mind a project that is historical in nature, and I intend to propose it as the second of two inductive-analyses for a graduate course in advanced qualitative research methods that I am taking at a local university. It is my first class with Dr. Kakali Bhattacharya, a new professor. The first of the two analyses is due to her this Monday. These are 20-page assignments that will represent a hefty percentage of our semester grade. So, am I drafting or revising a paper I must submit in two days? No. Instead, I sit in the local history section, scanning through film of the local newspaper, month of February 1968.

As I browse through pages that were composed and typeset many years ago, I note the changes that have occurred between now and then – not just the comparatively low prices on groceries or clothing, but the discourse used by reporters and editorialists – specifically, expressions that today's readers would find objectionable on grounds of xenophobia or sexism. Thus, the word "Negro" appears odd and out-of-place, whether experienced in a 1903 essay by W.E.B. Dubois or in a 1968 front-page story covering a speech by Dr. Martin Luther King, Jr.

While advancing the film to the issue where I wish to begin, the 8th of that month, something familiar on the front page of the February 2nd edition catches my eye (see Figure 7). It is an Associated Press wire photo of a Vietcong prisoner, dressed in civilian clothing, being executed at close range by a South Vietnamese police general. Then, as I briefly examine the rest of that front page – the U.S.S. Pueblo is still in tow, thanks to its North Korean captors – I note a small headline toward the bottom of the page in medium-sized, bold print. It reads, "Only One in the Nation: Schools Here to Try Bilingual Experiment," and the article's content informs me that in 1968,

Figure 7. Front-page of Corpus Christi Caller, *February 2, 1968*

"[t]he Corpus Christi school district ha[d] been selected as the only system in the nation to operate…a two-year bilingual reading program" (Goodwin, 1968, p. 1A).

Further, the district would receive $40,000 from the federal government to finance a bilingual reading experiment in which 600 first-grade students in five local schools would participate. The story also reveals that "[h]alf of the students [would] be taught to read in Spanish" while the other half would learn reading in English. Once the Spanish-reading group accomplished its goals and objectives, they would then switch over to English (Goodwin, 1968, p. 1A). According to one district official, it was to be the first time anywhere that a school system had ever attempted such an experiment. Repeat: *ever*.

I pull out a big, red spiral notebook from my canvas bag and commence taking notes from the article's beginning. Why? Because I have recently secured consent from a veteran college teacher to act as participant in the next inductive-analysis project I will propose for class, and I anticipate that bilingual education may become a significant topic during the interview. The participant is a Latino woman whose first language was Spanish. Her name is Angie.

***

Dr. Caroline Sherritt, my academic advisor, informs me during a meeting that she is aware of my topic and chosen participant for Dr. Bhattacharya's second inductive-analysis assignment. She thus cautions me to identify my reasons for wishing to explore the experiences of someone who is neither White nor male. I nod my head in the affirmative. This, I have been told, is how doctoral students behave. When they are told *what* to do by graduate faculty, doctoral students say "Yes," and then go about doing it.

To me, though, this insistence that I examine my own Whiteness in relation to another person's non-Whiteness is just so much busywork, nothing more. The reasons for engaging in such a maneuver elude me. It is a job I find not only tedious and unnecessary; it is a downright inconvenience. To be blunt, I am not certain *what* is being asked of me – nor can I fathom *why*. To write about…about *what*? I don't know. And until I do know, I cannot even *begin* the job in the first place. But I'll do it – because I have been told to. So I tell myself, "I'll think about all this when the time's right" – or, more precisely, when I damn well feel like it. I have more pressing matters; so for now, I decide that thinking and writing about being born White is a job that will be best tackled at some time in the future. Besides, it is only a minor task, one that I can always confront…just not now!

This is the first time I delay in doing anything that a professor has demanded. Why? Because only now have I *begun* to realize the task I have set before myself. Some in the field of ethnography might even consider it inappropriate. So perhaps I should extend my historical gaze beyond the 1950s and 60s go back even further in time.

Naturally, I *was* aware of historical injustices committed by White Europeans as well as White European-Americans the world over, but I was *not* aware of such practices in relation to qualitative research. As Denzin and Lincoln (2008) have noted, "[r]esearch provides the foundation for reports about and representations of 'the Other.' In the colonial context, research becomes an objective way of representing the dark-skinned Other to the White world" (p. 1). Thus, colonial researchers acted as social scientists carrying out a mission of reconnaissance for Queen/King and country – a recon job that extended its goals, in fact, to that of the manipulation of native peoples by European colonizers who used inquiry for their own economic goals. Research became, thus, a means toward an evil end, which was the subjugation of an indigenous population to the extent of their being transformed into slaves for Western exploitation. These are horrible truths, and I accept that some of my own forbearers were responsible for such evil – in the Far East, South Asia, Australia, New Zealand, as well as colonial America, and later, the ante-bellum South and the American Western frontiers. True, this all occurred in the past; but it is a past that should not be forgotten. Such atrocities *need* to be remembered. After all, how can I forget that those of my own ethnic faction, those of my own blood enslaved, raped, and murdered native inhabitants who had lived on these lands for centuries before our arrival?

This was *not* the version of history I was taught in the early 1960s while attending the public schools of Denton and later, Corsicana, Texas, grades four through six. That version truly *was* an indoctrination – but not a permanent one. I shed myself of American history – the state-mandated version out of fifth-grade textbooks – while witnessing events transpiring at Wounded Knee during the early 1970s as well as in Chicano communities in the Great Southwest just prior to my graduation from high school.

Yet my exposure to such events resulted in no epiphany or awakening. I viewed them from the safe distance of a television screen. Thus, those besieged men who represented the American Indian Movement were just abstract figures on a CRT monitor with poor resolution. The words they spoke were, for me, an attempt to make connection with my conscience and that of everyone else's. But it was difficult to feel or make sense of the reasons behind their anger – because (a) if you factor in the consequence that their words were filtered through the mainstream communication tools of corporate America, and (b) if you realize that perhaps after all these years and after all the atrocities committed for the benefit of the Dutch East India Company and the British Raj, then perhaps we have not progressed at all.

I am also aware that historically, Angie, the participant in my next inductive analysis, represents a population maligned by the oppression of not just the American (White) political system but by an Anglo-centric purveyor/ complex of popular culture. Clive James may have put it best. Writing for the *London Observer* during the late 1970s, this Australian critic noted that in American motion pictures:

There were two kinds of Mexican, the bad-teeth and the straight-teeth. The bad-teeth Mexican, who usually had a name like Gonzalez Gonzalez-Gonzalez, said: "Hey, gringo, you throw down the gon and we no hort you [sic]." The straight-teeth Mexican wore tailored suits and said, "Senorita, since you have come to our hacienda I feel lightness in my heart for the first time since my sister was trampled by her horse." (James, cited in Kael, 1979, p. 509)

These were two examples of male caricatures, chosen to represent those of Angie's culture and heritage. They too were distorted, abstract images, foisted on the mass American audience for generations. As representative icons from below our border, they were projected onto huge screens – figures reduced to incompetent, clownish behavior, not deserving of anything more than our jocular contempt. As for Latino women, they were either saintly Madonnas occupying private spaces or women of highly doubtful virtue found in more public venues (Franco, 1988, pp. 507–508). And while it is true that those who worked in Mexican popular culture held guilt for similar characterizations in their own literature and film productions (Berg, 1992, pp. 56–71), leave it to Americans to cannibalize and excrete even less palatable versions of someone else's mistakes.

Yet Angie has consented to allow *me*, a White man who represented that oppressive history, to interview her and ask questions about her lived experiences, to have access to her memories and stories, and to make available artifacts such as old photographs and decades-old high school yearbooks.

A few years ago, I knew of Angie only by sight. As I stated before, we rarely exchanged words during my first two years teaching full-time at a local community college. However, in 2005, Angie and I found ourselves classmates at the local university's doctoral class in educational leadership. As I will soon learn, it is a subject in which she is well-versed. At that time,

I had abstained from driving my vehicle, using instead the city's mass transit system. But the service provided no transportation from the university at 9:30 in the evening, when our leadership class ended. Upon learning of this, Angie offered me a ride home after each week's session, wherein she and I often talked shop and shared gossip about colleagues. Sometimes, she would discuss the "bad old days" at the college – i.e., the male-dominated administration, the oppression that she and her female co-workers often endured in order to remain employed there. It reminded me of what my mother must have gone through years earlier after she had accepted a position at the same institute.

These conversations were the extent of my association with Angie. Other than what she revealed about herself during these discussions, I knew nothing of her, beyond her close association with one of the campus's non-profit organizations, set up to assist poor but deserving students. In South Texas, a great number of those who rely on such benefits are Latino college students, many of whom have received public schooling under woeful conditions in facilities suffering from lack of financing and maintenance.

We have never discussed our personal histories, the similarities or differences of our cultural and educational experiences, family allegiances, religious preferences, or even what motivated us to become teachers. In other words, our interactions were professionally cordial, strictly non-argumentative, and tacitly, decidedly impersonal. I do not realize it at the time, but as of the beginning of the interview process, all of that unfamiliarity will cease; and part of me reacts with discomfort. If this were not a requirement for Dr. Bhattacharya's class, I would never have thought of engaging in what I was about to do. I needed a participant for a class project, and it took overcoming more than the usual fear of imposing on the free time of other people – especially a busy, committed professional like Angie – to ask them to contribute to an extended inquiry into their educational experiences.

***

For our first session, Angie and I have agreed to meet on the first floor of the university's library on a Wednesday morning during Spring Break. I arrive first, heading for a row of computers, where I log on to the website of my advanced qualitative methods professor. Dr. Bhattacharya has set up discussion pages for various topics so that the class can contribute comments during the week-long holiday. After twenty minutes, I notice Angie entering the building. After greeting me, she looks at my computer screen and asks, "Is that your professor?" She points to a small photograph of Dr. Bhattacharya, which appears on her home page. I reply in the affirmative and then ask if we might conduct the interview in one of the small conference rooms upstairs. She agrees.

We take the elevator up one floor, where we locate a small, unoccupied cubicle with table and chairs. After taking seats across from one another, I make certain the recording level of my new analog-taping device is properly set and tested. I then begin our first interview, the purpose of which is to examine how a Chicana growing up in 1950s–1960s South Texas characterizes her public-school education. Foolishly, it turns out, I have prepared no more than three or four questions to start with. From there, I plan to just wing it – a truly open-ended endeavor that may result in moments of embarrassment for an inexperienced interviewer, but I am nonetheless confident I can carry it off.

ME (*reading from a small list of questions*):
> I was wondering if you could relate a timeline involving your education starting with Kindergarten and pre-K, or (*looking up and facing her briefly, just long enough to finish the question*) what level did it begin with, specifically?

ANGIE (*quietly*): Well, I started first grade. I did not get to go to Kindergarten or pre-K. I started when I was 7 years old, my birthday being in October, so I had to wait. I didn't start at 6. So I started first grade in, gosh, 1956, '57? So, let's see, I went to [name of school withheld]. It's just a small town. Thirty miles from here. And continued and never did get retained. I went through all my years and then…

ME (*interrupting*): By retained, do you mean, get held back a grade?
ANGIE: Right.
> (*Silence*)

ME (*Consulting my list of questions*):
> And, uh, what was the ethnic makeup of your classes in elementary and middle school?

ANGIE: Well, in [my town] at that time, it was made up mainly of Anglo students. There were, I would suggest, not even a third, maybe a fourth of the population was Latino. And we had just maybe a couple of students who were black. There were very few black students.

As Angie responds, I silently recall that Latinos did not become the majority ethnic group in Corpus Christi until the 1980s (Osborne, 2000). I wonder if this was also the case in Angie's neighboring town. In the ensuing silence, I debate with myself whether to ask; but then I decide the question may lead away from the topic of Angie's schooling. I struggle now to think of another follow-up question. More silence.

Why do I feel such discomfort? Do I fear I may ask a question that might be offensive? Let's see, what would be defined as offensive, beyond that which is obvious? Or perhaps my uneasiness arises from the tentative way I brought up the issue of race with my last question? What if Angie feels that her attitudes on such things are too personal? Would she tell me to mind my own business? Would she become angry and abruptly leave the room?

However, a few seconds later, Angie breaks the tension.

> ANGIE: If you want me to tell you about my first-grade experience, I do have something that relates to the treatment, if you'd like me to explain.
>
> ME: Certainly.
>
> ANGIE: Okay…

I behave as if nothing out of the ordinary has occurred, maintaining a matter-of-fact tone. Those feelings of discomfort have been somewhat abated. At least for now. Yet inwardly, I must acknowledge gratitude for her suggestion. She continues speaking while I nervously pretend to take notes on a legal pad I have brought. And I do take notes, most of it just busywork – writing down a significant phrase here or there. It is just a way to concentrate on what is being said.

> ANGIE: …Um, I am the 4th of four children, and when I started at that time, I did know English. My brothers and – I had one brother and two sisters, two older sisters – taught me when they started school. Of course, they did not know English, just only Spanish. So in a way, they prepared me for this.
>
> So on the first day of class, I remember being put in a particular classroom with a lot of students that I remembered and recognized from church and different communities. One particular boy was the child of the woman my mother worked for (see Figure 8). An Anglo. My mother worked in houses. She was a housekeeper. So I recognized *him*.
>
> So anyway, that first, I guess, maybe that first couple of days of first grade, we had tests given to us and, uh, those

tests determined, I guess, our ability to speak English. And I do remember being put from that room into another room where there were more Latinos. And we were all tested for the ability, I think, to speak in English. So once we completed those tests, then we were re-assigned, and I returned to that first room I started in. By that point, a lot of the students that I remember seeing that first day were no longer there. So I was one of maybe, I don't know, five students who, of Latinos, who were staying in there.

And, uh, later on, in the playground, I would run into those other students I remembered seeing. And that was the problem that I think I understood, because some of them...I remember one particular little girl did not speak any English at all. Her parents had been from Mexico. And so I spoke to her, and she was always crying, and so I spoke to her. And I remember her telling me that nobody understood her, she, she didn't have any friends and all this. So I kind of took her under wing, and it turned out that she lived down the street from me. So we became really close friends after that. But she was never really in any of my classes until maybe middle school, junior-high. That's when I remember seeing

Figure 8. Angie's mother, circa 1964

her in a classroom with me. But…and again I think a lot of that had to do with her being able to speak in English…

They kind of separated us, you know, the A room, the B room, the C room…I basically stayed with the A room. And a lot of it, again, had to do with the ability to speak English. And then even in the classroom, they would divide us up into the different rows. You know, they had the, like, the bluebirds, the redbirds, the yellow birds. And again, having to do with, uh, having to do with the ability, I guess. Skill. And I remember being in that first row, uh, and they would move us within the row, like, you know, first chair, second chair, third chair. (*Laughs*) I remember going through these series of, okay, today you're going to move over here, just maybe you're going to move over there…

ME: Like a band, or a…
ANGIE: Right, it was very, uh, well, you know – very structured…

I notice Angie appears more relaxed than when we began. I also realize she is offering interesting testimony in the form of an uninterrupted monologue that I wish would go on and on. Yet I would prefer more exchange between us – more dialogue. Thus, I attempt to inject my voice into the conversation without interrupting the flow of data or veering into irrelevant chit-chat. However, the entire time she is speaking, I keep my eyes focused on the legal pad. I never look up or make eye contact with her. She is revealing something very personal, but she does it in such a way that she even laughs at some of the incidents she is recalling. I sense that these are events she has not thought of in years and years.

ANGIE: …But like I said, there were like a handful, maybe, of Latinos, and I remember seeing them. The yellow birds were the low birds, and so if you were a yellow bird, you were on the last row. And so a lot of times, I would see them. My goal was never to be a yellow bird. My goal was to always be a bluebird. (*Laughs*)
ME: Blue was the top echelon.
ANGIE: The top. (*Laughs*)
ME: Your mother was a housekeeper, and your father was…
ANGIE: He died when I was two years old.
ME: I see.

Figure 9. Angie at age five

ANGIE: My mother was a widow. She had four children. My grandmother lived with us, and she took care of us for a little while…

At this point, I resist making an interjection regarding the death of my own father when I was three. I almost wish this were not a case-study interview situation at all so that I *could* offer my own personal anecdote as – what? Some kind of confirmation that I had been through something similar? Naturally, I fear this will send the conversation on a tangent from which it may not recover. So I carry on with my nonsense-note taking, staring at the legal pad at all times, while rarely making eye contact with the participant. I struggle quickly to think of a question I hope will steer the exchange back onto the topic of her public-school education:

ME: Uh, the, the language you spoke predominantly at home during the first grade or the years leading up to that (see Figure 9) – which language predominantly was spoken?
ANGIE: Spanish…At home, it was Spanish. My mother also used Spanish, but…she spoke both. But we were more at home with Spanish…
ME: What was the ethnic makeup of the faculty in elementary school?
ANGIE: Oh, they were all White. All White.
ME: So there were no role models for you to look up to.
ANGIE: No, there wasn't…

ME: What was the attitude in your family during your K-12 years regarding higher education? Going to college?

ANGIE: Never. It was never discussed at all...I always associated college with high income, which would never have applied to me because my mother was a housekeeper. She barely made 50 cents an hour to work. So that I knew I would never be able to expect my mother to send me to college.

ME: When did you decide to go to college?

ANGIE: It wasn't until I was 33, 33 years old.

ME: And when you entered college, uh, was this locally?

ANGIE: Yes, it was [name of a local two-year college]. It wasn't until later I realized I wanted to go...I started looking at the classes I really enjoyed, and the classes I really enjoyed were English literature classes.

ME: Why was that?

ANGIE: It was the reading. I liked the stories. I loved reading fiction and the stories. I just enjoyed it. To me, it was very...I could see the humanity. (*Pause*)

ME: What was the content of the reading matter...?

ANGIE: Well...in American Lit, we were asked to find a writer whom we had not studied in the class – to read a book and then give a report at the end of the semester. So I remember thinking to myself, I sure would like to see what's out there, other than just Hemingway or Faulkner...So I went to the public library and just went down the row. And the first name that popped out was Anaya (1972). And so I pulled the book, *Bless Me, Ultima*... I took it to [the teacher], and I showed him the book and asked if it was okay to do my report on this one. And he said, "Is he American?" And I said, "Well, it says New Mexico," you know, so he says, "Okay, well, I don't know who he is, but if you want to do that, that's fine." So I did. I read the book; I read the whole time. And I reported on it, and I was in love with it ever since...

ME: (*pause*) Uh, when did you make the decision to teach?

ANGIE: After I finished my Associate's...And it was at that point that someone mentioned I didn't have to teach in the public schools...in order for me to teach at the college level. I could bypass that. So when *that* occurred to me...I realized, okay, I don't have to really just be teaching grammar...I can focus

on classes that I like, like literature…So that's what I decided
to shoot for: this idea of teaching more literature courses…

So this was Angie's motivation in becoming a teacher – to communicate
her love for literacy. And she wished to do so by connecting what she had
discovered in Anaya (1972) and, later, other Latino writers. In years to come,
she would become the driving, influential force behind a successful effort to
implement a Mexican-American cultural-studies degree program that offers
an alternative Latino-centered view of literature, history, and other disciplines.

As an English graduate student and teaching assistant some 15 years prior
to conducting this interview with Angie, I was of course made aware of
the silencing of minority voices in American literature, a practice that was
carried on for practically the length of the nation's existence – a time when
women authors were urged to use masculine pseudonyms. Thus the novelist
and short-story writer Georgiana Craig (1908–1957) was listed on her works'
front covers as "Craig Rice," to take just one example (Haining, 1994, p.
94). As far as the works of Latina/o writers was concerned, they were not
included in the traditional canon until the very tail end of the 1900s. Even
now, Angie has just related an account of a college English professor who in
the 1980s was shown a work authored by a writer with a Hispanic surname
– and this was his response: "Is he American?"

Naturally, Angie's teacher may have wished to make certain that her
chosen author for the class project would fall under the category of American
Literature, which after all was the course's title; yet Angie also reveals a slight
impatience with her teacher's adherence to the standard old curriculum, with
its particular homage to "just Hemingway and Faulkner" – a condition she is
now helping to remedy with her own efforts as a member of a college faculty,
seeking to address and eliminate the marginalization of Latino and other
minority voices from the American literary learning tradition.

At the time, however, I am thinking of none of this – not even in whether
I have heard or learned anything here that might help to confront my own
Whiteness or to carry out Dr. Sherritt's insistence that I reflect on how I, a
White male, must come to terms with the differences between me and those
of Angie's background and experiences. Instead, I am unaware of anything
related to gender or race or of how listening to the participant's story can
put into effect such awareness – even after hearing Angie's testimony of her
upbringing, of the impoverished childhood she endured, of the way she and
other Latino learners were shunted to the side by those who administered the
pedagogical duties of her hometown in a way they (mis)understood as showing

"tolerance". Instead, I know only of my disappointment that this afternoon's interview has come to an end. There is more I wish to ask Angie, mainly having to do with a 1950s public education program that was not geared to accommodate the learning needs of its Latino students. I want to cover her middle school and high-school years in more detail. But we had both agreed today's session would go no longer than 90 minutes. Before we part company that morning, I ask if I can follow up with another session later. She agrees.

***

A day later, while at home transcribing the interview, I come upon a part of our dialogue where Angie off-handedly recalled an episode in high school where she and someone else had successfully "crashed" (to use her verb) the membership of an extracurricular club. As I rewind and play back the tape, listening to her glancing reference to the event (mentioned as though it were mere trivia), I now remember that I interpreted the incident as a typical hazing stunt, and I forgot about it instantly. However, it is not until today while playing back the recording several times over that I recognize the significance of what she had told me. I immediately e-mail her my request for a follow-up interview. She suggests we meet in her office the Friday morning of the week classes resume after Spring Break.

In the meantime, Dr. Bhattacharya's advanced-methods class resumes following the week-long holiday. During our time off, we were to read Johnny Saldaña's (2003) article on "Dramatizing Data," which describes the reduction of qualitative data into a theatrical format for presentation to an audience. Thus, arts-based research will be the subject of tonight's session. I have read the article only once, but I feel intrigued. Yet I also find it difficult to believe this method is an accepted format among qualitative researchers for a report of findings.

Dr. Bhattacharya explains the process of writing a data-representation piece: (a) illustrating how we "chunk" the data together into a creative format, (b) describing how we enter and exit out of the chunks, inserting a constellation of interpretations and meaning making (from various perspectives that include but are not limited to Angie, me, people we carry within our consciousness, etc.); and then (c) demonstrating how a data-representation piece actually makes works on the data itself, inscribing layers and layers of interpreted, dynamic meanings. For example, what themes (arrived at by coding, categorizing, connecting, disrupting, interrogating, writing around ideas, codes, hunches, emotions, etc.) and motifs from the data are settled upon and how are those themes used by the author/researcher in describing the significance of what and how a participant reveals her/his fluid, messy, contradictory, contextualized "stories?" The purpose of an upcoming assignment in Dr. Bhattacharya's class, the inductive-analysis project then, is to explain how an arts-based process informs the interpretation of data.

***

Follow-up interview with Angie, morning of Friday, March 27, 2009, in her campus office. I decide to bring up the hazing incident first. Before actually recording this follow-up interview, I ask Angie to explain what she meant by "crashing" a club during our initial interview, and she tells me the story in fuller detail. I ask her if she would repeat the story here.

The taping, thus, begins:

ME: What sorts of extracurricular activity did you, uh, participate in, in school?

ANGIE: Well, um, I was in the pep squad…I was in the Spanish Club (see Figure 10)…

Figure 10. Angie's high school Spanish Club, 1969

And uh, and then there was one, uh, particular one that was the [name of homemaking club] that I joined…Because I had heard this particular group had never had any Latino girls. So I took Homemaking. You had to be enrolled in Homemaking to be in the club (see Figure 11), so…so I talked to one of my friends – the one I talked about earlier that she and I remained friends throughout the years – and, uh, talked her and another girl into joining this club. So that we *could* be the first Latinas.

And I remember going the first day they met and the girls who were involved in that, were just very standoffish. They didn't speak to us. You know, usually when you join a club, the first thing you do is stand up and say who you are, and like that. And, uh, I remember the stare-downs we got. Very cold...

Figure 11. Homemaking Club, Angie's high school

...And I think that the reason for that was that their main draw, they had a dance for the football players. And so, at the end of spring or whatever, they would have a dance. And it was a semi-formal kind of dance, and so people dressed up... And again, it was exclusively for the ones, the members who were in this group, for the football players. And it was usually the girls with high income. And of course they were all White... But I just wanted to prove a point: *they* knew we could join if we wanted to. It was not...we were *not* going to be held back.

This territory feels all too familiar, but always worth revisiting – it is like experiencing the history of South Texas over and over again, listening to Angie recount a variation of a saga repeated by other people of color. Two

Wednesdays ago, she described herself as a student with no role model in school. Now, I am given to understand she modeled a role for herself. A Latina, one of the few who said *no* – and said it loudly.

ME: What year was this?

ANGIE: Let's see, 19, uh, '64 or '65 maybe. It was after the Beatles had arrived. *(Laughs)* I remember there was that sense of freedom in the air, where, I don't know, I think it was the Civil Rights Act went into play. And as a kid, I didn't realize there were other things going on socially in the U.S. to help us feel this sense of "Oh, I can do anything!"

Listening to her speak is like reading John Staples Shockley's (1974) *Chicano Revolt in a Texas Town* for the first time. That book had chronicled the concerted effort by some of Crystal City's Latino high-school students in 1969 to organize a walkout, protesting everything from outmoded curricula to the paving of the school's parking lot (pp. 232–250). The movement soon mushroomed, and eventually all of the Chicanos (who made up over 80% of the school's population) joined the strike. Among their grievances was the inclusion of more than just one token Latino on the school's cheerleading squad. Up until then, the town's all-White school board had mandated that the cheerleaders should be comprised of 3 Anglos and just 1 Latino woman to be elected – not by the student body but by selected members of the faculty (p. 120). No one had complained to the school's administrators until the spring of '69. Predictably, the town's White numerical minority probably considered this a fair "compromise." But the Sixties signaled big changes, even in a remote southwestern small-town setting like Crystal City – or in a small village on the Gulf Coast, like Angie's.

ME: Do you still visit your hometown today?

ANGIE: Constantly. My mother lives there, and I have a sister who lives there…

ME: How would you summarize the changes over the past 40 years?

ANGIE: Black and White. *(Laughs)* I mean, opposites. Total opposites. Day and night. In fact, I've had students now, Anglo students, who come to me and say, "Oh, I feel so out of place in [my hometown] because basically the boys don't want to date us if we're not Latinas." And it's the Latinas and Latinos who have, pretty much, the control of [my hometown]…Of course, it's 40 years later. *(Laughs)*.

71

As we conclude the interview, I am reminded of Dr. Bhattacharya's data-representation assignment. Angie's story of how she "crashed" her school's homemaking club sounds like the "juicy stuff" that Saldaña (2003) had written about in his article (p. 224) – an episode worthy of staged performance, something tailor-made for ethnodrama.

One drawback, however, is the fact that there is no verbatim dialogue to incorporate. All the actors' lines must be invented. But Dr. Bhattacharya recommended that "verisimilitude" – a sense of realism and "truth" that pervades a narrative – can take on an overriding value. So how will I accomplish the injection of this sense of reality into make-believe?

And there is, of course, that other factor – the issue of a White investigator conducting a case study of a Chicana – of which Dr. Sherritt has pointed out. Will this negatively affect the legitimacy of a data-representation piece? It is one thing for a White man to research and write about a Chicana's experiences. But now comes the question of whether a man/White author has any legitimate business writing dialogue/scenes based on interviews with that same participant. I know that to complete this feat, I will be required to immerse myself in Angie's situation, to feel as she must have felt as a marginalized person. But is that even possible? Many researchers would say no. And I suspect they might be right. So what would justify such an effort?

To answer that question today, I would refer to the transcript of Angie's interview responses and cite the participant's words regarding why she was drawn toward literature classes in college: "I liked the stories. I loved reading fiction and the stories. I just enjoyed it. To me, it was very...I could see the humanity." Humanity, as in that which is largely concerned with human culture, our strengths, our weaknesses, our pride, our misgivings, our ignorance and so forth – the stuff of drama. Moreover, the *ethno* of ethnodrama would relate not only to Angie's struggles within an oppressive White-dominated public-school environment, but also the tension inherent when a member of that establishment tasks himself with writing such a play from a Latina character's point of view.

I make a decision. Unless I am prevented by faculty edict from attempting such a work, I will carry on with it. Dr. Bhattacharya's enthusiasm for the arts-based tradition has been enough to convince me. So has her encouragement. I will write the play, and the climax of that play will center on Angie's crashing the homecoming club.

NOTE

[1] The site of this class was Corpus Christi, Texas, where the demographic representation of people of Hispanic heritage is higher than in many parts of the U.S.

CHAPTER 3

FINDING SELF IN ETHNODRAMA

Trying to find the other by defining otherness or by explaining the other through laws and generalities is, as Zen says, like beating the moon with a pole or scratching an itching foot from the outside of a shoe.

(Minh-ha, 1989, p. 74)

KAKALI'S NARRATIVE

The first time I even heard of the term *ethnodrama* was when my dissertation advisor in graduate school told me to attend a workshop by Johnny Saldaña at the University of Georgia, which was hosting a qualitative research conference. Johnny had been invited as a special guest to work with students and attendees to host an ethnodrama workshop. I had no idea what "ethnodrama" was or how I would use it in my work. But my advisor believed that I should be exposed to as many approaches as possible to have a depth and breadth of understanding of qualitative inquiry. I walked in and there was Johnny in one of our classrooms in Aderhold Hall, asking us to rearrange our chairs in a circle.

I do not remember a lot of specific details from that workshop, but I do remember Johnny wearing a black t-shirt, a black leather motorcycle jacket with a zipper in the middle, and black pants. Johnny alerted us that his terminal degree in theater was not a doctorate but a master's degree. Later, I would find out that he identifies as a Hispanic, gay man. I only mention this because several of Johnny's plays focus on this aspect of his life, and he teaches us to pay attention to the "juicy parts" of our narratives and find the strongest, most compelling truths within them. The workshop was titled, "From Page to Stage" and Johnny asked us to write a story about a critical moment in our lives. Then we had to perform the story to a partner, who would give us feedback. We would then have to consider a compelling first and last sentence for the story with the middle part filled with well-paced action and development. As we repeated the process at least five times with five different partners, I began to see the story sharpening and how much of my own vulnerability and authenticity I had to put in the story for it to be accessible and engaging.

Ethnodrama, I learned, was the theatrical rendition of research data, where we would take interviews, observations, documents, and other data we collect in our studies and convert them into a play with dialogue scenes, props, music, and other multisensory details as appropriate. I did what Johnny suggested we do if we were drawn to writing ethnodrama – i.e., attend a lot of theatre productions. For the next year I witnessed as many theatrical plays as my budget would allow. For my own purposes, I figured out ways to balance creativity and scholarly work in one space that could appear as an engaging and entertaining play. Eventually I created front and backstage plays (Bhattacharya, 2009) to represent my findings from my dissertation, to demonstrate how we show up in the different spaces we occupy based on who else is present in that space, who we trust, and how safe we feel.

Since then I have carried this sense of obligation, where if students wanted to integrate something creative in their research, I would support them but also remind them to balance the artistic appeal and the scholarly elements in order to justify the work. In other words, if someone were to use ethnodrama in his work, I would want it to be not just entertaining from a creative aspect, but also have scholarly value by illuminating different insights gained from data collection and data analysis during the research. I have tried to cultivate a love for creativity in my classes, yet I have also been mindful of not creating a mini-me. I prefer that students discover their own space of scholarly work. I want to educate and not indoctrinate students.

Imagine then my surprise when I first met Kent and found out that he has a creative-writing background. I knew he would be open to integrating his artistic side with his scholarly interests. On this particular day in my Advanced Data Analysis Methods in Qualitative Research class, I am teaching students how to take their interviews, observations, and document data, and create a theatrical scene in a way that is scholarly, creative, and illuminating. I then give them time to write their own scenes based on their research. Kent leaves the classroom to write his scene in a computer lab, which is located on the second floor of the building in which I am teaching. When I visit Kent there and alert him to return to class, he shows me the scene he has written. The scene is vivid creatively with engaging dialogue, a sassy character with whom the audience could identify, good pacing of events, and even some humor. But Kent misses some key details. I cannot tell if he understands the pain in Angie's childhood where she was constantly discriminated, ridiculed for her Mexican heritage, where her mother was a maid in some of her own White classmates' homes – whereas Kent's mother was a teacher, and he was never discriminated or ridiculed for his heritage. It feels as if Kent is unaware of his privileges and so he falls into this familiar sense of complacency by just creating a "fun scene".

Still, I think the students could benefit from hearing Kent's entertaining work; it might enable them to understand the creative elements that can make a scene engaging. So I ask him to read it aloud. I fully expect him to read his narrative the way he usually speaks in class – monotone and sagacious. Kent is usually quiet and will speak only when spoken to, with brief sentences that would be delivered in a stoic voice with enormous depth and wisdom. Yet when Kent reads his scene, I feel as though I am witnessing an alter ego that has come out to perform. Just like Beyoncé has her alter-ego performer Sasha Fierce, it seems like Kent has an alter ego, whom I secretly tag "Sgt. Pepper," the name of the alter-ego band of the Beatles, when they did not want to perform as the Beatles or go on tour because of the loud mob-like behavior of their fans. This allowed the Beatles to experiment musically and to break away from their regular routines. It was as if Sgt. Pepper had a life of its own, different from the Beatles, and became a wildly successful experiment. Even though this is a messy metaphor, I like thinking of Kent's alter-ego as Sgt. Pepper. It is a persona that comes out to disrupt Kent's normal disposition, allowing him to be experimental and take risks in his performance. Plus, I cannot help thinking about how the word "sergeant" also connotes someone who is a leader, in control of his surroundings, which is clearly on display when he is performing the scene. And "pepper" is just spicy, a departure from the usual stoic disposition which Kent uses to interact in class. Sgt. Pepper just plays on different levels for me, and I am secretly amused and pleased with naming Kent's alter ego.

Sgt. Pepper stands in front of the class and reads out his scene. It is as if there is a one-man play being performed, where Sgt. Pepper would move in and out of his characters. His body language, dialogue delivery, intonation of voice, and other nuanced details would change as he would interpret the different characters from his scene. For a moment, I am shocked and mesmerized. Who is this guy and why haven't I seen him before? After the initial shock subsides, I realize that by being Sgt. Pepper, Kent is masking something. As engaging as Sgt. Pepper is, Kent's play is too easy, too wildly entertaining, without actually reflecting the gritty nature of Angie's experiences and Kent's struggle to understand those experiences. It is as if a nice scene has been written, performed, and offered as a gift to the class, all wrapped up with a neat, entertaining bow.

Kent simply could not see the large blind spot that distanced him from understanding Angie's experiences; either that or maybe he was not even aware of it. The best way to understand this blind spot is by imagining a big room with a horse that is larger than life and people (with sight) standing around it from differing angles and viewpoints. Imagine that from one person's individual vantage, she can only see a small part of the horse. So a person standing at the front of the horse would recognize that the horse has a mouth, but would have no sense of the horse's posterior or whether it even had one. Or worse, someone standing toward the rear of the horse would have no clue as to the existence of a mouth at the animal's other end or its function to fulfill a critical need – to allow the intake of food and water, for thirst and hunger. As far as that person knows, all she can see and know is a horse's ass.

Kent is situated in such a place with Angie's stories. He cannot sense that there is something further beyond what he has narrated, something that demands interrogation. Kent's own sociocultural location creates such a lack of awareness that he has no inner mechanisms to alert him to the most glaring differences between himself and Angie. They grew up in two different parts of the same area. One of them is White, of Irish heritage; the other, of Mexican heritage. Kent was raised by a mother who was educated. Angie grew up with the fear that her brother would be in jail any day and that she would not be allowed to go to school, let alone finish her education. Angie's house did not even have the convenience of running water while Kent, on the other hand, had no such worries. Angie lived in a crowded, small house with her widowed mother and her brother and sisters. Kent lived in a house where there was ample space to retreat into his own world of books, reading, and games. These gaps between their experiences, if left unattended, can only create a scene that would at best be superficially entertaining. And yet, because Kent is such a reflective, voracious reader, I have faith that he will sort out these differences as he reads and writes more. Thus, if Kent/Sgt. Pepper only knows the proverbial horse by its rear end, how would he know what the entire horse is like or that the horse might have other needs that are not connected to the horse's ass?

I engage Kent in a series of conversations about how we could publish the pilot study (Gillen & Bhattacharya, 2013) he is conducting in my class and the appropriateness of using ethnodrama for his larger dissertation study. However, no matter how many conversations I have with him, I cannot help him to see that blind spot or even acknowledge its existence. I optimistically believe, though, that by the time he prepares his proposal document,[1] he would have done more reading, thinking, and writing to sort out these ideas before proceeding with his dissertation.

***

Even though Caroline has asked me to work with Kent, she has stayed on Kent's dissertation committee as a co-chair with me. It would not be until much later after Kent's proposal defense that Caroline would step off the committee as a chair, and remain as a member, to acknowledge the work that I had been doing with Kent. But for now, as the lead supervisor, Caroline calls for a proposal defense meeting for Kent. I had seen a copy of the proposal and offered him some feedback much along the same lines as I had done with him before. Unfortunately, when I received his updated copy, I was disappointed to find out that Kent had not addressed my points sufficiently. The work is incomplete, but the date has been set and Caroline is convinced that we can sort out the gaps in Kent's work. So we move forward with the meeting.

By now, I am puzzled at Kent's reluctance to address what I consider the most salient issue in his dissertation. I try to gauge whether this is some kind of resistance, or lack of understanding, or just something he does not deem important. At the proposal meeting, four people are seated around the conference table: Beside me is Bryant, a seasoned professor, specializing in educational philosophy, representing Curriculum and Instruction; Caroline, at the head of the table; and Kathleen, a professor of English. When Kent finishes his presentation, Caroline starts the inquiry, "Kent, what exactly is an ethnodrama?"

Kent responds in his regular stoic disposition. I cannot tell if he is nervous or if he is unprepared. I decide it has to be the former because Kent is never unprepared. If anything, he is always over-prepared. Kent offers a canned answer to Caroline's question, focusing more on how to write a drama based on field research and very little on the integration of research and other scholarly elements in the resulting data-representation piece. I am not sure if Caroline is convinced about what Kent will do for his study and how that would be considered research.

A few more rounds of questions continue and when the discussion steers towards Kent's research design, as in what is his plan and how will he execute it, I start with my questions. "Kent, that's really just one of many things missing from the methodology chapter of your paper. What I'm really concerned about is that your Chapter Three is inadequate for this and many other reasons. There's too much here that is missing. You have no breakdown of procedure, the steps you are going to take in processing the data, or how you intend to transform that data into a report of your findings. I know you can write a methodology chapter. You've done it before in class. All that missing information needs to be here, and it's not." I am not sure if my irritation is transparent, but I cannot help but wonder if Kent is trying to bypass all the scholarly elements to just situate himself in the creative writing part of his study because the scholarly elements require him to reflect on some difficult, unsettling questions.

Kent attempts to offer a justification. "Well, it is difficult. I haven't done this before. I don't know what these steps will look like in advance of actually doing the study. How can I say what I would do without doing it? It feels like I am trying to predict the future and I don't know how to do that. If there are step-by-step procedures to be written, I can only do so after I have conducted those procedures, but not before."

I am at once puzzled and impressed by Kent's answer. On one hand, yes, he cannot be expected to predict step-by-step procedures in advance of conducting the study. On the other hand, he cannot expect us to approve his study if he cannot articulate some broad outline of a plan that he has to conduct his study. I tell him, "I understand, Kent. But we have to know what your plans are so that we can guide you, help you become aware of some gaps in your thinking, challenge your assumptions a bit, and have a meaningful discussion about your study. If you do not show us what you know about research design, we do not know if we could be confident in your ability to conduct a study."

Before I can continue, Bryant chimes in, "And at some point, you're going to have to deal with the fact that a White male is inquiring into the life of a woman of color. That's something you must address as well…"

Finally someone, other than me, pointed out what I have been trying to show Kent. "That's right." I support Bryant's comment.

Bryant continues, "…and furthermore, I can guarantee you that if or when you present these findings to a conference, and you haven't acknowledged that difference in ethnic or gender orientation, they're going to tear into your presentation and they're going to tear into *you* on that one point alone."

I am excited that Bryant has explained the consequence of not attending this big gap in Kent's thinking so I agree enthusiastically. "Right. You *must* discuss how you have situated yourself as researcher in relation to the participant. That is a requirement. It cannot be avoided. That is something that must be addressed in the beginning, in the middle, and in the end of your proposal." I sincerely hope Kent understands the seriousness of this issue.

After a few more rounds of questions, Caroline asks Kent to leave the room so that we can discuss our decision about his proposal. Once Kent is outside, we talk about how critical it is for Kent to address what Bryant and I have outlined. We talk about the missing details in his research plan. We agree that for Kent's dissertation to be rigorous, he has to understand that these are key pieces that need to be present the next time we meet, which would be his dissertation defense, after he would have conducted his study, analyzed his data, and presented his findings. Caroline invites Kent back into the room and tells him of our decision and the work that lies ahead of him. We then congratulate him for achieving this milestone in his academic journey.

I suggest to Kent that he should present part of his pilot study at the annual meeting of International Congress of Qualitative Inquiry conference held at the University of Illinois, Urbana-Champagne campus. Kent agrees to the presentation. I am hoping that by trying to put together the conference presentation, Kent will be able to identify the distance that exists between Angie and him. Plus, maybe the audience members could ask him certain questions that would allow him to attend to what he is bypassing.

***

International Congress of Qualitative Inquiry Conference. Urbana-Champaign, Illinois. I know that Kent has arrived after a two-day bus ride from Corpus Christi, Texas. He does not like flying. He does not have a cell phone. But I receive an email from him that he has reached Urbana safely and has been memorizing his lines. Kent would not attend any other talks prior to his presentation so that he can be fully prepared. I have seen a version of his presentation and I know that Kent would continue to revise his presentation script till the very last minute.

Kent and I walk together to the classroom where he is scheduled to present his work. The classroom looks like just any other classroom one might see across America's college campuses – beige chairs with desk, arms attached, organized in rows. As other people arrive, they start to rearrange the furniture in a U-formation so that a group of presenters can deliver their talk and move about as they would like. No other presenter/groups indicate any preference for furniture arrangement.

Kent walks into the class. He is wearing a green suit with plain White shirt. To me, the image of Kent in a jacket is a radical novelty. He carries a cloth White bag with straps attached and with the conference logo embossed on it. I suppose the bag contains his presentation materials. He opens the bag, shuffles through some papers, brings out a thumb drive, and loads his presentation to the computer at the front of the classroom behind the rusted brown podium.

However, for some reason, the classroom projection screen will not display images from the computer. I try to help Kent out, and we have to go through several rounds of fighting with the gods of technology to even get the images up there. Then, he pulls out some more papers and places them on the table located next to the computer. As more people arrive, he settles behind the desk while the screen behind him displays the title slide of his presentation.

Kent barely says anything to me and does not ask me to look anything over. Perhaps he is nervous. Maybe he thinks any suggestion from me at this late hour would throw him off.

Instead, he says to me, "Well, I have been to Johnny Saldaña's workshop on Thursday. Other than that I have just mostly stayed in my room and memorized my lines."

"Lines?"

"Yeah, you'll see. Thanks for being here, by the way."

With that, the chair of the session declares that there will be four presenters, and Kent, who is already seated at the desk up front, will be first. He takes off his jacket and walks in front of the desk. He stares at the people sitting around the room, finally saying, "Hi. My name is Angie. I have given Kent permission to tell my story of going through the desegregation movement in schools in South Texas in the 1950s and 60s."

Hmm. I am a little puzzled, amused, and intrigued. Kent, who is now Sgt. Pepper, is talking as Angie? Really? He can now just speak for Angie without any trouble or hesitation? I hope at some point he would address the awkwardness of having to speak in a Latina woman's voice as a White man. After Kent introduces himself as Angie, he returns to his seat behind the desk, and starts reading from his notes, as Kent, the researcher. In this reading Kent frames his research purpose and questions and recites some more academic stuff. But still no discussion of what is so visually apparent and cognitively dissonant, Kent performing as a Latina woman. Next, Kent comes up in front of the desk and starts to deliver his lines as Angie. Make no mistake, in those moments, Sgt. Pepper comes out to play. Kent is skilled in memorizing his lines, inserting pauses, making eye contact with the audience members and emoting effectively. All eyes are on Sgt. Pepper. We are mesmerized by his storytelling performance. But no mention still of how Kent, the researcher, reconciled the differences between Kent's and Angie's lives. The screen behind Kent automatically rotates between slides that contain a series of non-copyrighted colorful images of various species of birds. The bird theme is meant to match Angie's desire to "never be a yellow bird, but always be a blue bird," something that would later become a title of a paper we publish together. The bird colors were used to separate Anglo students from Mexican students when Angie was a school-going young girl. Small significant snippets of quotes from the script are printed over some of the images. I get the feeling that each picture is carefully selected to match the mood of each portion of the transcript.

***

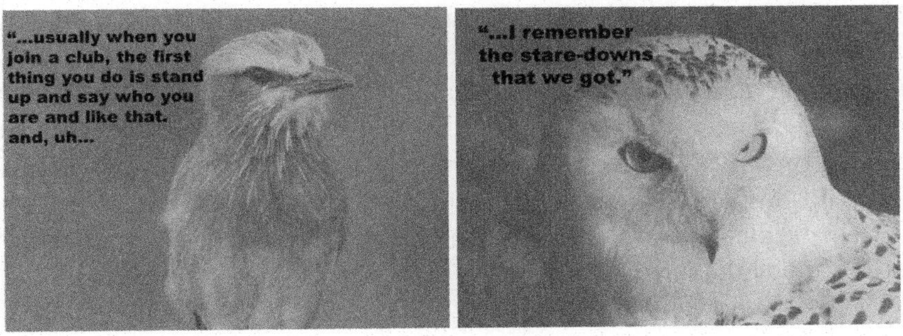

Figure 12. Images from Kent's presentation in Urbana-Champaign, IL, May 2010

Yet nothing here explores what I want Kent to address—how is he able to tell a story of a woman who has lived such a remarkably different life from his and what is he able to hear and understand beyond his scope of understanding? Instead, Kent postures as this researcher who can (albeit illusorily) take on the role of a neutral observer discussing academic topics relevant to the research and adopt the voice of Angie and move effortlessly between the researcher's voice and Angie's voice without ever experiencing any conflict. It is as if he has free access to both of these voices – or worse, he cannot see what might be problematic in believing that he has free access to both of these voices. Can anyone really speak *for* anyone else? When we tell a story, how we understand the story, what we choose to tell, how we choose to tell, reflects how we have made sense of the story through our own cognitive filters, past history, background, experiences, etc. To even assume that the storyteller can somehow be this detached narrator, absent from the story, is inaccurate and intellectually dishonest. My hope is that someone from the audience will raise this issue.

After all four presenters have finished, the chair of the session invites people to ask questions in the remaining fifteen minutes. Inquiries are posed to different presenters, with a few directed at Kent. One audience member jokes with Kent about the notion of a White man taking on a Latina's voice and asks if he would perform in drag the next year. Kent politely bypasses the remark and states that perhaps he will have moved onto something else by then. And that is that. No other discussion about Kent's performance or the discrepancy between the lived experiences of Kent and Angie. The session ends.

Afterwards, Kent and I speak briefly after the session but we are joined by other students, so we do not get a chance to fully analyze his presentation and reflect on the event. I praise him for his idea of demonstrating the difference in speaking academically, showing creativity with his slides and performing with a larger audience, beyond academia in mind. I ask him to think about how he might have addressed a question that could be asked about his ease in taking on Angie's voice and if there might be some problems implicated in that posturing. Kent nods meaningfully and leaves to take a bus. And I anticipate that he would address the issues I am raising by the time he presents me with his writing.

***

When I wrote my dissertation in an ethnodrama format, I did not have any trouble inserting myself into the plays. My study focused on international graduate students' negotiations in higher-education culture in the U.S. during their first year in academia. My participants were women. I am not stating by any means that I was better at creating ethnodrama than Kent. I experienced several roadblocks and struggles myself. However, finding self in ethnodrama was not one of them. Perhaps the need to insert myself in the plays came from the fear that I would be accused of "having an agenda" and not making it clear what that agenda would be.

Does Kent worry about such agendas? Or does Kent think that his similarity or differences with Angie would never be an issue because he could speak from an authoritative and trustworthy researcher-perspective, where he would never be accused of being an angry minority researcher, or a researcher with a crusading agenda as many scholars of color have often been accused of doing? In my ethnodrama, sometimes I inserted myself as a character, sometimes as a transparent narrator, and sometimes as an observer. However, I never thought of hiding behind the curtains and being a puppeteer of the characters in the play that I was creating. Holding that kind of responsibility, that kind of power, without being vulnerable would have felt unbalanced to me. I would wonder about the ethical implications of putting the participants under the gaze of the audience, which could be folks from and beyond academia, and remaining hidden from the very same gaze myself while gaining academic mileage. I try to extend some benefit of doubt to Kent. Perhaps Kent's introverted nature makes him write plays where he does not expose himself. But I am not fully convinced that if a person were introverted, then he would be absolved of certain ethical responsibilities of transparency, power sharing, and vulnerability. Or is it my feminist subjectivities coming out to play?

Generally speaking, I meet two types of students in my class – (1) those who are open to the critical issues I raise in class and engage in those issues actively; and (2) those who resist them. If the students in the latter group continue to resist me throughout the semester, then they choose to work with someone else, in a different area, and move on. Students in the former group generally either work with me directly or consult with me as needed. This group of students might have moments where they struggle to understand certain concepts, but generally they do not completely ignore my advice or bypass it. So it was difficult for me to understand Kent's reluctance to address my suggestions since I imagined that he belonged to the first category of students.

I take pride in the fact I do not spoon-feed students. I provide them with directions, suggestions, and feedback. I allow them to explore such issues on their own and come to their own critical conclusions. But with Kent, I am getting increasingly uncomfortable that someone, with my guidance, is not addressing one of the most salient and critical issues in his research. Who can tell whose stories? Whose voices are really "captured" when we engage in qualitative research? With which of Angie's narratives does Kent find resonance, dissonance? Why? What do these feelings of resonance and dissonance indicate about how he is reporting his research results? Which part of the data is he choosing to highlight? Which part is he bypassing? These are critical questions and have serious implications for how well thought-out his work is and how people will assess the rigor of his work.

Even though I have not seen Kent in any negative light, a part of me begins to wonder: Has Kent fully faced the fact that he benefits from a huge social system of privileges as a White man? Does Kent realize that the repeated dismissal of my suggestions could be considered microaggression? Would Kent have taken the same path had I been a White man who was his faculty mentor? And yet I know that to even present these questions to Kent would possibly break his heart and spirit, because he is genuinely a good person with a gentle spirit, no matter how much work he still needs to do to become aware of the entire horse instead of just parts of the horse. So I do not share with him these questions. I continue having faith that Kent will address my suggestions, perhaps at his pace, and perhaps what is necessary for me here, is to practice more patience.

Months after the conference, when Kent finally completes his ethnodrama, I find that there is one significant character that stands out for me, and I am curious to see how Kent would address the relevance of this character in relation to his own experiences as a human being and as a researcher. That character is named "Johnny," and he, like Kent, is Angie's contemporary. Johnny is a student in Angie's class. He interacts with Angie in two crucial scenes. Moreover, Kent narrates a form of segregation that teachers practiced most likely not being aware of such a transparent bias, where they would ask students what they had for breakfast and if the students mentioned anything that sounded Mexican or non-Anglo, then they were sectioned off, away from the White students when Angie was going to school as a little girl. This was an inadvertent form of racism. The sectioning-off was based on how well students could communicate in English, the colonial Mother-tongue. As a result, Angie learned to say that she had oatmeal for breakfast, without fully understanding how people might eat oatmeal.

On the other hand, the character Johnny responds to the teacher's prompt playfully, describing how he shunned his meal of bacon and eggs (a "typical" Anglo-Americanized repast), so he gave it to the family dog instead. Johnny's teacher and classmates react with amusement. That very same teacher, however, would press Angie with several questions to really determine if she had oatmeal or if she was simply fibbing. For Angie, this was a deeply meaningful moment. The incident would later become the inspiration for part of Kent's dissertation title. Toward the end of the play, an older version of Angie tells her contemporary Anglo counterpart, Johnny (who has now attempted to save her from a different kind of embarrassment) that she did not need saving from anyone and that she could fend for herself.

I found that insight quite revealing in terms of Johnny and Angie's interactions. This made me curious about how Kent saw himself in relation to Johnny. Was he similar, identical to Johnny? Was Johnny inspired by Kent's sociocultural space in relation to Angie's? Or does Kent relate to Johnny in a different way? These answers require Kent to be vulnerable and honest with himself and I do not know how to create the path for this authentic inquiry into self for Kent or if it is my responsibility to do so. But my discomfort remains.

KENT'S NARRATIVE

Theatre's primary goal is to entertain – to entertain ideas and to entertain for pleasure. (Saldaña, 2003, p. 220)

Spring Semester 2009. Reading Saldaña's article a second time, I am inspired by the words above. They stirred my excitement over a month ago. But today, that challenge to "entertain ideas" with ethnodrama is like a dare – an open invitation to commit an act of subversion against the conventional. I am also drawn to the back-and-forth dialogical format of narrative – an easy, accessible means of communicating stories and ideas. I thus wade further into the theatrical format of data-representation. The pull toward experimentation is too strong, and I cannot resist going further.

I have completed two scenes thus far, both based on the interview sessions with Angie. So I draft a third scene that jumps from 1957 all the way up to the 1960s. This final segment of the one-act play centers on the Future Homemakers United (F. H. U.) club that Angie had referenced in her interview. (In reality, there was a Homemaking club, but not with that particular name; it is more fictional contrivance.) I set the scene at the club's annual spring dance to honor the school's football team. Angie and Linda make their appearance as high-school girls. To open the scene, I dress the Anglo club members in cheerleading outfits and compose a song-and-dance routine for them to perform:

Every year about this time
We feel the need to go sublime...
To bare our hearts and naked souls
To those who strain for useless goals...
Our parents want us home by ten,
But oh my God, we'd rather sin...
Our teachers want us reified.
Idolized! Beatified!
But we just wanna be bad.
Is there nothing really so rad
As a vicious, righteous, totally obnoxious
Coterie of clucks like we (we) (we) (we)...?
F. H. U! F. H. U!
Wash, rinse, dry and spin.
F. H. U! ...

From there, I focus on Angie and Linda, who play the roles of reluctant wallflowers. No one at the dance will interact with them, so they are anxious to exit early. But not before an altercation erupts between Angie and one of the Anglo girls, who is slightly tipsy and believes our heroine/participant has been giving the eye to her boyfriend, a White senior student named Johnny. Angie acquits herself quite well during the argument, and Johnny even steps into the fray on her behalf. However, before departing the dance, Angie tells Johnny, "I guess I'm supposed to thank you for sticking up for us, but we can fend for ourselves. It's not your fight anyway." The End.

As I write that concluding speech, I am vaguely aware of the issue of "speaking for others" that must be addressed by researchers in cross-cultural endeavors (Alcoff, 1991/2009; Phillips, 1995). As previously discussed, I have been warned by Dr. Sherritt to include a discussion of these ethnic intersections between the researcher and the researched. And as stated before, I am dispirited at the notion that my intentions would be questioned – based on the fact I am not of the same cultural background as the person whose life I wish to investigate. Yet it seems a complex, burdensome, unnecessary task to fulfill the requirement of clearing myself of – what? Something other than performing a case study with a Chicana educator who has led an interesting life? Why would anyone feel I have ulterior motives in doing *that*?

Nonetheless, I press on with the inductive analysis by focusing on the idea of ethnodrama itself. Thus far, I have not researched the background and history of performative writing. I presume that since theatre is considered a "cutting edge" technique in research – a recently employed method of presenting findings to an audience – I may dig up few articles on the subject. But I am wrong on both counts: (1) the idea of performative text has been around for decades, and thus (2) there is plenty of literature already published on the subject of artistic data-representation, including opinions both pro and con.

Saldaña, of course, is one of the most frequently cited proponents, but I quickly discover others – Dwight Conquergood (1985), for example, whose article, "Performing as a Moral Act," includes the warning that "[w]hen one keeps intellectual, aesthetic, or any other kind of distance from the other, ethnographers worry that other people will be held at an ethical and moral remove as well" (p. 399). Researcher detachment, in his opinion, is deemed a strategy to dispose of early during any qualitative procedure. So do I refuse to heed the warning?

Later, I discover Maso's (2003) assertion that researchers (such as I) unwittingly "bring with them their own emotions, intuitions, experiences, meanings, values, commitments, presuppositions, prejudices, and personal agendas, their positions as researchers and their spontaneous or unconscious reactions to subjects and events in the field" (p. 40). That's quite a mouthful. But it makes sense. And according to the author, it all affects the way we make implications about what we study. So do I address the issue? I know now it will be necessary, and I also know why. Beyond Angie's parting shot at Johnny, there is nothing I have added to the subject. So I ask myself: Do I really believe Angie's concluding line is sufficient enough to address the issue of "speaking for others?" And I respond, "Yes." Yet I know I deceive myself. I am guilty of intellectual laziness for avoiding the matter. There are also certain implications about myself with which I am not ready to face. Thus, I avoid the issue. I even wish it, pray it away. I dare not cope with it – not now, when there is so little time left to complete a class project that accounts for 20% of a final semester grade. Such a burden, therefore, must await another day. It will require much headwork; and I already have enough to deal with.

Just before the semester ends, I finish drafting and revising an inductive analysis centering on Angie's experiences for the advanced methods class. What with quotes from the transcript and the resulting mini-play, it comes to 30 pages total. Dr. Bhattacharya's prompt had set the ceiling at 20. But it is mid-May and she has to turn in grades, and so I send it to her by e-mail attachment. She replies the work itself is good enough, though among her comments, there is this: "So the third scene is not so much about the tangible truths but about truths of desire. The desire to be quick, present a witty mind, use humor to reject boundary-based discourses."

I take the remark as a back-handed compliment, but her criticism rings true. I have engaged with Saldaña's challenge to write a diverting piece. But what *ideas* have I entertained? Beyond a historical recounting of ethnic resistance against "boundary-based discourses" of the past, what have I really contributed to the *universal* dialogue – the scholarly conversation on the significance of arts-based social-science reporting?

In the end, I receive an A for the course – but not before Dr. Bhattacharya urges me to complete the project for submission to a journal. Therefore, during the summer break, I produce even more pages of reflection, referencing everything from Dwight Macdonald's (1969) essays on early Russian cinema to Moss Hart's (1959) remembrances of co-authoring his first Broadway comedy. I have generated enough content already; but instead of organizing, editing, and condensing, I keep going further, adding more and more. Finally, in November, after 53 additional attempts at revisions and multiple condensations, I submit a completed draft with a note: "I've gone about as far as I can go with this." I have reached a point where I can no longer bear to look at it. Dr. Bhattacharya agrees to take over from there as both co-author and methodology consultant.

***

Christmas Break 2009: I have not prepared a proposal for my dissertation study, but I now realize it will focus on ethnodrama. Further, I suspect Dr. Bhattacharya knew this even sooner but withheld it from me. I must discover such matters for myself. I purchase a blue, five-subject, 200-page spiral notebook in which I plan to make daily entries during the four weeks I have off from classes. I intend that these notes be in the form of dialogues centering on ethnodrama and the proposal. The entries will reflect on the possibility of extending the inductive-analysis itself into a full-blown dissertation. One entry reads:

*Rationale of the Study:

(WHAT WILL BE STUDIED?)

Specifically, the K-16 experiences of a successful Chicana academic will be the target for ethnographic inquiry; and ultimately, data elicited from interviews, observations, examination of artifacts, photographs, and other similar objects of interest, along with field notations will be transferred within the creative framework of a data-representation piece.

(WHAT IS THE RATIONALE FOR ENGAGING IN THE STUDY? WHAT ISSUES, INTERESTS, OR CONCERNS WILL THIS STUDY ADDRESS? WHAT IS THE EDUCATIONAL INTEREST OF THE PROPOSED STUDY?)

This study will explore the issues of:
Chicana feminism in a South Texas venue – but will do so within the context of an arts-based approach. That will be the study's contribution to the educational field.

QUESTION: *But how would this differ from, say, Gloria Anzaldúa's essays, which themselves, can be considered arts-based?*
ANSWER: *Did Anzaldúa ever engage in ethnodrama, per se? Poetry, yes. Autobiographical fiction, yes. But play-writing? (Don't think so.) There's the (unique?) difference.*

QUESTION: Maybe, but it's not all that unique. What is the "educational interest" of the study?

ANSWER: Part of the study will ask the participant to explore the sociological barriers she overcame on her way to becoming a successful academic and to reflect on internal and external factors that may have facilitated her success.

QUESTION: Then what has the ethnodrama component got to do with the rationale? Why is it the subject for study?

ANSWER: Has anyone explored the issue of ethnodrama as related specifically to the experiences of a South Texas Chicana who became a successful educator?

QUESTION: Not to my knowledge.

ANSWER: It's certainly worth investigating. There, then, is the rationale.

At this stage, I have not yet contacted Angie about extending our researcher-participant relationship. I am, however, working under the assumption that she will give her consent. In the meantime, I inquire into the nature of what I have already attempted with the three-scene play for the inductive-analysis:

Leavy (2009) summarizes Saldaña's (2003) suggestions regarding the writing of ethnodrama:

a. *Recommends that researcher cull down the data to "the juicy parts," but warns of certain ethical issues that may emerge (such as the unintentional revelation of a participant's name or identity.)*

b. *Recommends that the number of actors in the piece be equivalent to the number of participants in the study. (I did not do this; should I have? Why? Are* these *"the rules?")*

c. *Recommends "in vivo" coding process. (I prefer line-by-line)* (fused *coding.) (Why?: Because I find it more conducive to work with.)*

d. *Also recommends condensing of cast to composite characters (where 1 represents many.)*

Again, I read Saldaña's (2003) "Dramatizing Data: A Primer," and I am reminded that the author also touched upon the issue of ethnodramatists casting themselves in their own work. I attempt a reflection on my desire to keep my presence offstage:

I would maintain that, while conceding the necessity for some self-disclosure on the part of the researcher, the extent to which "you" are involved can be freely and flexibly determined. ~~by oneself~~ For example, there are varying degrees to which one may wish to inject their presence (physically or in spirit) into an ethnodramatic presentation. Ultimately, it all depends upon a researcher/author's discretion. Additionally, such an issue may be determined by factors related to internal (ethical, moral) as well as external (~~physical~~ personal comfort) issues.

At this point, I attempt to create another "rationale" – a reason for distancing myself from that which I seek to explore. In other words, I have convinced myself to perform research in ways that contemporary investigators would strongly object. Yet, I reason that I am not part of Angie's world. I do not belong there. I do not belong in anyone's world except my own. This is how it is. This is how it *has* been since growing up in Denton, when I would venture underneath that highway bridge and hold imaginary conversations with imaginary friends. In a like manner, my sole intention during Christmas break is to see no one. Instead, I isolate myself in my second-story bedroom and work six hours daily, reading and making a large amount of notations, some whose meanings appear hazy the day after I wrote them.

The only rationale this unfortunate, novice researcher can devise to defend his own wish to keep solitary distance and omit any involvement with those whose lives he purports to explore reveals itself ashamedly in the following passage:

ISSUE: *Would autoethnography-drama create a larger pitfall for self-indulgence on the part of the researcher than ethnodrama? (Because of the conscious injection of self in the former? Would not ethnodrama involve the same pitfall?)*

A: *Yes, but to the same degree?*

Q: *I don't know...doesn't the "creative act" of ethnodrama involve self, as well?*

A: *In the sense that the creator is the central guide for the conception, the structure and everything else, yes it does.*

In other words, I have mistakenly convinced myself that as an artistic tour guide into the research of others' lives, the "self-indulgent" act of injecting my own presence will serve as a sort of...confounding factor? Even for an inexperienced researcher, this is a bit naïve. Confounding factors are a chief concern for *quantitative* researchers designing cause-and-effect studies. Nevertheless, in overlooking this simple fact, I invent a rationale for my denial and avoidance of what I would realize later should have come first – a confrontation with my own Whiteness. At this pre-writing stage of the project's development, this was where all that thinking and reflection and writing was taking me – on a self-delusional trek, devoid of good, sound thinking.

***

Spring 2010: A dissertation committee is chosen, with Dr. Sherritt and Dr. Bhattacharya as the two co-chairpersons, and a date is set for proposal defense – April 15. It is a day to be enjoyed by neither the beleaguered taxpayer nor the fledgling researcher.

I arrive early and head straight for the room where I will be heard by the committee. I make certain the handsomely designed PowerPoint program I have prepared is ready to play through. Minutes later, the committee members arrive, each with copies of my proposal in hand. The first member to be seated is Dr. Caroline Sherritt, who has been my most ardent supporter and champion. A week before the proposal, she predicted what might happen today. Confidently, she presented a scenario where I was to give my presentation, answer a few questions, and then leave the room while they all discuss last night's baseball scores. Then, I would be called back into the room, and the committee would give the okay. However, her prediction turned out to be the most inaccurate forecast this otherwise intuitive, highly perceptive, well-travelled educator has ever put forth.

The proposal hearing turns out to be every bit as grueling as an inquisition – omitting the physical torture, of course. I am put on the hot seat for what seems like an hour, taking a good grilling. One professor wants me to define just what ethnodrama is, and I am unable to provide a suitable answer. Another professor desires to know if I have written my proposal with a specific participant in mind. This is a particularly disarming question because I did secure consent in writing from Angie just last week. She has now agreed to continue as the lone participant in the larger project I am now proposing. There is just one problem: I may have disregarded protocol by signing up a participant before the proposal is even approved. I wish I could ask, "Have I violated any rules? And if I have, are there any serious repercussions?" Nevertheless, I begin my reply, "Well, strange you should mention that because…"

Fortunately, Dr. Bhattacharya interrupts to deliver a scathing review of my methodology chapter, while another professor weighs in with a lengthy diatribe criticizing my nonexistent examination of the self in relation to those I endeavor to research. (Where have I heard that before?) I attempt few answers during this embarrassing ceremony. For the most part, I am there to listen, learn, and obey.

After a few other questions, Dr. Sherritt offers me her thanks and then asks me to leave the room while they mull over their decision. Once outside, I remark to myself, "They're certainly not discussing baseball scores." But as Dr. Sherritt assured me, they call me back into the room and, their criticisms notwithstanding, verbally sign off on the proposal. I may now proceed with the study.

Before I leave campus that afternoon, Dr. Bhattacharya confides to me that years ago at the University of Georgia, just before she defended her own proposal, she had experienced the feeling of "Fried Kakali, coming right up!" I know what she means. Proposal defense is not a ritual I wish to re-live. I then say nothing more, but I feel thankful she interrupted me as I was about to reveal my possible departure from protocol by selecting a participant before the proposed study was approved. Perhaps I should be more than thankful. Maybe I should be *grateful*. I wonder now if she suspected the truth. Did she inject herself into the conversation in order to keep me from implicating myself before the committee? I am too afraid to ask.

***

May 2010: Just before the beginning of Summer Semester, I take a 25-hour bus ride north to Urbana-Champaign, Illinois, and an international convention for qualitative researchers, where I am scheduled to present findings from my pilot-study, the not-yet-published inductive analysis I completed last year as a student in advanced qualitative methods. As part of my presentation, Dr. Bhattacharya has convinced me to stage a performance of excerpts from Angie's interview-responses; in other words, I am to stand before an audience of research professionals and perform the role of Angie. So before the trip, I prepare a monologue consisting of the most interesting quotations from transcriptions of her remembrances. I have no intention of donning a costume or applying makeup. I am not a professional actor, and I have no training as one. But my teacher and new mentor has urged me to try this risky maneuver, and I have reluctantly agreed.

The convention takes place on the flagship campus of the Illinois university system. It is an imposing setting, with a huge quad surrounded by classroom buildings that must be a century old. I am scheduled to give my presentation in one of them – an ancient, musty three-story science building. Outside, I meet with Dr. Bhattacharya, who has flown up from Corpus Christi and has already participated in two panels. After proceeding inside and up a flight of stairs, we discover the room where I will present has a wall of shadeless windows to let in the merciless four o'clock sun. "No place to hide," I whisper. And it is true. Why did I ever agree to "perform" in front of an audience of my peers? But then I remind myself that I made the commitment, so I must go through with it. Before the panel commences, therefore, I attempt to summon internally what Angie feels as a marginalized Chicana who resents being held back. Someone other than I must have decided that if this method – right out of Victor Turner's (1982) playbook – of "acting out" the part of the researched did not eradicate the emotional distancing of a researcher from those whose lives he desires to study, then what else can?

The panel includes four other presenters, and it is decided I will go first. Good. I can get this over with fast and fret about it later. Throughout the week, when not attending a workshop or buying new clothes, I have holed up in my motel room with coffee and fast-food carryout, memorizing the lines I will soon deliver. Now, the chair of the panel introduces us and then calls on me to begin my presentation. I approach the front of the room and sit behind a long table, facing an audience of two dozen other researchers, mostly young graduate students. I read from a prepared introduction of what I am about to perform. Then, I stand up, walk in front of the table where I take a seat, and begin my performance, reciting each sentence with the calculated emotion and enunciation I have planned, while trying not to engage in any unnecessary physical movement.

Do I feel the intense anger and bitterness of a person who is oppressed by a dominant culture intent on preventing her from accomplishing personal and professional goals and anything else of significance? No. I am suffering from a slight case of stage fright. I am trying not to forget my lines. I am struggling to keep eye contact with the audience. In other words, I am so busy managing my own performance that in the end, there is no performance at all – just a nervous doctoral-level student delivering a conference presentation.

When I finish the monologue, I dismount from the table and walk behind it to take my chair. Once again, I read from a prepared script that offers theory and rationale for what I have just done. But they are words. On paper, they may have been the result of careful, deliberate reflection on arts-based research. But here, they are only tools to complete an additional entry on a vita. And when I finish the presentation, there are no applause – only dead silence. Dr. Bhattacharya, however, appears delighted. She lauds my decision to perform astride the table and sit behind it afterwards. To her, it was a theatrically artful move. But for me, it was a desire to place something between myself and the audience. I was seeking a way to re-establish distance from everyone in that room.

During the question-and-answer session, one member of the audience jokes that I should return next year and perform the part of Angie in drag. Everyone laughs at his remark as I resist the impulse to crack a two-word rejoinder. Instead, I smile in the gentleman's direction and reply, "Well, hopefully by then, I'll have moved onto something else." Indeed.

***

Two weeks after returning from Illinois, I begin work on my study. I e-mail Angie, and we meet the second Friday of June in her office. I tell her about the conference but make no mention of my misgivings about the presentation. We then begin the interview – our third now. I start with questions about her extracurricular activities in high school. There was the Homemaking Club, of course, and the Spanish Club and the pep squad. I was curious if there were any others. So I begin by asking her if she had other experiences in school related to actively resisting established rules based on ethnicity.

ANGIE: My senior year – we were having our Who's Who elections...I noticed that very few Latinos were ever nominated for Who's Who or Homecoming Queen or any of those kinds of elections and activities. So I formed a little group and I took the name from La Raza Unida, and I called it La Raza Party...And I started approaching people to run...I went to one who was very athletic, who I had seen in sports many times, and so I asked her if she would run in Who's Who in Athletics. And then another person who had been, pretty much, a very good student. She had been in the National Honor Society – and I asked her if she would run as well.

At this point, I allow my mind to wander while a reel of cassette-tape dutifully records her words. As Angie speaks, I am already thinking of ways to stage the events she describes. The La Raza Club, for example. How can it be written theatrically as part of an extension of the three-scene inductive analysis into a larger work with many added scenes for a dissertation chapter? Perhaps, I can follow Prendergast's (2003) example and have Angie's character stand in front of the audience and read from a series of monologues, all in the form of diary entries, using much of her own words from the interview transcripts concerning how she resisted the political structure of her high school. Maybe I could call the entire play *Diary of a Mad Chicana*...No, that would make her sound insane...Hmmmm...

ANGIE: ... And so I made little buttons, you know, out of paper, cardboard, construction... I asked them if they would wear their little button (*laughs*), so that they would show solidarity with the rest of us and show that we would promote Latinos. And sure enough, the Latinos got three, I remember clearly. Two girls and a boy, running with this little tag that I asked them to wear, again, to show that we were a separate group and we wanted to be included in these activities. So in our senior album, here we have these students showing under Who's Who.

ME: Were the boys athletes?

ANGIE: Yes, football. Football's the main thing here in Texas... definitely football.

I pause here and ponder the theme "resistance." I ask myself in silence, what other subjects do I want to touch upon? And then I think of one.

ME: What was law enforcement like in [your town]? I'm guessing it was a small constabulary. Do you recall any discord between the police, the local constabulary, and minorities in the community during that time when you were in school?

ANGIE: I think fear. There was a lot of fear to some of us, I think. I was always afraid of doing something wrong because I was going to be arrested. I mean even so much as being tardy to school, I thought I would be arrested. I always had that feeling of, you know, that tardiness was going to cost me jail time. (*Laughs*).

ME: How old were you at the time?

ANGIE: Oh, gosh, I was a little kid, maybe elementary level. Of course, I have an older brother. He's a year older than me, and that was, you know, he was a very passive person also. And so he used to fear that. So most of the time, I went to school with my brother. And I used to always worry about that. "Don't go to the stores because they were going to accuse us of shoplifting." So things like that, we just avoided it.

But, of course, we had the rougher boys, the wilder boys in the community. Uh, they would have the weekend drinking parties at their homes or whatever, and we were not allowed to go. (*Laughs*). We all knew where we belonged. I was a church girl, so church activities we did…but those were the only kind of parties I would be allowed to go to anyway. Church and school. That was all…

Another lull in the conversation occurs. I realize now I should have prepared a list of questions, but I have none. For the second time in two years, I catch myself flat-footed. I was so confident. Boy, was I wrong! I am also aware that these are her office hours, and if any students from her summer courses knock on her door, I must halt the interview. So I now ask her about something regarding English – not as a course discipline, but as a second language. I now recall something she told me in one of the interviews I conducted with her last year.

ME: You mentioned being taught English by your older siblings. And I was wondering how that came about?

ANGIE: I don't remember an actual lesson or anything formal. But instead, it was just a communicating, speaking. We played games together, we sang songs. Our songs were English songs. We'd put on little plays; we'd perform to each other and to friends around the neighborhood, singing a lot of, you know, you remember that song, "Alley Oop?" (*Laughs*). And, so we'd take turns singing songs. Uh, the Everly Brothers, you know, that kind of song, very simple. But, uh, we'd sit on our swing and sing songs, and that was our stage, and the next person would sing on the swing. And we'd just take turns. And we'd have Kool-Aid and cookies and that kind of thing (see Figure 13). It was a lot of fun…

Another possibility for an additional scene. I smile as Angie continues.

…but that was just it. It wasn't just us; it was the neighborhood kids. My mother was very strict, so if anybody wanted to play with us, they had to come to *our* house or our yard. So, here, we wouldn't be in the house, which was too little. We'd be outside, and we'd play games.

ME: Was there a bilingual education program in place at your school?

Figure 13. Angie (extreme right), Kool-Aid and friends

ANGIE: No, no...

ME: It was immersion?

ANGIE: Oh, yes. It was all-English. All-English. The expectation. Like I said...my friend who spoke only Spanish, uh, I think she did really well, because within the year, she ended up passing, I mean, gradewise. But she was always able, she was able to learn English by the end of that year. But I'm sure it was difficult for her because she had to go home and continue with the Spanish, and then change over for English in school.

Another scene. This one could feature Linda – the girl Angie discovered crying on the school playground – at home, speaking Spanish, then switching to English when in school. How could I work that into the play? I'll have to think about it later as I attempt to keep the interview going. I try to recall my own first- and second-grade experiences. What did we do in class?

And then I remember Tina, a pint-sized moppet with dark hair who lived down the street from me in Denton. One of the first girls, maybe the very first, on whom I had a crush. One morning, she brought her black kitten to class for show-and-tell. I remember how the animal's fur matched perfectly with the dark sheen of her own hair. Show-and-tell. First grade. So I ask Angie:

ME: In first grade, just as an example of activity in the classroom, I would imagine many might tend to recall a day the teacher may have set aside for, say, "show and tell." Was there anything like that in your first grade or elementary grades?

ANGIE: I do remember a certain episode. Not necessarily show-and-tell, but we did have to tell how, you know, what kind of breakfast we had. And I remember thinking, well, that morning, I had had a taquito. And, uh, probably beans. And my mother used to put spam. Spam and beans. It was the greatest thing ever. But I knew that if I told them that, they would laugh at me. At least, I felt like they would. So I told them I had had oatmeal. And, uh, I thought oatmeal was acceptable. (*Laughs*). It was plain, it was, you know, uh… and, you know, they left me alone after that. But that was always my fear, you know. What do they want to hear? So I would try and figure out, well, what do they want to hear? And that's what I would say. Now, looking back, I think to myself, I was lying a lot. But to me, that was my way to protect myself from being ridiculed. And, you know, it did not hurt to tell them something that was not true. Of course, I had eaten oatmeal, but not that morning necessarily (*Laughs*).

Show-and-tell, I don't know what I would have taken. Again, it would have been something that I would take that they expected me to take, and it wouldn't be anything having to do with being ridiculed.

ME: So you were conscious of a feeling of wanting to be included?

ANGIE: Right.

ME: Was there a time when you may have felt *excluded*?

ANGIE: Going back to…we were learning how to read. And, uh, the first time I ever encountered this word written down… They always told us, of course, break it down. Into syllables – so that you can learn how to pronounce it. So, I saw the word, and I broke it down: "To get her." Well, of course, the teacher laughed. And she says, "No, no, no. It's 'together.'" And, of course, I was humiliated and I remember being very embarrassed. And it got to the point where I wanted to cry. One thing I learned straight, right from the beginning was never let them see you cry. That was always something in the back of my mind. I don't care how insulted I felt, or embarrassed.

I was never going to let them see me cry, and I found that very hard. It was difficult. Then I'd go home and cry. Or on the way home, I'd cry, but they were not going to see me cry. And I carried that for years, and even today, I, people who know me, they're my friends, say, "You're so stiff, you don't cry." And I say, "Not in front of people." (*Laughs*). So that was one episode, uh...there was another episode...

Episode! She has used the word "episode." Not once, but twice! Does Angie read minds? Or does she think this is what *I* want to hear – a series of possibilities for expanding my play? If this is what she suspects, then she is right of course. And I realize that in the last minute or so, she has just given me two more possible "episodes" for adaptation. Let's see, that makes how many in all this morning?

ANGIE: ...I guess, it was in, maybe the fifth grade, sixth grade. Before I started middle school or high, or junior high. They had had a party for one of the children at their home. So everybody was supposed to be invited. And...and I remember not wanting to go...and, uh, my mothers[2] told me, "Yes, go. It will be fun. You'll have a good time." So I thought, okay, I'll go. And I did. I did go. And the party was held outside; we never went inside the house. So, uh, probably the first time I had gone to an Anglo house for a birthday. No piñatas. *(laughs)*. And I kept waiting for something, something more than just cake and cookies, or whatever, you know. I thought it was just a bit boring. But okay, I was there. But I was included. I do remember that.

And in junior high, that's where I really noticed "the shift." I was not going to be included in anything. They were not going to invite me to anything. Uh, there was no such thing as an 'A room' any longer in junior high. So they just put students, I don't know how they decided to put students in what sections or whatever, but, uh, that's when we did move from class to class, course to course. We had homeroom, and then after that, we would divide up. But that was in junior high.

Once, we were running for whatever elections they had. They were friendly only when they were running for something. But after that...

99

ME: The cheerleaders were all-Anglo in junior high?

ANGIE: Yes...until, possibly, my senior year when a little girl, a Latina, did become a cheerleader as a freshman. She was a freshman, I was a senior. And she was a daughter of one of the teachers in junior high, [last name of teacher]. They were not in our class, they had more money than the rest of us.

Up until now, Angie and I have not explored the issue of class – at least, not overtly. But as I think of a question to follow up her last response, there is a knock on her office door. I turn to open it, and I hear the voice of Angie greeting the student behind me who desires to consult with her about an assignment. Angie asks the student to come inside, and I turn the recorder off. Before leaving, I thank Angie and ask her, "Next week? Same time?" Angie smiles her consent, and I walk out, feeling pleased with myself. I am thinking, "Episodes...Right!"

***

Before I draft additional scenes for the play, I must transcribe Friday's interview. So when I arrive home, I locate the blue spiral notebook I used six months ago during Christmas break to record notes and thoughts regarding ethnodrama. Opening to the first blank page, I begin playing back the interview, stopping every second or so to write down each phrase, sometimes each word. I must be as accurate as possible.

Then, I compose a scene based on one of the "episodes" Angie mentioned yesterday in her office – the one regarding the spam-and-bean for breakfast.

(Lights fade in. ANGIE enters from the left, appropriately dressed for school in (ask Angie about this in next interview). To her right, a series of pictures are projected Pictures of???...

PICTURE: A large black question mark, on White background.

ANGIE: Ask me, and I will tell you what you want to hear. *(Pause)* Trying to find out what people want to hear in Elementary and then telling them? This is something I am just learning. Comes in handy on days when they want to know stuff. Like what we had for breakfast. I had a taquito and some beans I fixed myself. *(Pause)* But I know if I tell them that, they will laugh at me.

Angie then takes her place in a CLASSROOM, stage right, as lights fade in.

Background: *PROJECTED PICTURE: An old-style one-room school house, illustrated the way a first-grader might draw it.* **(the idea of projected pictures may be dispensed with; it's become a cliché, after all)**

Stage right – lights fade in. ANGIE takes her place in a seat with other students in a typical classroom setting. A young woman, MISS CARTER, perched on a stool, center and down stage, facing slightly away from audience and directly toward students who are in chairs upstage. One student is already standing and speaking to the rest of the class...

Here, I pause typing. I have to think of a name for this student. Should I make this first-grader a boy or a girl? I then recall the title of a classic hit tune, "Johnny Angel," that was popular during the early Sixties. I guess "Johnny" seems an appropriate name... Johnny Angel... Johnny/Angie... All right, I decide, the student speaking in class will be an Anglo first-grader named Johnny. So I continue typing:

... We catch him in mid-sentence.

JOHNNY	...but I didn't like the eggs. They tasted all runny. So when Dad wasn't looking, I gave 'em to Skippy. That's our dog. But my sister snitched. *(indignant)* So I got punished – no more *Whirlybirds* or anything else on TV. For a month! *(Laughter from most of the children.)*
MISS CARTER:	I'm sorry to hear that, Johnny. You may sit down. Now, Angie, it's your turn. Would you please stand and tell us what *you* had for breakfast this morning?
ANGIE *(hesitantly and looking down)*:	Uh, I had oatmeal. *(Long pause)*
MISS CARTER:	Okay. Anything else?
ANGIE *(still looking down)*:	No, Miss Carter. Just oatmeal. *(Shorter pause)*
MISS CARTER:	I see. Well...uh, did you have it with sugar? Butter?
ANGIE:	No, Miss Carter. Just oatmeal. *(Muffled laughter from one or two students)*
MISS CARTER:	Oh. Uh. Well, what did you have to drink with it?
ANGIE:	Oh, I can't remember. Milk, I think.

> *(Laughter from the children. Angie tenses, tightens her fists)*

MISS CARTER: I see. Well...okay. That's all, Angie. You may sit down.

> *(Lights fade to dark on classroom stage. ANGIE walks stage left and she continues speaking to the audience...)*

ANGIE: So I told them I had oatmeal. It's plain, it's, you know...they left me alone after that. *(pause)* What do they want to hear? So I try and figure out, well, what do they want to hear? And that's what I say. I guess I lie a lot. But to me, that's my way to... *(Pause)* And, you know, it doesn't hurt to tell them something that's not true. I *have* eaten oatmeal, but not this morning...

The scene is too short, but I can add to it later. In the transcripts, Angie had described being laughed at in first grade for reading the word, "together" as "to get her." Maybe I can work that in. Perhaps Johnny can be the chief instigator and ringleader, encouraging everyone to laugh at Angie for mispronouncing the word. In doing so, he could represent...what? A symbol of mindless oppression? (Was oppression ever instigated with nothing in mind?) Maybe he could be the son of parents for whom Angie's mother cleaned house. In our first interview session, she had remembered recognizing such a boy among her classmates during her first day in school.

In the end, though, I decide Johnny has been given enough attention. It is not *his* story. He is a White youngster, and as such, he is a peripheral existence in Angie's life. I conclude that his continued presence will amount to no purpose or consequence. So I decide to keep little Johnny off stage for the remainder of the play.

I neglect the fact that a year ago, there was already another "Johnny" – the one who appeared in the last of the pilot-project's three scenes. He was the character Angie had told off at the Homemaking Club's dance when he tried to intercede for her in an argument: "We can fend for ourselves. It's not your fight anyway." I have not looked at the inductive-analysis draft since last November, when I turned it over to Dr. Bhattacharya. I had worked on it so much last fall that even now, I find it unbearable to read through again.

As a result, I have forgotten all about that older "Johnny." I will not be reminded of his appearance, or his unexpected thematic significance, until months later when the play will be completed.

NOTES

[1] A proposal document involves writing three chapters of the five chapters of a typical dissertation, where the student explains what s/he wants to study, the literature that exists in the field in the area of the student's research interest, and how the student wants to execute the study (methodology).

[2] The word "mothers" is used here by the participant in referring to both her mother and grandmother.

CHAPTER 4

DIALOGUES WITHIN DIALOGUES

In our conflicts, we must sometimes put certain aspects of our identities backstage; otherwise, we'll be so busy asserting and protecting those identities that we will miss what's really going on, miss the opportunity to become or gain allies.

(Anzaldúa, 2015, p. 77)

KAKALI'S NARRATIVE

When Caroline decided that I should work with Kent, I was excited because I enjoy working with deep thinking creative scholars. But within each of my conversations with Kent, there were other dialogues, histories, memories that were intersecting, that continuously informed how I would mentor Kent. These intersecting dialogues were the result of the complicated positions in which we found ourselves – student, teacher, minoritized woman, untenured faculty, qualitative researcher, privileged, man, woman, White, Brown, etc. Several years ago, I wrote up my dissertation as front and backstage plays similar to how Goffman (1959) discussed the performance of self. The basic idea behind such plays is that we show up differently in different spaces, we reveal different things about ourselves in different spaces, and such ways of showing up are directly related to how we understand our power and privileges with the people in those spaces. For example, what a student would say to her peers about a class would not be the same as what she would say to her professors because she is aware of the power difference, how power could operate for or against her interests. Similarly when I am talking to Kent, Caroline, or my colleagues, I am not just having dialogues with the person in front of me. I am carrying with me dialogues I have had before, dialogues I imagine having as a result of my current interaction, and dialogues I want to have strategically so that my place in higher education as a minoritized woman faculty is not severely jeopardized. What follows next is a series of front and backstage scenes where I interact with various aspects of my relationship with Caroline and Kent, where Caroline is at once an older White woman, mentor, ally, and a gatekeeper, and Kent is a White man, mentee, student, introvert, and had lived in Texas his entire life.

105

BACKSTAGE SCENE

Act 1 Scene 1

CAST OF CHARACTERS:
CAROLINE 1 – Older White woman
CAROLINE 2 – White woman who is not concerned about unpacking privileges
CAROLINE 3 – White, liberal social justice ally
CAROLINE 4 – Academic and institutional gatekeeper
KAKALI – Brown, untenured, woman academic

Scenography: *A coffee house in Corpus Christi, Texas. There seems to be an alcove separated from the rest of the coffee house where the different versions of Carolines are sitting down and having coffee in plush mismatched chairs. On the wall there are paintings of a local artist who focuses on the use of blue and green in various compositions. Soft lounge music plays in the background. Kakali enters the alcove with her coffee, and sits down in one of the chairs. Beside her is Caroline 1. Kakali sinks into the chair, looking visibly shorter than all of the Carolines except for Caroline 1 who is beside Kakali. Caroline 2 is leaning back on her plush chair, looking fully relaxed. Caroline 3 is leaning forward on the table, drinking coffee, and looks alert. Caroline 4 is sitting in a tall chair, with a stoic expression on her face while she sips on coffee.*

CAROLINE 1: Hey, welcome Kakali. (*Pats on Kakali's back*)
KAKALI: Thank you. How are you? (*Smiles back at Caroline 1*)
CAROLINE 1: Good, what brings you by?

Kakali takes a sip of her coffee, gulps, and straightens her posture

KAKALI: Well, I want to talk to you about Kent's proposal. I don't think he is really discussing how he is going to study someone's experiences who is so remarkably different from him.

CAROLINE 2: (*still leaning back on her chair, fully relaxed*) Oh, that's not a problem. Students learn as they write. I am sure he will learn how to do what we are asking him to do eventually.

KAKALI: (*leans forward*) I think it is critical though that he unpacks his privileges and the ways in which he is trying to create an entry point into this study. How else would we guide him to do this work if he doesn't know what his entry point might be?

Suddenly Caroline 3 slaps the table with her hand and talks in a loud voice. Caroline 2 and 4 appear unphased. Caroline 1 is startled.

CAROLINE 3:   Look, this is social-justice research. And isn't it time that now in South Texas we stop doing research that centers on White folks and sheds light on the oppression of Hispanic folks? People here are usually so provincial. Besides, this is not even a deficit narrative. This is about how someone made it in academia even with all the oppression. This is a great story to tell. I think Kent can and should tell this story. We need to tell these people's stories. It will be good for this community.

Caroline 1, 2, 3, and 4 nod their heads aggressively in agreement. Kakali takes another sip of her coffee. They all stay quiet for a minute before Kakali starts to speak.

KAKALI: I agree that this is a story that needs to be told. But who tells the story has a lot to do with how the story is being told and how he understands the story.

Caroline 4 gets up from her tall chair and walks over to Kakali. Kakali looks even shorter to a standing Caroline 4 beside her.

CAROLINE 4:   Listen, Kakali, you know I have been sitting back and saying nothing until now, so let me say a few things. You know I am your ally. You know that I like you.

Caroline 1 leans in and pats Kakali on the back while Caroline 4 speaks.

KAKALI: Yes, Caroline, and I completely respect that and appreciate it too.

Caroline 4 moves in closer.

CAROLINE 4:   So know when I say this. As someone older to you. As someone who has seen a lot of academia. As someone who is chair of your tenure and promotion committee, since you are submitting materials later this year. You don't want to come across as a firecracker. No one would want to work with you and in academia, you don't want that kind of reputation or perception about yourself.

Caroline 1 holds Kakali's hand.

KAKALI: Okay.

Caroline 3 stands up, leans in, slams the table again, and points at Kakali. Caroline 2 still seems relaxed in her chair. Caroline 1 carries on holding Kakali's hand. Caroline 4 appears to be surprised at Caroline 3's outburst.

CAROLINE 3: (*points and wags her finger*) And if I may interrupt, another thing to be careful of is to know when to draw the line so that you are not making other people feel insecure based on what you know about race, culture, or research. People might think that you are showing off. And then no one would want to work with you.

CAROLINE 4: (*nods*) And you know what *that* would mean for tenure and promotion.

CAROLINE 1: (*squeezes Kakali's hand*) And really, as a friend, I don't want to see you do all this hard work and then not get the recognition you deserve.

CAROLINE 2: (*leans forward slightly*) And think about it. We still have time. We can make things work out. We just don't have to be so aggressive about it. It will happen.

KAKALI: Okay…well…thank you.

Fade to black.

FRONT STAGE SCENE

Act 1 Scene 2

Scenography: *Kakali is seated behind her desk working on her computer. Caroline comes in and sits down on the blue couch against the wall in Kakali's office.*

KAKALI: Oh, hello! Wasshappenin?

CAROLINE: Let's get Kent's proposal defense done. He needs to be working on his dissertation and left to his own devices he will start thinking about studying the Corpus Christi bus system again, or pick another random topic out of nowhere. That boy needs to be focused; so if we move him along, he won't get distracted.

KAKALI: Okay, but he is not where he needs to be. He is missing a few pieces theoretically and methodologically.

CAROLINE: (*leans back on the couch*) Oh, that's fine. The proposal is never perfect anyway. We will just give him feedback and it will be all right.

KAKALI: You sure it won't be embarrassing for us?

CAROLINE: (*stands up to walk out of the office*) Nah. He will just get good feedback. It will be good for him. Don't worry, it will be fine.

KAKALI: Okay, if you think that's what needs to happen.

CAROLINE: (*at the door almost exiting the office*). Yes, let's do it. I will send out the emails today.

Fade to black.

BACKSTAGE SCENE

Act 2 Scene 1

CAST OF CHARACTERS:
KENT 1 – Introverted, socially uncomfortable man
KENT 2 – White man who is not concerned about unpacking privileges, never left Texas to be anywhere else
KENT 3 – White, liberal social justice ally
KENT 4 – Mentee, graduate student
KAKALI – Brown, untenured, woman academic mentor of Kent

Scenography: A coffee house in Corpus Christi, Texas. There seems to be an alcove separated from the rest of the coffee house where the different versions of Kents are sitting down and having coffee in plush mismatched chairs. On the wall there are paintings of a local artist who focuses on the use of blue and green in various compositions. Soft lounge music plays in the background. Kakali enters the alcove with her coffee, and sits down in one of the chairs. Beside her is Kent 3, smiling, and drinking coffee. Kakali's chair is visibly taller than other chairs

*so that when she sits in it, she is almost as tall as Kent,
who is at least 5'8". Kent 2 is leaning back on his plush
chair, looking fully relaxed. He is leaning forward on the
table, drinking coffee, and has a yellow notepad on the
table, which looks well used with many written pages.
From time to time Kent 3 starts to write something on
the pages. Kent 4 is sitting across from Kakali, slightly
fidgety, drinking coffee faster than the rest of the Kents.
Kent 1 is sitting in a corner chair, almost blended into the
chair. He is drinking his coffee and reading a book. He
makes no effort to chime into the conversation between
all the other Kents or anyone else.*

KAKALI: Hey, what's happening?

KENT 3:   Nothing, just thinking about finishing this dissertation.

KAKALI: Have you given any thought to what we talked before
about your entry point to this work?

KENT 4:   (*sips some more coffee*) Yes, yes, we have been reading a
lot.

KENT 2:   (*stands up and starts pacing in the alcove*) Okay, yes, I
have been thinking, but here's the truth. I read a lot. I
think a lot. I don't go around oppressing people. I have
lived in Texas all my life. I have been around people of
color. I have never oppressed anyone. I don't know what
the hell kinda privileges that I have had that made things
so bad for people of color. Besides, does anyone know the
kind of stuff I have had to go through? Just because I am
White doesn't mean that I didn't have my own struggles
or suffering.

KAKALI: (*turns around to face Kent 2 who is still pacing. Gets up
and leans against a wall where she can see everyone and
watch Kent 2 pace back and forth*) Well, of course you
have your struggles and suffering. I think it is possible to
hold your suffering in the same place with the suffering
of a group of people because of a system that fails them.
They don't have to erase each other. They co-exist.

KENT 1:   (*looks up nervously from his book*) I don't want to be here
anymore. Can we just go home?

KENT 3:   (*Points at Kent 1, raises voice, Kent 1 looks surprised,
Kent 2 leans forward*) See, that's what I am talking about.

I would much rather just go hide in my apartment and barely talk to anyone, let alone oppress anyone. So why do I have to start listing my privileges? I don't support prejudice. I don't support bigots. I have been on the right side of issues. I have always hated when I have read about oppression. How am I the bad guy?

KAKALI: You're not the bad guy.

KENT 4:   Then I just don't understand what it is that I am supposed to do.

KAKALI: Well, first you have to read some more. Then think about privileges more than something you personally enjoy or deny people. Then think about the fact that if Kent 1 wanted to go back to his place right now, he could, and he has a place to go back to, instead of being dead, or being in jail. Think about how you learned, when you were young, who belongs in jail. Who did you see behind the bars? Think about how that made you form an idea of who belonged where. (*Pause*) Now think in terms of Angie's perspective. What would Angie have learned as a child? What could have destroyed her goals and ambitions? What kind of strength and resiliency is needed to overcome that? Here you are, never having to think what you want to become, because you know whatever it is, if you really wanted to be that, you could. Angie, on the other hand, is thinking of her brothers and uncles ending up in jail, of how doing well in school may not be a good idea for her, especially in Math. Very different realities. Why is that? Why is Angie not growing up thinking the world is her oyster?

KENT 1:   I don't think the world is my oyster either, I would rather not even participate with the world (*returns to reading*)

KENT 2:   This is tough.

KENT 3:   Well, Angie's story is a powerful one and I am trying to tell the story. I am not oppressing her.

KENT 4:   (*Stands up, picks up everyone's coffee cups and puts it on the table by the garbage can*) Guys, guys, guys. Look, she is asking us to read some more. Let's just go home and do that. Obviously, there is something here we have

> overlooked. We are not getting anywhere right now
> anyway. Let's go home.
>
> KENT 1: (*gets up first*) Yes, good idea.
>
> KAKALI: (*stands up*) I agree. I will see you later.

Fade to black.

The front stage performance relates to my conversation with Kent in my office. He will detail this later in the chapter. I describe the narrative of the front stage performance below and then pull together all the performances to explore how these dialogues-within-dialogues functioned as Kent and I worked through a tough terrain of learning and unlearning things we had known or taken for granted.

At some point after defending his dissertation proposal, Kent comes into my office. We have been meeting somewhat irregularly to see the kind of progress he has made with his writing. Sometimes, I chuckle to myself in the ways I shock Kent, or think I *might* be shocking Kent? I have wondered if my students think I am the perfect representation of a nutty, quirky, and sometimes wildly crazy professor. This day, when Kent presents me with his writing, I begin to see how Angie is reflecting on parts of herself, as who she is currently as an educator, who she was as a Chicana student, discriminated against in her school days, and as a girl with enough agency to question patriarchal norms. It becomes clear to me that we should tease out these parts of Angie, and then see if we can understand how these parts of her separately and collectively work together to make sense of Angie's journey.

I suggest to Kent that he should divide Angie into three different people depending on her age and then have the Angies talk to each other. This may have been a good moment for Kent to back away, choose another mentor, thinking his current one suffers from dissociative identity disorder or at the very least projects some kind of split-personality issue on his research. However, Kent does not bolt from the office or resist or reject the idea. Instead, like always, he remains seated and just falls into deep thought. In my experience, this is common with Kent. I would ask him a question or make a suggestion, and then he would immediately start thinking about it. To the untrained eye, it would appear that a question was asked, but an answer was not offered. But he is not being disrespectful. In fact, he is actually being quite respectful and thinking deeply about what was posed to him.

Perhaps several minutes have passed while we share the space in silence. Something about Kent's movement and body language makes me feel that he is ready to engage in a conversation again. I start to talk. "It would be interesting to have Big Angie talk to Little Angie and tell her that it's okay for Little Angie to do well in school, to do well in Math. And that Little Angie doesn't have to worry about going to jail or be worried about her brother going to jail."

There is some deep pain in me as I suggest this rhetorical device for Kent. It is the pain of thinking about "Little Angie," who was being trained to believe that men who look like her brothers, cousin, and father would very likely end up in jail, and women who look like her would not belong in school. I do not know this pain because I grew up in India and Canada and my family modeled higher education for me. I did not have to worry about anyone in my family going to jail. I only had to worry about whether I could meet the high expectations my family placed on me. So when I put my privileged upbringing against Angie's, I feel pain in my heart. What is it like for a little girl to grow up and resist her own family's patriarchal norms and society's racist, sexist norms? I admire the agency it takes for someone as young as Angie to decide that her path will be different and have the resiliency to stay the course and challenge stereotypes.

Based on my years in academia, I have learned about academic bullying during various stages of my career. Early on I was naïve to think that if I did my job well, then I would be successful in higher education. Soon, I found out that our dialogues-within-dialogues, our backstories, play a huge role in how we understand and interact with others. Unknowingly, I made people uncomfortable by simply doing my job well because some of my colleagues felt that their performances might be compared to mine and they would then be regarded as less than competent. As a result, their insecurities rose to the surface, and their actions reflected those insecurities. I was at the receiving end of some of those actions, so I carried them with me into my front and backstage conversations with Caroline.

The backstage conversation with Caroline did not actually occur. It was an artistic representation of how my dialogues-within-dialogue informed the ways in which I interacted with Caroline in the front stage performance, which did occur. What I carried with me was the fear of how far I could push without being vulnerable myself and jeopardizing my sustainability in higher education. Caroline has always been a friend and never acted maliciously towards me or anyone I know. But because of the stories I carried with me, I always saw her as a mix of gatekeeper, ally, mentor, and older White woman.

And from seeing her in those positions, I found myself arguing with two White people, urging them to understand the value of unpacking privileges when working with people of color. For Caroline, it was not that critical an issue and could have been worked out gradually through feedback and revisions. For Kent, it was not difficult to unpack privileges. It was just difficult for him to think that he had any privileges or that he benefitted and continues to benefit from a system that has been set up in his favor. And here I am – someone who is also privileged to be in academia, someone from a minoritized position, asking folks to put the agenda of unpacking privileges as the key threshold to cross before conducting any inquiry. And based on my power relations with Kent and Caroline, I express myself differently with them. With Caroline, I am deferential. With Kent, I am much more assertive, even authoritative. Perhaps at some point, I even use my position of power to insist he accomplish what I think is the most critical piece in his research – to situate himself in relation to his participant. Interestingly, at Kent's proposal defense, another White ally, Bryant, brought up the same issue of Kent's position as researcher, which then legitimized further the necessary influence over Kent and his work. As a committee, we made it clear to him that we expect to see that work done before he completes his research.

KENT'S NARRATIVE

Yesterday, I conducted another interview with Angie. I now transcribe the dialogue into my notebook. I began the session with a query designed to expand on Angie's recollection of her warning not to go into the shops of her small town for fear that White storeowners would accuse her or her brother of theft. I asked her if she ever overcame that fear.

> ANGIE: In [my hometown], no. *(Laughs)*. I never really did…the [storeowners] were very suspicious, even of the salesladies, because I know my mother had a friend who was a saleslady in one of the five-and-dimes. She would tell us stories of how her boss constantly, constantly, checked them, their pockets, checked their purses coming and going home – and constantly just be looking. I remember one time [my mother] went to buy some material at this particular store. And her friend was cutting the yards. The woman, the owner was, like, right on her to make sure she didn't cut an inch more of material…Just like I'm saying, there's a fear that the, the, just a sense of not belonging, you know, I'd go in, I'd go out. I never really liked shopping in [my hometown].

ME: I'm surprised they didn't lose clientele.
ANGIE: Well, it's a small town. A lot of people didn't have cars to
           come shopping in [name of nearby city]. And that was our
           only other place. So we either shopped there, or we didn't
           get anything. So people had to live with that if they had no
           other options.
ME: I guess the storeowners knew that. And played on that...
ANGIE: Sure, sure. Yes... We went to [the city], possibly, once a week
           because my aunt had a boyfriend who could drive a car. So
           he would bring my aunt and my mother and possibly the
           kids. So we'd go downtown and we'd go to the groceries,
           and we'd just kind of, it was on Saturday, an all-day kind of
           shopping thing...
ME: She bought things for herself and for the family as well?
ANGIE: Yes, her main shopping – here's another option she did have
           for shopping – was catalogs. I remember it wasn't Sears so
           much, but the National Bellas Hess catalog. We'd sit there
           and just go over the clothes we wanted – and then we'd have
           to choose one outfit. My mother had credit there. And that
           was another reason. She would order C.O.D. We'd have just
           a little different [clothes] from the regular stores down the
           street...

But exclusion from shopping in her hometown was not the only evidence of
cultural stigmatization during her youth – as I learned when I followed up
with another prepared question.

ME: Can you describe more about "the shift" that occurred
           between elementary and junior high school? And how did
           this "shift" affect you personally?
ANGIE: Well, uh, again in junior high...we were, I guess, integrated
           with other students. So that was really the first time that
           I got to be in the same classroom with students who had
           been in other classes, in other kinds of rooms...I liked it,
           there was no problem with me...As far as the Anglo group,
           I knew that they would not even sometimes acknowledge
           me. You know, we'd pass each other in the hall. Here's
           these students who had been in classes with me since the
           first grade and – they would pass me in the hall and just

115

ignore me, like I wasn't even in the hall and just ignore me, like I wasn't even there, you know. Not even a hello or a good morning or whatever. So I realized, okay, this is, this is it. And then, because I think sometimes, uh, they were, at that point, starting to date Latinos. Maybe they saw me as a threat, I don't know. Uh, competition…I never felt that I was pretty, and I didn't think of myself as, you know, popular, I mean, so…there was a lot of negatives and so I think, looking back, well maybe, maybe it was more me than them. But I did remember…the only time they did talk to me was when they were going to be running for some kind of cheerleading or student council or whatever it is that they were running. *That's* when they would talk to us.

As I listen to Angie's voice on tape, I wonder what it was like to be deliberately excluded by the dominant culture of one's school. If this had been me, how would I have endured "the shift" and the treatment that came with it? I know, of course, I will never discover an answer. I can only imagine experiencing such marginalization. But what if I had? Would I, like Angie, have taken the initiative to engage in active resistance? When did Angie determine she could no longer accommodate such long-established norms of behavior? When did she decide enough was enough? What was the catalyst that led her to infiltrate the exclusive, all-White Homemaking Club? Or to enlist and organize other Latinos to run for Who's Who? To discover that turning point, I asked the next question.

ME: I was wondering if there was ever a time when you began to cease anticipating what others "wanted to hear," in particular with respect to teachers or other authority figures.

ANGIE: Closer to my senior year, I would suggest, because, you know, again, as an A student, I was always looking for the right answer. There's, there was always a right answer and a wrong answer, and there never seemed to be a gray area. But in my senior year, I remember getting assignments in English class asking for essays. You know, what do you think about, you know, pick a topic and write about it. And that was when I remember writing constantly, one paper after another after another, about our rights, our civil rights not being given. I wrote about Vietnam. I wrote about everything that bothered me.

And I remember getting a paper back from, from that teacher… And she wrote on the side: "Well, aren't things getting any better?" She had a question mark. And I thought, "No! No! Don't you hear the news? Don't you see, listen to the radio? No, things aren't getting better." Because I guess she got tired, but maybe not tired, but she kept wondering, "She's so negative. She's just writing about everything *bad*." But no, I never felt like it was, uh, getting better – *but* that was when I realized, "Hey, I *do* have a voice, and I *can* be assertive. Even if I can't be vocally assertive, I can *write* it." And to me, that's something where my whole life changed. This idea of writing. Writing was my forte. I could, I could be anybody I wanted to be in writing.

ME: Did you speak with her about her [written] comments on your essays?

ANGIE: Never. No. That's one of the things about that setting – at least, I didn't think so at the time – [it wasn't] like we do in English class today. I'll ask my writing students, "Well, really think about this." And, uh, "What do *you* think about this? So I try to get them, to engage them in "oral," so that their "written" will be a little stronger. But at that time, it was not like that. You know, you raise your hand and give me the right answer, and let's move on. More stifling, I guess. It's still, uh, our education system had not gone into group learning or anything like that. We were still very – controlled. But yes, I think [the teacher] probably thought: "You all have civil rights now. Yeah, you can go to a, a theatre, you know, any theatre you want to. You could go eat at any restaurant you want to. You, you're not going to be denied service. So, isn't that better?" *(Laughs).* No!

ME: The point of view from those born with privilege?

Suddenly, I press the stop button on the tape recorder – and I am compelled to ask myself a question: "Did I say *that*?!"

It sounds the sort of question Dr. Bhattacharya might pose. Even the same words. Where had I heard the word "privilege" used in that manner before? From reading Gloria Anzaldúa? Gloria Yamato? Possibly. It is a strange experience, listening to myself form a question like *that* in mid-conversation.

I rewind the tape and play back the question again: "The point of view from those born with privilege?" Then, I press the stop button and ask, "What did I mean by the phrase 'born with privilege?'" Was I referring to privilege bestowed by class? "No, Kent," I tell myself. "Privilege born of race?" But, but...I look upon this kind of privilege as a remnant of the past. Things *have* changed...But wait...Am I taking sides against Angie here? Am I aligning myself with her 12th-grade English teacher?

Well, after all, this *was* 40 years ago. Perhaps her teacher was mistaken about the speed with which things changed in 1969. But if she were still around to make that statement, would she be correct in today's context? And had not Angie herself observed how "things have sure changed" in an earlier interview when she discussed how radically the demographics of her hometown have altered since those times we are now discussing? ...

I press the play button. As I listen to Angie speak, it is almost as if she is addressing my thoughts.

ANGIE: It's difficult. And I, I do understand that, and I do, you know, see people and I try to explain how I feel about certain things. And basically, unless a person's gone through something, it's difficult to understand how the others think. It's difficult for me to think what it's like to be privileged all the time, you know. And I can never imagine living on [name of fashionable street in participant's locale] with a fancy house and servants all the time, you know, I, it's beyond my scope. I'm still cleaning tables after I eat, you know, at a restaurant. You know, this is my thing here.
           (Pause)
ME: Uh, these were written essays for a grade?
ANGIE: Yes. They were, they were called themes. I don't know if you remember that, but they were called themes, not essays. And so I, you know, I loved that. It was, that was, like I said, my voice. They said, "Pick a topic." And I did.
ME: Were you encouraged by the grades you got?
ANGIE: Oh, yeah. I, I was an A student, right? I still maintained, maybe not my A level. But, uh, I was still high B, A. And I was always on the honor rolls. But I didn't make it in the National Honor Society. And, uh, that always affected me... Why not? And somebody told me that it was because I was one-tenth of a grade, one-tenth of a point away. So okay, I

didn't make it. I hadn't made it for other things, so it wasn't
going to tear me up.

End of session, end of transcription. But not an end to my thoughts. I cannot
help but reflect on Angie's response. Was her failure to obtain recognition by
the National Honor Society the result of just numbers not falling into place?
Or was another factor involved? Like her race? How did Angie feel about
this then? Even now, what inferences does she draw from the incident? Is this
an issue from the past that she still questions today?

Afterwards, I begin the process of coding and theming Angie's responses
in our last two sessions. I use methods recommended by Charmaz (2006)
in order to "curb [any] tendencies to make conceptual leaps and to adapt
extant theories" prematurely (p. 48). Coding is the breaking down of the
participant's responses line by line before they are fused later into "chunks"
in order to widen the focus into a "more conceptual" view and thus enable
the researcher to examine any general ideas or recurring themes that may
result from interviews (pp. 48–57). This is how I intend to infer meaning
from Angie's narration of her public-school and hometown experiences.

I apply this procedure throughout the two interviews. The resulting sub-
themes reveal a pattern (or motif) surrounding the dichotomous idea of
inclusion/exclusion. No surprises there. But at least I have assured myself I
did not make any "conceptual leaps" or postulate any "extant theories." After
coding, I plot the ethnodrama's next scene. I decide to base it on the incident
described by Angie at one of the local dress shops, where the White woman
storeowner kept a close eye on her employees to make certain they were not
stealing from her inventory.

Scene Title: A Dress Pattern of Oppression.

Mrs. Pillory's five-and-dime store, Fall 1962.
From stage right enters ANGIE. She addresses the audience.

ANGIE: In our town, a lot of people don't have cars. People
                like us. But my aunt has a boyfriend who can drive a
                car. So he brings my aunt and my mother and the kids,
                depending on how much room they have in his car, and
                we go to the city to shop. First, we go downtown and
                we go to the groceries. It's a Saturday all-day kind of
                shopping thing. *(Pause as lights begin to fade in stage
                left area)* We never like shopping in my hometown.

We're always told by our mothers, "Don't go into the stores. They will accuse you of shoplifting."

ANGIE exits, as the curtain raises on a five-and-dime store, where among other items, the local people shop for material to make their own clothing. The store is just opening for business. MRS. PILLORY, the storeowner, is currently the only character on stage. She is tall, very slim, very stiff, and walks with a carefully measured stride as she meticulously inspects and counts the number of items on the sales floor. After a short while, she examines her wristwatch to check the time; then she glares in the direction of the extreme left of the stage, where we notice three LATINO WOMEN lining up and facing in MRS. PILLORY'S direction, as if waiting for something to happen. It soon does. The storeowner marches toward them and then halts quickly.

MRS. PILLORY: Assume the position, ladies!

She then proceeds to frisk each woman thoroughly – or, at least as thoroughly as propriety will allow. As they are being searched, the women display no emotion, no outward resentment. Each does as she is told without complaint. It's a routine that they must put up with every day.

MRS. PILLORY: All right, ladies. Now man your stations!

The women go to their assigned places and begin the day's business. In the background, we hear a church bell signaling the half-hour. MRS. PILLORY turns stage left.

MRS. PILLORY: Come on in, folks. We're open.

At this point, I realize some conflict is needed to distinguish the way Mrs. Pillory interacts with White customers in relation to her behavior with those of color. So I decide to introduce two rustic, small-town Anglo-Americans into the scene.

Two CUSTOMERS, who have apparently been waiting outside all this time, enter from the left. They are a middle-aged Anglo couple, a short man and a tall woman. The man wears a neck brace and moves very gingerly. The woman, on the other hand, is definitive, purposeful in her movements and very decisive in speech. It's quite apparent who wears the pants in this family.

MRS. PILLORY: Why, hello, Chester. How are you, Maudie? I didn't recognize you out there, otherwise I woulda let you in ahead of the kitchen help *(gestures toward her women workers)* What's it yer lookin' for?

MAUDE: The old goat here *(motioning toward CHESTER)* needs another tin of boot polish. Won't buy nothin' but Kiwi, he says. Hell, boot polish is boot polish for all I care. Got any, Hester?

MRS. PILLORY: Right over here. *(Walks to the wall counter and addresses one of her clerks).* Hey, you! Lainie! Get up on that ladder there and pull me down one of those canisters of shoe polish.

The clerk does as she is told and delivers the container into the hands of her boss, who gives it to Maude.

MRS. PILLORY: There ya be, Maudie.
CHESTER *(stuttering)*:
B-b-b-b-b-ut th-that ain't K-K-K-Ki-wi.

MAUDE: Clam up, Moose Breath. You'll take it and you'll like it. Thanks, Hester. Just stick it on my tab, will ya?

As CHESTER continues to complain, they both exit the stage.

After finishing this part of the scene, I wonder if the pathos is a bit excessive, exaggerated. Is it necessary that Chester stutter? Could this not be interpreted as insensitivity toward those who suffer from speech disabilities? I realize now I need to be careful. In earlier times, I might have felt that audiences would accept this as legitimate farce. Today, however, such characterizations may appear cruel, cheap, gratuitous…Nonetheless, I continue writing:

ANGIE and her MOTHER enter from the same direction. At first, MRS. PILLORY ignores them. Then she thinks better of it.

MRS. PILLORY: Lainie! Gotta pair of live ones for ya.
LAINIE: *(quietly, as if not to disturb the oppressive atmosphere)*: Ah, hello, *amiga*. How *are* you? Hey, Angie, you're getting taller every time I see you.
MOTHER *(laughs)*: That's why we are here, Elena.

At this point, I stop. Lainie and Angie have entered the store to buy a dress pattern, but I have no knowledge of the wording a customer would use in such a transaction. Is there a specific jargon? I must remember to consult with someone about this. I then write a description of the action that will conclude the scene.

As LAINIE unrolls the fabric onto the cutting table, we notice that MRS. PILLORY is now practically leaning over LAINIE from behind to make sure she does not scissor off more than she is supposed to. LAINIE tries to ignore her, but she is noticeably tense, as she cuts the fabric off before folding it into a neat parcel for wrapping...As the curtain closes on the store scene, ANGIE steps out of the store and in front of the curtain to address the audience.

ANGIE: I never really like shopping in my town. In the city, I can go into places, and I almost never feel that attitude of "You don't belong here" or "What are you doing here?" But in my town, if you don't have a car, you either shop here, or you don't get anything. We have to live with that.

After I have written this far, I have no idea what to put down next. I also realize there is more in the way of mental logistics to writing a scene than I anticipated. So I stop short and begin a new scene with Angie still in place.

Scene Title: Shifting into Irrelevance.

Angie continues addressing the audience in front of the closed curtain.

ANGIE: It's only my first week in junior high, and I am already wondering how they decide to put students into what sections. They just move us from class to class, course to course, so that we're not with the same kids all the time. We have homeroom, and then after that, we divide up. *(Pause)* That's where I'm really noticing "the shift." *(Pause)* I can already see that I'm not going to be included in anything. The Anglos are not going to *invite* me to anything.

Enter AN ANGLO GIRL, who constantly chews gum the entire scene. She looks excited and enthusiastic as she approaches ANGIE quickly from the right. She carries a shoebox filled with purple ribbons.

GIRL: Hey, Angie.

ANGIE: Dawn?

GIRL *(giggles)*: Yeah, it's me.

ANGIE: Dawn, I know it's you.

DAWN *(still giggling, but finally gains control)*:
           Well, I just wanted *you* to know I'm running to be
           cheerleader next year.

ANGIE *(quietly)*:   I might have guessed.

DAWN: Huh?

ANGIE: Nothing. I just wondered what's in the shoebox.

DAWN: Oh, this? Oh! *(giggling again)* Right. Well, I just
           wanted to ask if you would wear this ribbon with my
           name on it.

ANGIE: Where?

DAWN: Yes, wear.

ANGIE: No. I mean, where do I wear it?

DAWN *(a fresh outbreak of giggles)*:
           Oh, wear it…oh, anywhere. Uh, school, home…

ANGIE: Dawn, I mean some of the girls running for cheerleader
           like their stuff to go on a blouse. Others prefer the skirt.
           Then there's the shirtsleeve…

DAWN *(confused at first. Then, dawn slowly breaks)*:
           Ohhhhh. I get it! Well…*(all serious now)* I really
           hadn't thought of *that*.

ANGIE: Never mind. I'll think of a place to put it.

DAWN: Well, you *will* vote for me. Won't you?

ANGIE: I don't know, Dawn. I've never seen you do, uh,
           anything.

DAWN: Oh. Well, let's see. I can cartwheel, and, uh, I can
           climb up pyramids, and, uh, I can even do the shimmy
           shimmy shake. *(Again with the giggles)*

ANGIE: Dawn. I tell you what. I'll see how you do at the tryout
           assembly next week. And if you're good, I'll vote for
           you. Okay?

DAWN: Great, great! *(proceeds to exit stage with a flourish of
           giggles)*. See ya!

ANGIE *(addressing the audience)*:
           Did you notice? *(pause)* That's the only time they talk
           to me – when they're going to be running for …

At this point, Angie is interrupted by the sound of a loud school bell signaling the end of a class period. As ANGIE continues her speech, the stage fills with junior-high school age students carrying books under their arms or in satchels, notebooks, supplies, etc. Shortly, the students become as high-school students. Some even wear mortarboards with sashes as if anticipating their name being called at a graduation ceremony. They stroll left and right across the stage as if in the hallway between classes. Toward the end of Angie's speech below, some even jostle or rudely walk in front of ANGIE while she's still addressing the audience.

ANGIE: As I was saying, that's the only time they talk to us – when they're running for some kind of cheerleading or student council or whatever it is that they're running for. *That's* when they talk to us. But the rest of the time? Forget it. The *bolillas* will not even notice me. You know, we pass each other in the hall. *(Now she points at or gestures to the students who walk by her on stage.)* Here are these students I used to play with during recess and even go to their parties. Kids who have been in classes with me since the first grade and all the way through elementary. Members of the A Room, just like me. I used to read with them, draw maps of Texas with them, help dress up bulletin boards... Look at them now! They pass me by and just ignore me. Like I'm not even in the hall. Like I'm not even here, you know? Not even a hello or a good morning.

At this point, ANGIE, clearly a dejected young girl, joins the other students, who make their exit, walking off stage.

This scene is my interpretation of "the shift" – the racially motivated exclusion of Angie by her Anglo classmates. But what about Angie's own "shift" – the point at where she ceased to negotiate around the unwritten rules that permitted such exclusion? How could the beginning of her resistance be dramatized? Up to this point, I relied on what she had told me thus far in our interview sessions. When I asked her about this yesterday, she had told me about her discovery of writing as an act of empowerment. Her themes for 12th-grade English class had offered her the liberty to write opinions on social and political issues. In that way, Angie was interacting with the changes that were occurring in the world, and she had every intention of making her presence and opinions felt and read. Her only audience for these themes, however, was her teacher – an Anglo woman who evidently believed that the passage of laws designed to end the denial of admittance of racial minorities into cinemas, restaurants, and other public venues was sufficient enough to "make things better." From Angie's point of view, though, her teacher was mistaken. How can this difference in opinion be presented in a theatrical format? I proceed to set up a new scene and find out.

Angie, again, is on stage addressing the audience directly. She opens a loose-leaf binder and turns to a theme she has just written. Meanwhile, a voice will be heard offstage, making intermittent comments about her writing. The voice, of course, will be that of her teacher.

ANGIE *(wearing eyeglasses and reading from her own English theme)*:
"White America – White kids, White teachers, White principals, and most of all, White parents. They all wake up one morning and discover that there are non-White faces populating their classrooms. And they freak."

VOICE OF TEACHER *(off-stage)*:
No slang please, Angie! How many times have I told you?

ANGIE *(continues reading)*:
"But then the Whites recover or they think they do and they say to each other, 'Oh, it's not so alarming as all that.' To them, it's all a subtle sort of surprise, a mild practical joke and they just turn and ignore it and walk away and 'they can take it' just like London during the Blitz."

VOICE OF TEACHER *(off-stage)*:
Now really, aren't you stretching the analogy? Bombs?! Why do you have to be so *negative*?!

ANGIE *(continuing)*: "But still they feel taken aback by the presence of students of a different color and they don't know how to react or what kind of face to put on it or what kind of voice to do it with. None of it registers. What do they do, do they give it the cool Frank Sinatra deadpan, the kind he uses to put down Sammy Davis Jr. to end a funny scene?"

125

VOICE OF TEACHER *(off-stage)*:

That will do, Angie! I'll not have you refer to my Frankie in that manner!

ANGIE:

"Or how about the old Our Miss Brooks kind of wisecrack, designed to wilt the bloom off any ambitious classroom cutup?"

VOICE OF TEACHER *(off-stage)*:

Hmmmm.

ANGIE:

"Then there's always the Don Rickles Insult Special, the kind where he screws up…"

VOICE OF TEACHER *(off-stage)*:

"Angie, I will *not* condone such language!"

ANGIE:

"…the kind where he *wrinkles* up…"

VOICE OF TEACHER *(off-stage)*:

That's better.

ANGIE:

"…wrinkles up the brow below that shiny bald head with the creases above the eyes that snarl in their own kind of negative scrutiny that most non-Whites I know can interpret…"

VOICE OF TEACHER *(off-stage)*:

Angie!!!

ANGIE:

"… his voice revved up to its most venomous, most fevered and breathless delivery – for the entire span of a *Hollywood Squares* – before telling the White studio audience that it was all a joke, a big joke, ha-ha, and he didn't really mean it and he loves you no matter what color you are – White, yellow, black, brown, purple, polka-dot, Pepsodent-stripe, lemon-lime Jell-O, burnt orange, burnt charcoal, Duncan Hines angel-food or marble-cake delicious?"

VOICE OF TEACHER *(off-stage)*:

Young lady, that will do!!

ANGIE:

"When I listen to White show-business wise guys tell me how cool the other folks are, I think I can do without the usual brotherhood-of-man babble."

VOICE OF TEACHER *(off-stage)*:

I said, that will do!!!

ANGIE snaps the loose-leaf container shut, bows to the audience, then bows toward the side from where the TEACHER's voice emanated.

After finishing the scene, I read through it and begin to have doubts. The problem here is that I have no evidence or artifacts of Angie's style of writing when she was a senior (see Figures 14 and 15). Would the participant be displeased with what I have done here? In a sense, I have veered away from data and made up an English theme as I feel she *might* have written it. What was that complaint her teacher had made? "She's so negative!" Well, yes, I would hope so. Thus, I consciously wrote the scene in a manner that one might consider "negative" – i.e., disrespectful of cultural norms. Still, is this really

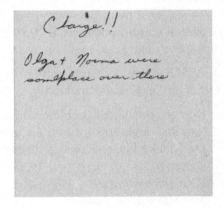

Figure 14. Angie's penmanship, 1969

Figure 15. Her school's football field, 1969

akin to a tone that Angie would have used to make her social views known to her teacher? It is not just "negative;" it is rude, sarcastic, and somehow I cannot imagine Angie as that sort of writer. This is the nature of the intersection – a case of someone's (my) voice overpowering the character's (Angie's). In the end, I consider chucking the theme and replacing it with another – or if not that, then at least rewording the theme to make it more the product of a girl genuinely concerned about the way the world appeared to her when she was 18 and less the pontificating of a White man high-school smart-ass, circa 1969.

I mention the year because that leads to another problem. Let us assume a theatrical troupe were to actually present these scenes. How would Angie be physically played on stage throughout the entire ethnodrama? Would she appear as the same girl (one actress) throughout her 12-year public-school tenure? Or would her character be interpreted by different actresses of different ages, all playing the same character at various points from 1957 to 1969? I have set a meeting with Dr. Bhattacharya next week. I will discuss the problem with her.

Fourth week of June. Graduate research section of the university's faculty building. Office of Dr. Kakali Bhattacharya.

ME:	I've got this small problem concerning Angie and how she ought to appear as a character in the play? Do I make her one person throughout? It seems a stretch to…
DR. BHATTACHARYA *(interrupting)*:	
	No. Make her several.
ME:	Several? How many is several?
DR. BHATTACHARYA:	
	Three or four… Let us assume you settle on three. You could have them intersect.
ME:	What? Intersect?
DR. BHATTACHARYA:	
	You would have intersecting Angies. They could meet each other at various junctures and interact. They would have conversations with one another.
ME:	You mean split up her personality? Or mix up each one's identities?
DR. BHATTACHARYA:	
	No, no…Naturally their identities would appear separate at different ages. But the audience or the reader would still know that the Angies are actually

the same character, situated within the same consciousness, as her awareness develops through multiple stages of experience.

ME: You're not kidding, are you? One participant divided…

Here, I have to stop talking and start thinking. Would this stage business of "intersecting Angies" really work? Or would it result in self-indulgent farce – a sort of "art for art's sake" free-style parody – so free, in fact, that it may threaten to dislocate the whole vision from those overriding themes of oppression and division and so forth…?

DR. BHATTACHARYA *(interrupting my reverie)*: You have interviewed her a total of how many times now?

ME: Huh?…Oh! Let's see. Five, if you include the pilot-project. The inductive analysis.

DR. BHATTACHARYA: How many times, excluding the pilot-project?

ME: Three. I did the second one two Fridays ago. The third I did yesterday.

DR. BHATTACHARYA: Have you transcribed all of them?

ME: Yeah. I have it here if…

DR. BHATTACHARYA: Let me see it.

My mentor takes the copy and begins reading through it. I soon notice she is not speed-reading, as she is often wont to do; instead, she is poring through it carefully, even going back and re-reading certain portions. I excuse myself in silence, sneak away from her office, exit the building, and then decide to wade slowly through the mid-summertime heat wave, all the way to the student center for something to drink. Upon returning a half-hour later, I discover she has progressed as far as the content of the third interview. She looks up briefly to comment.

DR. BHATTACHARYA: This section here is very powerful, the way she describes this.

ME: Where are you?

DR. BHATTACHARYA: Where she discusses her math class.

Yesterday, while interviewing Angie for the third time this June, I had asked her to describe any specific K-12 teachers that stick out in her memory. She

129

had related anecdotes about two. The first was an obese French teacher who preferred playing the latest top-40 records in class to teaching the language of French. She eventually eloped with a boyfriend midway through the spring and was subsequently fired. A second anecdote, the part Dr. Bhattacharya refers to, concerned a math teacher, as described below by the participant:

ANGIE: I had an algebra teacher, and I remember she was very, very, very old. And, uh, mainly there were boys in that class, and I was maybe one of two girls…And I, I was maybe a sophomore. And I remember being so intimidated because there was a room full of boys and they were all loud. And again, I tried to be as quiet as a mouse and look good. But I did know math and embarrassingly so…I remember thinking to myself, "Oh my God, I wish I hadn't passed the test!" so that I could be in the regular math with, you know, with my friends and stuff. But they had put me in this algebra class. Of course, I passed. But that was, you know, it wasn't a fun class. But she…she taught math. And then I took Geometry 2 with her…

ME: Why do you suppose just you and one other girl in that algebra class?

ANGIE: Math was hard. *(Laughs)* Math was hard. And uh, I don't know. Again, it was a time girls tended to dumb down. It was just part of an idea, that if you're too smart – can't get a man. *(Laughs)* Or wear eyeglasses.

ME: Do you suppose it's still that way today?

ANGIE: I hope not. I hope not, but you know, in some of our classes, I do ask the students that question. And, you know, I get an occasional one that says, "Yeah, it's still like that." In general, of course, I think especially in college now, a majority are women in the classes. And so they're more willing to talk. It's the guys that I'm worried about because there's just so fewer, fewer… maybe two or three in each section. But now, I'm seeing a little more…Let's see, something about not wanting girls with glasses…

ME: Boys don't make passes…

ANGIE: Yeah, yeah, don't make passes at girls who wear glasses. And I thought, yeah. *(Laughs)* Of course, you know, here again, wear glasses. I was, and I knew that even then, my sisters were always saying, "You're gonna…," because I was always reading.

Dr. Bhattacharya is as well-versed in feminist and post-feminist literature as anyone I know. Last year, on that inductive-analysis paper, she commented that the scene I wrote of Angie and Linda at the Homemaking Dance reminded her of a quote from an essay by Audre Lorde. I promptly interpreted this as a cue to incorporate the passage into my paper, which I did. Therefore, I understand how this part of yesterday's interchange with Angie might make some impact on my professor.

DR. BHATTACHARYA: The idea of girls doing badly in math, not excelling in science, being discouraged from reading…How would you go about dramatizing the way she resisted such ideas? How would you stage this in your play?

ME: Well, I already have. Want to see it?

DR. BHATTACHARYA: If it is not too much trouble.

ME *(Handing over a copy of the scene)*: Good. Tell me what you think.

DR. BHATTACHARYA: I intend to…once I have read it.

…Which she proceeds to do. It is a three-page scene, but almost seconds after she begins her perusal, I can detect the sounds of her stifled laughter. Very soft, but very distinct. Should I be alarmed? Impulsively, I attempt to find out.

ME: What? What is it?

DR. BHATTACHARYA: Quiet. I'm reading.

Immediately, I have visions of trashing the scene. Very frustrating. But once I calm down, I begin to come up with new ways to stage the episode. What follows is the scene I fear will be jettisoned.

SCENE TWO: Muzak to the Ears.

High School algebra class, Fall 1966.
A classroom with a bulletin board on which are tacked the display of various algebraic symbols and equations. The teacher, female, appears old. Very, very, very old. One might suspect she will one day expire in the middle of explaining a problem to the students. Speaking of the students, there doesn't appear to be too many girls among them. Maybe

two or three. But that's it. One of them is ANGIE. The rest of the class consists of boys. They're really quite demonstrative too. And the girls? Well, they're just there. Yet, it is apparent they wish they weren't.

MRS. CONSTANT: ...and so your word problem for today is as follows: *(The text of what comes next is spoken very quickly)* Peter Piper picked a peck of pickled peppers. A peck of pickled peppers Peter Piper picked. If Peter Piper picked a peck of pickled peppers, how many pickled peppers did Peter Piper pick? Please prepare a precise response for points. Protests? Problems anyone?

JIMMY: Uh, just one, Mrs. Constant. How much is a peck?

At this point, MRS. CONSTANT pulls out from under her desk an oversized ear trumpet and places it close to her left ear.

MRS. CONSTANT: What's that? Repeat please?

JIMMY *(practically shouting)*:
I said, "HOW MUCH IS A PECK?"

Laughter from the class.

MRS. CONSTANT *(in a normal tone of voice)*:
Master James, you should know by now about the peck conversion chart located in the back of your textbook. See if you can find it.

STEVE *(shouting)*: MRS. CONNNNN-STANT?

MRS. CONSTANT *(normal tone)*:
Yes, Stephen?

STEVE: *(Here, STEVE enunciates each syllable carefully, slowly, and loudly)*: IF WE WANT TO KNOW HOW MAN-Y PICK-LED PEP-PERS PE-TER PI-PER PICKED, DON'T WE NEED TO KNOW THE WEIGHT OF EACH PICK-LED PEP-PER?

By now, most students in the class are in hysterics.

MRS. CONSTANT: Oh, really, Master Stephen! You're making the problem much more difficult than it sounds. Check the average weights of all alphabetically

	listed foods and vegetables located in the same section of the book as the conversion chart. You'll find two entries under the word "Pepper" – "Pickled" and "Unpickled."
STEVE:	YES, MA'AAAAAM! I SEE IT NOW. THANK YOU VER-Y MUCH!
MRS. CONSTANT:	Thank *you*, Stephen. Now, if there are no other questions, you may begin work immediately.

Class commences to work on Peter Piper's peppers. However, knowing that the teacher is oblivious to all sounds, the BOYS in the class begin whispering to each other. As a result, ANGIE and SYLVIA find it difficult to concentrate.

ANGIE *(softly)*:	This is driving me up the wall.
SYLVIA:	I know. I *hate* peppers. Especially the ones they put in the diner's cheese sauce…
ANGIE:	No, no. I mean this class. It's crazy sitting here day in, day out, listening to all that shouting.
SYLVIA:	I know what you mean. Sometimes, I think *she's* "pickled."
ANGIE:	Boiled to the gills.
SYLVIA:	I'm bringing cotton to put in my ears tomorrow.
ANGIE:	And that ear horn! Every time she pulls that thing out, I want to be locked in an elevator, forced to listen to Muzak.
SYLVIA:	I know what you mean. And the guys in here give me the creeps.
ANGIE:	I wish I had never passed that entrance test; I know it would have meant a lower-level math class if I didn't, but at least I would have been with my friends.
SYLVIA:	You're a girl. You're not supposed to be smart, remember?
ANGIE *(smiling)*:	I'm even worse than that. I'm a girl who wears glasses.
SYLVIA:	And boys don't make passes…
ANGIE:	Yeah, yeah, we know all about that.
	(pause)
SYLVIA:	Did you get the answer yet?

ANGIE: Yeah, I got it about the time Mrs. Constant put away her horn. A world's record.
SYLVIA: Show me.
ANGIE: All right, but be careful.
SYLVIA: I will.

But she's not careful enough.

MRS. CONSTANT: Angie! Sylvia! No cheating! ... *(pulls out her grade book, waving it in the air)* Just for that, I'm docking you both 5 points off your next six-weeks grade.
SYLVIA: But Mrs. Constant, I was only looking at Angie's grocery list...
MRS. CONSTANT *(pulling out the old trumpet once again)*:
                    What? What? Speak up!
SYLVIA *(enunciating carefully but softly)*:
                    I said, in a tone of voice loud enough for all to hear, I was looking at Angie's grocery list. And I noticed that she had written down "peppers." And so I asked her, "Is that pickled or unpickled?" And she said...
MRS. CONSTANT: Silence! That will do. You will both report to me after class. I am writing both of you up for referral to Mr. Carstairs for disciplinary action.
ANGIE *(in as nice a tone as you please)*:
                    Will you be witnessing the flogging, Mrs. Constant?
MRS. CONSTANT *(standing up and approaching ANGIE)*:
                    No. You just go about answering the day's problem.
ANGIE: But I've finished, Mrs. Constant.
MRS. CONSTANT: Oh, *did* you now! Let me see it.
ANGIE *(handing her teacher the work)*:
                    Here, Mrs. Constant.
MRS. CONSTANT: Hmmmm. You didn't get any help from the boys, did you?
ANGIE: Oh, no, Mrs. Constant.
MRS. CONSTANT: You're sure?

ANGIE: Oh, yes, Mrs. Constant.
MRS. CONSTANT: All right.
ANGIE: Is that the right answer, Mrs. Constant?
MRS. CONSTANT: Mmmmmmmmm…possibly…

End of scene.

Yes, it will certainly be the end of *that* scene. Curtains. Nonetheless, I await Dr. Bhattacharya's reaction.

DR. BHATTACHARYA: Good. The extreme age of the teacher could represent outworn patriarchal notions – that women don't possess the minds to retain, understand, or accommodate the complexities of mathematic or scientific principles, that they are better suited for less intellectual pursuits. And the nursery rhyme she uses to teach with. That could signify the simplistic thinking that seeks to justify the colonizing tendencies toward women that much of the current structure has internalized and clung to historically and today.

ME: I was thinking maybe of tossing that ear trumpet. It might come off as a bit too insensitive. Do you think I should get rid of it?

DR. BHATTACHARYA: Can you think of a good reason, one related to the theme of resistance, to leave it in the scene?

ME: I was thinking it might be symbolic of the refusal of some to resist the idea that women *can* perform in math as well as men. Yet there are still some today who turn a deaf ear to that kind of thinking and so forth. It's just that the algebra teacher, here, seems like such a one-dimensional, cartoonish figure…

DR. BHATTACHARYA: I will leave it up to you. If you feel discomfort about the ear device, then take it out. When are you seeing the participant again?

ME:	At the end of next week. Her summer English class finishes after the first week of July. Then she's off until August.
DR. BHATTACHARYA:	But you're not. Your Chapter Four and Chapter Five need to be drafted. And you still have not rewritten your methodology section.
ME:	I promise…
DR. BHATTACHARYA:	Writing seminar begins this Friday. Don't forget.
ME:	I'll be there.

As I leave her office, I consider various excuses to justify avoiding the act of writing. After all, as Margaret Mitchell's (1936) Southern belle observed, "Tomorrow *is* another day" (p. 1037).

And August is another month. The insertion of multiple, intersecting Angie's proves a tough stunt to accomplish. On the first such occasion, an older Angie appears on stage to console a younger Angie who is coping with the fear that she or her brother may inadvertently be arrested by the local white-dominated police force of her small town. She also frets over the shame of not enjoying what were considered by many to be the essentials of living – like a home with indoor plumbing. When I finish the scene, I am nearly taken aback by the sentimentality in the lines spoken by each character. It seems to border on Maudlin-ville. But Dr. Bhattacharya seems pleased with it, so I leave it in. Even now when I pore through it, I feel the tears well up – my tears – and I have to speed-read through the rest of it just to maintain an emotional equilibrium as a means of distancing myself from what I have created. This distancing, I learn later, will turn out to be the central, troubling problem with the dissertation as a whole.

At the beginning of the summer, I had proposed finishing the content of the entire study. That way, I could devote autumn to revising and editing the work. Instead, I have succeeded only in completing the ethnodrama; as a result, I have neither rewritten the inadequate description of methods nor described the implications of my study. Yet, I have scheduled a date in early November to defend the study before the committee of professors who approved the proposal last spring.

I meet with Angie for one final interview. Long ago, she had expressed approval for what I was doing – the transformation of data into the format of a play. For her, it was reminiscent of the theatrical author Luis Valdez and the plays he had staged throughout the Southwest with his troupe, El Teatro

Campesino (Elam, 1997). Valdez's works examined the Latino experience in contemporary America, cleverly infusing satire with sociology in a way that resulted in something akin to Expressionism. I had e-mailed the scenes I had composed for her perusal and comment. With only minor comments correcting important accuracies in the way her character interacted with others, she had maintained her approval of the concept.

For this concluding interview, I decide to focus on the one factor of her upbringing that we have not touched upon yet. I begin by reading from a prepared list of questions.

ME: At that time, your life seemed situated in three places – there was home, there was school, and you mentioned church, right? What sort of church functions did they have that you recall attending? And was there an intersection between home and church and school? Was there a time when one may have affected or influenced events in one or the other location?

ANGIE: Well, yeah, my mother was a church-goer. Big time. And we would get up many times at 6:00 in the morning and go to Mass…Uh, I belonged to, of course, went to catechism. We had catechism maybe once or twice after school. So yes, from school we would head over there. And…I belonged to this other church group, uh, that was formed by the nuns there. The Schoenstatt Sisters…

ME: How do you spell that?

ANGIE: S-c-h-o-e-n-s-t-a-t-t. Schoenstatt Sisters. Uh, I don't know if you know this, a convent. There's a convent at [a small Texas coastal town]. And they would send some of the sisters to [our town] and to the different areas. And so they formed these "little-girl" groups, uh, where we would sit and talk about life, you know, basically. And I really loved that. I mean, I was involved in that since I was in the second grade. All during junior high, I think. And it was a club. We talked about a lot of issues, you know, things that bothered us, school. And I remember being very vocal there. People there used to, you know, little girls would come in, and they'd say, "You're always talking!" Because that, to me, *was* my format. I may not be able to talk in school, but I could talk here, with that group.

ME: You could be aggressive.

137

ANGIE: I could be aggressive. I could be assertive…we had an annual trip where we'd spend a week at the convent, you know, praying and talking and doing activities…For a whole year, we would collect money to be able to go. I remember it was only ten dollars; and to me, that was a horrendous amount that I had to collect all year long just to go. Because my mother couldn't just hand it over to me. But that was a good thing to me. So yeah, I would do other kinds of things like, you know, clean church altars and do that kind of stuff, and for Communion, I would help prepare the kids. Prepare them, walk them through on how you're supposed to do it. Uh, I even taught summer school in church, summer classes, Bible classes – I remember teaching it in junior high to the elementary kids. And that's the first time I ever felt like a teacher, but still, you know, I never thought I could be a teacher. I just, it was just a little, you know, too much fun.

ME: "Now why didn't I see that back then? Why did it take so long?"

ANGIE: Right, well, because, uh, I knew that – I guess I just felt so sure of myself in that setting. But not in a school setting. I just couldn't see myself as one of *those* teachers.

ME: Yet you felt sure enough, as a freshman, your first year… you dared to break into this all-Anglo [Homemaking] club. Would you credit your experiences with the Schoenstatt Sisters…?

ANGIE: I think I can say that at this point, because I do remember a lot of that confidence-building kind of attitude…It did give an edge that I didn't know I had anywhere else.

Here, then, was the intersection between church and school – the seminal point of her transformation from a shy, eager-to-please elementary-school child to the increasingly aggressive, more socially-aware high school activist. This change was due in large part to her enthusiastic participation with a group of young girls, organized by a Catholic order known as the Schoenstatt Sisters.

Suddenly, I realize the ethnodrama I finished last month is, indeed, not finished at all. Not without this one important element I have just discovered – a scene, or a series of scenes devoted to the Schoenstatt Sisters' influence on Angie and other members of these "little girl" groups. I mention this to Angie, and she suggests that perhaps we could visit the site of those childhood retreats later in the week.

And so two mornings later, I find myself seated in Angie's late-model SUV, travelling north along a coastal highway to a location approximately 50 miles north of the city – the headquarters of the Schoenstatt Order, and the site of those retreats that she and other girls experienced some 40 years ago.

We turn onto a paved country road, the entrance to the site of the Schoenstatt convent and surrounding estate. The property which houses the Order, I now discover, also contains a gift shop. Angie pulls into a parking space in front of it. We disembark from her vehicle and walk toward a grassy area near a structure that serves as a residence hall for the sisters. The convent overlooks a small waterway, one of the many inlets that appear along the southern Texas coastline. Occasionally, in the distance, we spot one of the nuns, in habits of bright, spotless white, walking quickly at various points between the buildings on the estate. Angie recalls, "A lot of the nuns were nurses. They were teachers, they all had degrees. And I thought for a while, 'That would be great. I could do that. I could get my college degree that way, and become a nun.' But then later on, I thought, 'No.' I wasn't going to make it."

Angie points out a small sheltered enclosure, situated on a pier, down by the edge of the inlet. This was the place where groups of girls used to hold their discussions, often supervised by the nuns. We walk down a hill toward the pier, and when we arrive, we find a small portrait is suspended from one of the wooden rails that were constructed as protection from falling from the pier into the water below. It is a reproduced painting of the Virgin Mary cradling a child in her arm, the baby Jesus. As the water laps peacefully against the muddy shore, Angie now recalls, "It was like a camp. We'd go, hiking, picnicking. We could go wading, but we couldn't go swimming because we didn't have bathing suits and we had to wear dresses all the time. We'd stay up all night and tell ghost stories. The kind of stuff that I hear people in camp…" Here, she pauses here and then continues, "I never got to go to a camp."

The Schoenstatt Sisters, Angie later informs me, no longer host these annual summer retreats. In fact, there is only one nun from those years who still resides at this site. She is usually found working in the gift shop we parked in front of earlier.

We walk away from the pier and uphill now, approaching a small chapel. Angie wishes to go inside and pray, but before entering the structure, she tells me, "You can wait here, or you can come inside if you like."

"They won't mind?" I ask, as I begin to perspire from the dense summer humidity.

"No, it's all right." So we both enter.

The interior of the chapel, thankfully, is air-conditioned. I also discover that we are not the only two people inside. There are around 20 others, a few of whom are nuns, while the rest are dressed in rather formal attire. Many are elderly and probably local residents. They sit in various spots along four long rows of pews, all facing the opposite wall, where there is an enlargement of the same portrait of the Virgin Mary and Jesus we had observed while on the pier (see Figure 16).

Figure 16. The Virgin Mary and Jesus, in the Schoenstatt Chapel, South Texas

No one speaks; everyone is silent, in prayer or in meditation. Angie sits among the others and begins to pray. I silently take a seat in another pew in the very back, next to the doorway. Intermittently, one person leaves, then another, and then someone else enters. Occasionally, one can pick up the soft whispering of prayers emanating from various parts of the chapel. After fifteen minutes, Angie rises and proceeds slowly around the edge of her pew in the direction of the doorway. She is a serious, solemn figure as I stand to join her, and we both exit the chapel into the summer heat, which no longer feels as oppressive as before we entered.

From there, we make a small trek to the parking lot and the return trip home. But before leaving, we decide to go into the gift shop. Angie approaches the sales counter and briefly greets the elderly nun who decades ago had watched over her when she was a youngster at the retreat. Angie introduces me to the sister. I debate whether to ask the sister for an interview, but I sense this is not the time.

As we return to the car for the trip back to the city, I realize it has been an informative outing. Angie, in fact, is already thinking of retiring from teaching in just a few years, and she has considered this area the perfect place to spend the remaining years of her life. For her, the "draw" is the solitude. As for me, I believe no other scene could prove more appropriate – in close proximity to the locale that, more than any other, facilitated her discovery of an awareness of self and a spiritual pathway for a life-long devotion to activism that has meant so much to her and those around her. I can now confirm what I suspected two days ago at the end of our final interview – that Angie's association with Schoenstatt had been the single most transformative event of her youth. To cite her own words, those "aggressive, assertive" nuns had indeed provided her with the "edge" that she would not have known she possessed at any other time.

The trip out of town has reinvigorated me, yet at the same time I am afflicted with a mild depression, as I am at the end of all summers. But why? Is this condition a hangover from school days, when I, like every other kid, mourned the loss of time off from reading, writing, numbers, and homework? Is it the closing of public swimming pools and the suspension from the freedom of doing nothing? This is certainly not the case now; I have accomplished a lot these past two months, and there is still plenty more to do.

What, then, is the basis for this sense of angst? Does it entail the unforeseen misgivings of future work ahead? Or is it my realization that a process I wish could go on and on will soon come to an end?

I feel now that there is some not-yet-visible roadblock that threatens to undermine the whole project. Should I discuss this now with Angie while she drives us back to the city? I think not. She has offered to buy us both lunch at a popular seafood restaurant located just down the highway and I therefore should not burden her with my emotional predicament. It is my problem, not hers. Should I broach the mystery of this sudden dread with Caroline Sherritt? I wonder what she would make of it. But no…What about Dr. Bhattacharya? Maybe, but not until after Fall classes are underway. And so, like everything else of importance that causes me discomfort, I shelve the problem until later. But this is not the only matter I have delayed in addressing. And in the end, the avoidance of facing my own fears and grappling with challenges to my own thinking about issues of gender and ethnicity almost derail the process before it reaches its destination. As a result, the study nearly becomes the study that never was.

THE BREAKDOWN AND COMING TOGETHER

Paying deep attention to irrational events, messages from the environment, dreams, fantasies, and other imagining processes are attempts to understand, to reach awareness.

(Anzaldúa, 2015, p. 24)

KAKALI'S NARRATIVE

Some time in October, 2010. I have read an early draft of Kent's dissertation. The product is still incomplete, missing several technical details that a dissertation should contain. And there is still the issue of who Kent is in relation to Angie, still unexplored. We meet at a local barbecue joint, because that is the sort of thing one does if one is in South Texas. The technical details are dull topics to a creative writer like Kent, since it should contain details about data collection, analysis, representation, ethics, trustworthiness, etc. Yet it needs to be done or he would not pass his dissertation.

Kent is more of a philosopher than a technical writer. Asking Kent to write a technical narrative might be the same as asking me to teach by lecturing *at* people and clicking on boring PowerPoint slides. I would even say I would rather eat my own vomit than just lecture *at* people and click through slides.

I show Kent some exemplary dissertations to point out to him what he might have missed and I can sense the palpable discomfort because in some way I am drawing boundaries around him and he does not like that. When I was close to finishing my dissertation, I stopped arguing with my advisor, justifying why I had done what I had done. I found Kent's lack of argument today the same as my behavior five years ago. He is close to being done. I feel some pride in playing a role in his journey thus far.

KENT'S NARRATIVE

Early October 2010. At a suburban barbecue restaurant, Dr. Bhattacharya and I confer on the study. Neither of us dines, and the scene is not pleasant. I am being read the "riot act" for my still-inadequate methodology section. Now and then, I gaze at other patrons, wondering if they can overhear. She finally ends her lecture by loaning me a copy of another student's dissertation. She feels it contains a model methodology chapter and suggests that I might benefit from incorporating a similarly ordered structure to my work. She then rips a sheet from a legal pad and we both collaborate on a precise outline for the chapter. I am determined to follow it to the letter. With the due date so close at hand, it is too late now to just continue "winging it."

The next evening, I begin a new draft of the chapter with a description of the study's research design and breakdown of data inventory. Composing this much of what will become a 40-page methodology chapter consumes all of four hours. If this sluggish pace continues, I may never finish. I begin to wonder if perhaps I harbor a hidden desire *not* to finish. In fact, could it be that I am subconsciously grinding down the pace of my work on purpose? If so, this circumstance parallels closely with the life-script that was forecast for me early on. Allow me to relate the following:

At the age of 16, I was for the first time in my life given the use of an automobile, a hand-me-down Ford Galaxie, which was in fact the same car my mother had bought brand-new in Denton. On Friday nights, I would take it out alone, beyond the city limits, into the outskirts of various unfenced farms. One evening, I deliberately drove into a cotton field and got the car's tires stuck, just to see if I could find a way to get them *un*stuck. My initial strategy involved flooring the accelerator, but as one can imagine, this only resulted in a deeper trench. At this point, I noticed an old quilt lying in the car's back seat. I took the quilt and placed it under one of the car's tires. Then, I got back behind the steering wheel and slowly pressed the accelerator while peering through my open door at the spinning tire. In a short while, the quilt provided enough traction for the car to maneuver itself out of the rut; and from there, I drove out of the field and back home.

Question: Why had I done this? Why had I deliberately plowed my car into the furrows of a muddy field? Back then, the best answer I could offer was situated in just-plain boredom. It followed, therefore, that the best way to alleviate the weekend tedium was to induce a problem. And when I discovered I could solve the problem, I felt good – not just relieved, but *good* – that I was able to successfully extricate myself from a dire situation without anyone's assistance. Besides, if Mom had discovered I was using the old Ford like a John Deere tractor, I might have been grounded – literally and figuratively.

In fact, escaping such consequences provided me with a marvelous sense of accomplishment – so much so, that I would repeat the same scenario on

144

succeeding Friday nights. It became a chief amusement, demobilizing my vehicle in muddy acreage and devising different procedures to navigate myself out of trouble. It felt as though a tragic fate would never intercede, and that there was no problematic situation I could not surmount independently.

Figure 17. Kent in his high school days

But I was a teenager then, not an adult doctoral student. Yet, here I am, years later, inviting trouble by jeopardizing a serious vow I took – to complete a major study in a given set of time. And what has happened? Foolishly, I have handicapped myself by ignoring the work. It *does* seem preposterous, not to mention irresponsible. What do I seek to prove anyway? Lack of maturity may partly explain the phenomenon. Some may refer to it as "fear of success." Others may label it "self-destructive behavior." Feel free to apply all possibilities. In any case, I struggle to complete the study's write-up before deadline, just two weeks before my defense in mid-November. Yet up until now, I have engaged in mindless procrastination. Why do I still play these games? Why do I risk trashing four years of a serious academic pursuit to indulge in such childish shenanigans? Am I still trying to prove my immunity to fate? Who's kidding whom?

KAKALI'S NARRATIVE

Many years ago when I was a newly minted graduate, I felt academically bullied in my tenure-track position. I was naïve and full of feminist sisterhood idealism. In my field, most of my colleagues are women. So, I imagined that we are all entangled in our struggles and liberation. I wanted to do well so that our department, college, and school would be seen favorably in academia.

In the beginning things were going well. My hard work was being praised. I won an Outstanding Researcher award.

What I did not realize was that by doing my job well, or at least trying to do it well, I was making people uncomfortable, unsettled, and unbalanced around me. We used to have Friday Research Talks, and take turns in being a speaker. I noticed when I was the speaker, a few of my colleagues would openly laugh at what I was saying, chat amongst themselves loudly while I was speaking, to the point of fully drawing the attention of everyone around. I felt insulted and invalidated. I approached one of them, Jane, who had joined the university just a year before I did. We were both early career academics. I thought maybe she was unaware of how her actions were coming across to me.

I walked into her office one day and sat across from her. A desk was in between us.

"Jane, I wanted to talk to you about my presentation last Friday. I noticed you were just chatting away, laughing, and at times talking quite loudly when I was talking. Other times you just edited your paper. It felt really disrespectful to me. If a student did that in my class, I would call her out. But I have a lot of respect for you. So, I wanted to see if there was something that we needed to talk about or clear the air."

Jane looked at me with coldness in her eyes. Her jaws tightened. She put her pen down on the desk and leaned across. "Look, I am busy. I went there to give you support. I was present and I gave you support. What else do you want?"

"I just want you to be present when you're present. If you have so much work that you have to talk to other people while I am talking and edit your paper, then people see that you are not supporting. So your goal to support me fails."

"In that case, I will just not show up at anything you do, or support you in anything you do. I will make sure you receive no support whatsoever." Jane sounded like she could rally people to her agenda of not supporting me.

From there onwards, Jane started forwarding any emails I had sent to her earlier in confidence (when we were in better terms) to our department chair without my permission. Mortified, I talked to a senior faculty, Bonnie, an older White woman, close to Caroline's (my colleague at South Texas) age, at the end of her academic career, who seemed uninterested in interfering. She reminded me that I should never write anything in email that I do not want the world to know. At a later Friday research talk, where I was the speaker again, Jane and some other colleagues did not show up. Bonnie did. And she challenged almost everything I stated in my presentation. The people in the room appeared to be stunned. There was no discussion. It was an attack on me and my attempt to defend myself. I looked up to Bonnie as my mentor. My illusion was shattered that day.

The bullying got worse. I was kept out of discussions. My students were unusually penalized in my colleagues' classes to the point where they were harshly graded, given no opportunity to meet with their professors outside of the classes to gain clarity on the work they needed to complete. One day I saw one of my students waiting outside a colleague's office. I knew he was inside his office, because I saw him in there only minutes ago. I asked my student what she was doing there and she said that she came by to see Dr. Tony during his office hours, as he would not meet with her at any other time. And she too saw him enter his office, so she knocked on his door, but he was not responding. Helplessly, she sat outside, hoping to catch him should he come out. I tried knocking too, but he did not respond, even though I could hear him walking inside, stopping or starting his music, and shuffling his papers.

One of my students dropped out of the program altogether, unable to deal with the bullying himself. Another one simply stopped working on her dissertation, and instead just focused on getting a job, hoping to return to the dissertation when she felt more capable of enduring the harassment.

Jane and Bonnie stopped talking to me altogether. This was hard to bear, since Bonnie was the chair of the search committee who recommended my hire. In earlier days, Bonnie used to say that I was the best hire that she had made in decades. But three years into the job, if I ran into Bonnie and/or Jane in the hallways, they would not speak to me or acknowledge my existence or respond to me when I greeted them. When Jane and Bonnie would not respond or make eye contact, I would remember that I am supposed to be in some sort of conflicting, oppositional relationship with them, and perhaps there was some protocol that dictated I should neglect their presence when around me. This oppositional-relationship protocol spilled into program and department meetings where nothing I said was even considered. Eventually, I just stopped talking altogether.

In the meantime, my classes, which were mostly elective research courses, were filling up with students so quickly that I had to start a waitlist. Jane's classes, which were required research courses, remained empty. Students would transfer credits from other universities to meet their research requirements rather than taking Jane's classes, or they would stay up till midnight when registration for classes would open, to enroll in required research classes taught by anybody but Jane. Those who would take Jane's

147

classes would offer strong critical feedback. Bonnie would lament and say, "Jane seems to only get the bad students."

The following semester, I was not given a classroom to teach my classes. I was told that Jane had booked a classroom and the computer lab. When she was not going to use the computer lab, I could use that as my classroom. Also, when she would need the computer lab, then I could use her classroom to teach, as both of our classes were scheduled at the same time. Stunned, I tried to speak with Bonnie and other administrators. I was told that there was no other option other than for me to not have a designated classroom to teach. And because Jane chose to not speak to me, she would not inform me when she would need the lab or the classroom. My students and I would go to the lab first, guessing that perhaps more often than not, Jane would use the classroom. The days she needed the lab, we would either find her already in the lab before our class would start. Or Jane would bring her students at the middle of the class, when she would need the lab, expecting us to leave. And we did, since both the classroom and the lab were designated as her spaces to teach. And I knew I did not have the support to correct the situation.

Tenure is our holy grail in academia. We are temporary employees for five years and then we apply for tenure, which allows us to become permanent employees. At that point, we are told that we have some job security, although such security is no longer permanent or without vulnerability. Before a faculty member goes up for tenure, we are to offer a mid-tenure portfolio so that tenured academics could comment if we are on track with our work and if we demonstrate the promise of being successful in earning tenure. My mid-tenure review was coming up and I was genuinely nervous about the kind of feedback I would receive and if it would be helpful or hurtful. I considered the option of looking for another job and debated whether it was better to do it before or after my mid-tenure review.

One day I received an email from Jane that was sent through our departmental listserv, which included all faculty members in our department by default. Jane thanked the department for being part of her wedding over the weekend and posted pictures. It was clear that I was the only faculty member absent from the pictures and I was also excluded from parts of several other conversations that were being carried on in the department, based on the exchange between my colleagues.

Truth be told, I was deeply hurt. I did not care that I was not invited. Jane was free to invite whomever she wanted for her wedding. But to use the listserv seemed like a deliberate way to remind me of my exclusion. As an educator of color, marginalization in higher education was and continues to be a regular occurrence. But this seemed more hurtful than it needed to be. I started to look for other academic positions and found a therapist to help me manage my depression, stress, and anxiety.

I received an offer for another tenure-track academic position. When word spread that I was leaving, a handful of faculty members privately said goodbye to me. My students held a party for me at a local coffeehouse. Mary, a Black woman in her 50s, was furious about my departure. I had not told anyone of the real reason for my departure, because I did not want my students to be penalized in any way for their association with me or support for me after I left. But Mary was intuitive enough to make a strong educated guess towards the reason of my departure. At the party, Mary started to talk about how the university made it difficult for students and faculty of color to be successful, and put extra, unnecessary, and unfair challenges in front of students and faculty of color.

Bonnie never said goodbye to me. I have mourned the loss of my relationship with her for years and have often wondered if there was ever a way to repair the relationship that I might have missed or overlooked.

***

Sometime in early October, 2010. Caroline comes into my office and plops on my teal blue couch. She looks around, leans her head back on the couch, and stretches her arms up.

"Hey, I think you should be Kent's chair."

"Okay, sure. What brought this on?" I ask.

"It's just fair. I have not done any work with him. You're pulling the load. I have no idea what he is doing, so I can't even tell if he is doing it right or wrong."

"Okay, so you just want to be a member of his supervising committee?"

"Yes, I want to still stay on, just not be the chair." Caroline clarifies.

"All right, I will tell him."

"How's he doing anyway?" Caroline seems genuinely curious.

"Not well. His work is at a rough stage and he is struggling to address what we told him to address at the proposal meeting."

"Well, he is in good hands with you. He will get there." Caroline stands up and walks out. I send Kent an email telling him of the change in his committee. Kent responds in agreement to the change. I begin to feel a bit free, because now I can tell Kent what to do without being worried about my relationship with Caroline. And I also realize that whatever fear I had about Caroline being a gatekeeper, it was my own. Caroline was not Bonnie. Perhaps Caroline would have always acted with integrity as she did today.

And perhaps the ghosts from my past haunted me long enough to prevent me from seeing that I could advocate for a strong study for Kent, and Caroline would have entertained my ideas without wanting to penalize me in any direct or indirect ways. I chose to put behind my earlier days of enduring academic bullying.

KENT'S NARRATIVE

In October 2010, I am working on the methodology chapter in the library when I receive a communique via e-mail from Dr. Caroline Sherritt.

Kent,

I do not feel right about sharing the chairmanship of your committee with Kakali. It strikes me as more appropriate to give her all the credit given the amount of work she's put into helping you reach your dissertation goals... We DO get credit for chairing dissertations and Dr. Bhattacharya deserves that credit in your case. I'm delighted she came along when she did...

So am I, dear lady, so am I. And I must admit her influence as primary guide through the study has been supplanted by yours. The situation was not planned that way; it simply happened. I sensed this for the past year, from the time of my first encounter with her and my amusement at those frequent one-dollar fines she levied against me in class for using positivist terminology when discussing research – words such as "valid" instead of "compelling," or "subject" rather than "participant." I realized Dr. Sherritt presents a convincing case. Soon after, another e-mail arrives from Dr. Bhattacharya.

Kent

Dr. Sherritt would like to recommend that I am the sole chair...since she has not worked with you on your dissertation. I have agreed with her request and I hope you do too.

I type in, "No problem," and click the Send button. I then return to the troublesome methodology section.

In nearly a week, I generate a complete draft of the chapter. I have met all demands of the outline Dr. Bhattacharya scribbled for me – or so I believe. But the committee's new chair raises a whole array of objections all bundled into one. Here, I refer to the one challenge – the one great hurdle – that I have avoided these past two months: My confrontation with the inevitable issue of researcher-positionality:

Kent,

There is something that has been bothering me deeply from the onset of this project. It is your refusal to identify the privileges that you carry with you as a White male. You are claiming to work with Chicana feminism and feminist thoughts in general. Part of the feminist work is to identify unearned privileges that people have as part of their subject position(s) they occupy in our social structures... You have made a bold choice to use feminism as your lens to understand the participants' experiences... Yet nowhere in your dissertation that I have read so far have you unpacked your privileges in relation to the participant's... Peggy McIntosh has an article of unpacking White privileges which is seminal in this area...

To fix this, you would have to:

1. *unpack your position, as a White male, and your privileges with which you process the world.*
2. *state why especially this topic interests you. What is your intersection with this topic? What is your intersection with the participants' experiences?*
3. *think beyond the drama, beyond the creative writing, beyond hiding behind the curtain, because you are directing this entire production and you have to make yourself transparent to your readers as to who are you in the context of this study. What baggage do you carry with yourself in this study? What milestones have you experienced that bring you to this intersection of White male and Chicana female experiences?*

Please know that I am extremely invested and committed to your success. However, I am also just as committed to the integrity of this project especially since it is such a valuable one. I hope you understand why these changes are necessary and address them appropriately in your work. Call or email me later today...

Call or e-mail her later. This I should do, and not later, but immediately – because, as of now, I feel the whole endeavor has become another vehicle grounded in the mud. The study, or what is left of it, has been mired there for longer than I care to admit. Each day, I feel the problem consuming me – a rather florid way of expressing the fear that I may never become unstuck. Next Monday, the project is due to the committee for reading – just four days away. I have Dr. Bhattacharya to fall back on for guidance. But then consulting her now would be like calling someone to come get my car out of the field. So I decide I will go it alone. I will pry loose the old Ford. After all, I put myself in this mess; I can get myself out.

The next day, Friday, I enter the college's library and begin work on the study's fifth chapter, determined to engage with the ideas my adviser has illustrated, the first of which is to list the privileges "with which I process the world" as a White male. But what exactly does that mean? Process the world? To me, this is unfamiliar language. How do I "process" the world? Does that mean, "How do I, as a White male, *see* the world?" Well, I would assume that I view the world no differently from anyone else.

"…as a White male." What does *that* mean? White male. What does she want me to write? – All kinds of incriminating things about myself? That as a White person, I view the world through a heritage of racism and discrimination and prejudice? Is this what she would have me say? If I were in a meeting with her right now, in her office, is this the line of thinking she would have me pursue? To admit to her that, deep down, I am a racist and there is nothing I can do about it? ("My name is Kent, and I am powerless to the influence of racism.") Is this what she envisions the study's concluding chapter to accomplish? Is this its purpose? To admit to characteristics which I feel are inherently untrue?

I must consider this. But not here, at the library, where I am working. So instead of writing or journaling about the problem, I go home. It seems much better to mull over a problem there than on a public computer. Maybe I can better concentrate in more muted surroundings. I know instinctively, however, that I desire neither to write nor to think. Thus, when I arrive home, I tend to other, more pressing matters – like supper. For if I am to brand myself a bigot on paper, I shall have to prepare psychologically on a full stomach. Maybe a few beers might hold the key. ("My name is Kent, and I am powerless to the influence of racism.")

No…Alcohol, no matter how light, will not solve the problem. So the next morning, I return to the campus library and proceed where I left off; but as one might guess, I am able to achieve very little. I am still mired in that damned cotton field. So I move on to Dr. Bhattacharya's second complaint: "State why especially this topic interests you. What is your intersection with this topic? What is your intersection with the participant's experiences?"

This appears an easier route to take – my intersection with the participant's experiences. So I begin to get my thoughts down on paper. The intersection, I feel, is the ethnodrama…

CHAPTER FIVE (FROM MY DISSERTATION DRAFT)

The ethnodrama in the preceding chapter is a narrative reporting on the political evolution and social development of a young Latina throughout the school years, culminating during a time that an early wave of the modern Chicana feminist movement was beginning to take shape in 1968 and 1969. The social awakening that Angie undergoes was duplicated within other Latinas, particularly those who wished to take a more active part than allowed to before in shaping the destiny of their culture while refusing to remain silenced in the background by the same Chicanos whose actions and hopes and dreams they supported…

While I ignore the "intersection" – which I have mistakenly interpreted as how our paths crossed, and not in terms of gender or ethnic positionality – I tie together the thematic elements that the study encompassed. I decide a recapitulation of those themes will be appropriate:

As a young Chicana, she witnessed the same inequitable conditions in her school environment that she experienced in the streets and stores of her own town. As a child…she was warned not to go into certain public places for fear that accusations of thievery by Anglo-American business owners may put what freedom enjoyed by her or her friends in jeopardy. She saw the baring of her own emotions – evidence of her own suffering, her tears – as a form of submission to the very people she feared. Allowing others to see her cry was interpreted by the young girl as representative of acquiescing to those in power or those she perceived as having power…The question here is, how does ethnodrama operate as an effective medium to present her story to an audience?

At this point, I make an attempt to tie the case study and the ethnodrama into a united endeavor. But after, three double-spaced pages, I can go no further – and just two more days to complete the entire chapter. Three days, if I include the day of the evening it is due. Let's see…How *does* a person go about "processing the world? …"

Finally, I decide it is no use. It is done. And so am I. I put an end to "processing" altogether. I save what I have written thus far and send an e-mail to Dr. Bhattacharya:

Postponement is inevitable. Writing a chapter takes more than 3 days. And that's on top of everything else that needs to be done…My apologies for having placed you in a bad situation. If you choose not to serve on my dissertation committee anymore, I will understand. Nothing else need be said. If you do continue, please inform me of any penalties I will suffer in addition to the humiliation of postponing…

I click the "Send" button. Then, I log out of the campus computer before succumbing to any temptation to await a reply. What kind could I expect anyway? Something laced with anger? – I dwell instead on the predicament I stumbled into by avoiding an issue I now feel unqualified and incapable of handling. Perhaps I simply am not good enough or smart enough to be a "doctor" or anything else beyond what I am. Maybe I was foolish in even aspiring toward such a goal. "Let's face it, Kent," I mutter to myself. "You don't have the brains, you don't have the discipline, you just don't have what it takes. So forget it. Go home."

This I do. It is easy. I feel competent enough to run away from the problem, but not fix it. Yet at the same time, it feels like the only route to take. At least for once, I am looking squarely at the truth. This will be my only worthwhile accomplishment for the rest of the day – the act of making a decision and following through on it. And such a simple decision too…I quit.

Once at home, I try and forget everything by watching a movie, an old one, a loud and noisy one, like a war film, to clear my head – James Mason as German Field Marshall Erwin Rommel in the movie, *The Desert Fox* (1951). After a lengthy, violent prologue before the opening title credits finally come on, there appears an off-screen narration by the voice of an announcer, informing the viewer that his name is British Brigadier General Desmond Young, and he is the person who authored the biography of Rommel (1950) on which this very film is based. As he continues to speak, there is an impressive montage of Young interviewing various sources after the war – former enemies and friends, including ex-soldiers who served in Rommel's Afrika Korps, as well as civilians who knew the late German hero personally. Young comments on the time and work it took for him to compile all of his transcripts and notes and then draft and revise the content for his book.

At this stage, I consider the idea of positionality – or at least, what limited knowledge I have of the term. Here is an author, an officer in the Allied Army, writing a biography that took years of his life to research. The subject of the book was an *enemy* of his country. What could a researcher make of *that* "intersection?" …

It is no good. I cannot forget. I am sickened. I feel remorse for betraying Dr. Bhattacharya, a person I trust and who trusted me in return. As a result, I feel a complete waste, a failure with no possibility of redemption. To be honest...

No, I cannot trust myself to be honest. This would require energy, and I have none in reserve. Besides, I am in no mood for self-confrontation. It is too late. It is over. I have given up. The situation is resolved. So why do I *not* feel the relief one might experience at the completion of a cycle?

"Kent, nothing has been completed."

Yes, nothing is completed. Only abandoned. I am now in exile – from work, myself, and those who mattered. Could it be that...?

No, I will not allow myself to ponder divine intervention or a last-minute plunge into grappling with the search for something more to write, even if another attempt will result in failure...Wait! Was that a prediction? Did I just forecast my own failure? Is this what I really wish? How do I know that returning to the problem at hand will "result in failure?"

Oh, give up. Just quit...If only I could get around this business of "processing the world" and dealing with "intersections of..."

My name is Kent, and I am powerless to the influence of ...

KAKALI'S NARRATIVE

Dorina is a colleague I trust. She is a Black academic in Counselor Education. She speaks her mind with me, even though with others she practices a lot of self-censorship. Dorina is in her early 50s, in fantastic shape, and she comes to work dressed in pant and skirt suits, with an impeccable sense of accessorizing her outfits. I have had a few tough weeks with Kent and I thought it would be fun to just go out for coffee with Dorina. We tend to laugh and feel lighter after we talk with each other.

It is Saturday, so Dorina and I have decided that we should hang out at a new coffee/drinks bar in the south side of town called, "Coffee, Drinks, and Me." I like the place because it has open chat areas and enclosed booths. I choose one of the booths and I order a latte while Dorina orders a cappuccino.

"So how's it going?" Dorina asks as she takes a sip.

"It's going... This place is pretty cool. Do you like the jazz they are playing in the background?" Dorina is a jazz snob, so her approval or disapproval is usually my indicator.

"Yes, yes, it is pretty good." Then Dorina points outwards to the center of the coffee bar. "Would be nice if they did a little performance in the middle there with a jazz band. They have the room to do it."

"Oh, that's a great idea. Maybe you should tell them."

"I would, but I don't trust just anyone with their jazz sensibilities. Too many White folks don't know what good jazz is, and a whole lot of them just appropriate it anyway."

"Speaking of White folks and appropriation…"

"Yes?" Dorina gives me a look.

"You know my student Kent?"

"The White boy that Caroline thinks is weird?"

"Yeah, yeah, that's him."

"What about him?"

"Well, he is trying to do his dissertation using Chicana feminism and looking at a Latina woman's experiences during the 50s and 60s in South Texas."

Dorina stares at me hard, mouth agape. "He *what*? Want to do *what*? And *why*?"

"According to him, his gaining access was that he asked the participant and she said yes."

"Yes, of course, indeed! What *else* is needed?" Dorina loads on the sarcasm as she continues. "Has he considered the ethics of this? How is he trying to understand her experiences?"

"Umm, he says using a Chicana feminist lens?"

"Oh, hell, no! That boy needs some tough talk. Why did you let it get this far and not do anything about this?" Dorina asks.

"Umm…I was with Caroline before as his co-chair, so I was trying to be careful so as to not mess up my relationship with Caroline and still hold Kent to high standards."

We both take sips of our drinks, and then Dorina waves the server over, "You know, we came here for coffee. But I think we need something stronger. What have you got?"

The server smiles and lists some wine and liquor options, and we both choose Long Island Iced Tea, as we know we might be here awhile.

"So where do things stand with Kent now?" Dorina continues.

"Ermm… I have been asking him to interrogate his privileges and discuss his entry point to the study. He has sidestepped the privileges and said his entry point to Chicana feminism was when he entered the library and got books on Chicana feminism."

Dorina slaps her palm on the table, startling the server who is about to serve our drinks. "No. No. No! He did *not* say that? Really, he said *that*?"

I nod my head. "Uh-huh. I think he is struggling with terminology."

"You straightened him out, right?" Dorina is expecting me to say yes, but I really cannot. I have never been able to straighten anyone out. I don't think I have the power to do that. People straighten themselves out when they are ready. I can only provide the stimulus.

"I have been talking to him, yes. I have been pushing him. And then he sent me a draft and there was no interrogation of his privileges. So I did write a really harsh and open email to him about how uncomfortable I have been with his sidestepping. The subtext of the email was that I was not going to approve his dissertation unless he addresses these concerns. Otherwise, both he and I would be chewed up and spit out by academia." I feel really heavy inside as I say this – because it was a difficult email to write.

"That's right. You can't afford that on your record. Is this your first solo dissertation chair gig?"

"No, I have two others besides him, but none of them have defended yet. So no one knows at the moment what the quality of my mentoring is like. No benchmarks." I say.

We drink some more. Dorina tells me about some of her students. We talk about our struggles of being an educator of color in academia. We talk about how hard it is to even make time for us to meet. Dorina then asks, "So what is Kent supposed to do now?"

"That's the thing. I sent him an email earlier this week, the harsh one, telling him all the things he needs to do before I can sign off. And then he just sent me an email which reads like he is quitting. He says we might need to postpone, and that he is sorry for this, and I can go off his committee if I like."

"Oh, dear. That's tough. Sounds like he is a bit drained." Dorina is putting her counselor hat on.

"Yes, it really does sound like that. So I have sent him some emails today, asking him to not give up, and that we would figure things out. But I haven't heard from him. I am thinking that he should at least respond back. It has been hours and Monday is his deadline to submit his draft to the committee."

"What do you think is going on with him?" Dorina asks with genuine curiosity.

"I don't know. I don't know much about Kent. He lives alone. I don't know if he smokes, does drugs, or if he drinks. I know he drinks a lot of coffee, almost like he needs an IV tube of coffee running into him so he could be pumped with coffee all the time." I just start thinking out loud.

"Do you think he is lying dead in his apartment?" Dorina takes a morbid turn.

"Oh, God no. I don't know. Could it be? Do you think…?" I am scared.

"Umm… since we don't know much about him, we don't know how he handles crisis. I am just thinking with you." Dorina's counselor hat is back on.

"I don't know. Am I pushing him too hard? I want to be sensitive to him. Unpacking privileges under such pressure is not an easy thing to do if you have never even been made aware of such things. It is a tight rope that I am walking. I want to encourage him, but I want to hold him accountable." I am thinking out loud again.

"That's what you should do anyway. You can't have your name on something that you don't believe. Also, seriously, back to that ethics thing. I think it is unethical that a White guy thinks he could just start telling other people's stories in a detached way, but use our framework to do that. How does that *work* even? I can't even compute this." Dorina takes a sip and finishes her drink.

"I don't know. And that's what I am trying to find out and get to the bottom of anyway. How does he think this is okay? And I don't know what buttons I am pushing by doing this, and what I might be triggering, or other harm I might be causing him." I am deeply concerned, hoping my counselor-friend can provide some insights.

"It is not your responsibility to know other people's triggers. If they do not communicate that with you, then you cannot go around wondering if everything you say and do could be a trigger. If someone is triggered, either they should tell you about it, or they should go see a therapist. But it is on *them*." Dorina is quite clear on this.

"Okay. Well, it is too late now. I am still worried about him. I better hope that what you said is not true, that he is lying on his apartment floor, hurt or injured somehow. Do I have to call 911 tomorrow?"

"Call him tomorrow morning. Do you have his number?" Dorina asks.

"Yes, I do. It is Sunday tomorrow, but I will give him a call." I am quite settled on this.

We carry on chatting for many more hours. Our drinks have long finished. Our conversations seem to linger on about anything and everything. We talk about our semester. We talk about our families. We talk about our careers. We talk about needing to do this more often. Finally, we get up, hug each other tightly, and then we go to our cars.

***

Next day. It is 9:00 am. I look through my records and find that I had stored Kent's phone number from a previous exchange on my phone. Calling Kent inevitably means calling him at home since he refuses to get a cell phone. I start to dial his number and wait for the rings. One ring. Two rings. Does he even own an answering machine? Does he believe in answering machines? Three rings…

KENT'S NARRATIVE

"Is this the number for Kent Gillen?" The voice is familiar.

"Yes," I reply, realizing who is on the line. I force myself awake. I try not to sound groggy. It is odd to hear her voice. She has never called here before, and I have spoken to her by phone only once while a student at the university.

"Is this Kent?"

"Yes."

"Kent, I have tried e-mailing you several times. Did you get my messages?" Messages? Plural? "No, I haven't been near a computer since yesterday."

"Are you all right?"

"Sure, sure."

"Then I'll tell you what I have been considering…Are you still there?"

Oh, no. The riot act. I brace myself. "Yes, go on."

"I phoned to tell you there is no reason for you to quit now. I just require that you let me know one thing. If you keep going with the final chapter, and that is all you need, what kind of time frame are we looking at to complete the writing?"

"I don't know. A week, at least."

"All right, I will work with the other committee members to see if we can pare down the reading time from two weeks to only one."

"Okay." I feel a sense of reprieve. Still, I wonder if she is angry.

"Kent, I realize you are feeling depleted and stressed. All I can tell you is this. I will negotiate around a few strategies I have in mind. But first you need to understand I am totally invested in your success, and there is no need for you to give up hope. You have come so far, and this is only the last stretch. Just hang in there, and I will do whatever I can to help you succeed."

If she is angry, she would tell me, wouldn't she? But then perhaps she is only containing herself. Maybe the eruption will occur later. Should I chance it? Of course I should. What choice do I have? She is offering that I step back into the fray. How can I turn her down, regardless of what she really feels?

"I appreciate that." I struggle to assume some semblance of coherency. "What are the chances, or uh, do you think the others will really agree to a shorter reading time?"

"I think so, but I will let you know. Can you come by the office tomorrow or on Tuesday? Maybe if we discuss the chapter face to face, this might ease the tension you're experiencing about what needs to be addressed."

"Tuesday sounds okay. It will give me time to put more on paper. I'll get right to work on it. This afternoon and this evening."

"Send me what you have when you are through writing. Tonight..."

"I will..."

"Kent...I want you to know that I am your biggest cheerleader and I am extremely proud of you. Just don't give up hope now, not when you have achieved so much."

"I understand...I'll get right on it."

"Good...Call me or contact my e-mail if you need to."

"I will. I promise." And we both ring off.

I told her, "I promise," several times before. And then yesterday I reneged. But this time I swear I will never let her down again. What is it about her that inspires this kind of devotion? ...Spending a Sunday in front of a computer is something that, up until now, has been completely foreign to my experience. But today is different. I am *not* looking forward to the work ahead, but it must be done. There will be no more delays, self-induced or otherwise.

***

I devote that Sunday to writing until 7 p.m. when I send the work to Dr. Bhattacharya. The next morning, I open my e-mail to find her reaction:

> *I am not sure if you understood my previous feedback...I am going to try to do this again here...*

My "biggest cheerleader" has returned to critical form, and I am strangely assured in sensing the sharp tone of her commentary:

> *...Chapter five is a place to make your points, connect all the dots in the dissertation, and show your reader that you did what you have intended to do. To that end a recapture of Angie's experiences without providing the reader a rationale for it seems confusing...*

But then, as if the challenges to "process the world" and interpret "intersections" are not large enough tasks to cope with, up pops another new concept to decipher – my "entry point."

> *YOUR entry point into:*

Chicana feminism (this is really important given that you are not Chicana and not female), and ways in which the findings within this theme respond to the research purpose and questions.

...Think how did ethnodrama create an entry point for YOU into Chicana feminism...This study is about your interpretation of Angie's experiences. Therefore you have to tell your readers transparently where this took your understanding, how this methodology created an entry point for you. What could potentially be exciting is that you might be making an argument...that outsider researchers could use ethnodrama as a way to negotiate their understanding, create entry points into these standpoint research topics even though the dangers of objectifying the Other loom high.

This may turn out to be the most important implication of your study – how do genuinely interested outsiders create an entry point into research like this that is unfamiliar and mired with differences in power relations?

Entry point? As in what? Gaining access to a participant? Is that the entry she is discussing? How did I gain entry into the life of a participant? Simple – I asked her...What is this term, this "entry point?"

Entry point? – Into Chicana feminism? The entry point was the library. There are whole shelves covered with volumes on Chicanisma. My entry point was to take books from those shelves and read them, cite them, quote passages from them. These are entry points that are there for the taking. Anyone has that ability, so what has "power relations" got to do with it? What does she mean, entry point?

I dismiss the notion for the time being and write a section for the final chapter, focusing on the connections between Chicana feminism and Angie's experiences concerning what she accepted in her role as a young Latina – an assertion of her heritage and the collective goals of the Chicano Movement – as well as her rejection of the limited expectations of Latino women – her refusal to remain silenced, in the background, confined to private spaces that were exclusive of behavior approximating political activism. I attach this to a message – "Is this what you have in mind?" – and send it. I am not in a pleasant mood. Afterwards, I receive a reply:

This is in the right direction but what you are still not addressing is YOUR entry point. So yes, you are on the right track but you would have to situate yourself transparently in the analysis and discussions. Hope this helps.

It doesn't. So I click the Reply button, intending only to request a face-to-face in her office. But before I get around to that, I write about everything I might possibly consider an "entry point." The frustration has built within me, and it takes a full-on lecture to purge just part of the tension:

Okay. Entry point as "personal." Just as Turner (1982) recommended researchers "act out" the role of those whom they researched and wrote about, researchers who create an interpretation of a participant's experiences through ethnodrama or poetry or other art forms are similarly engaging themselves with the work. They (We) are interacting with their (our) findings on a personal level.

So yes, I can see the act of creating in itself as an entry point. The entry points are in the drama, and the data and events of the past that I worked with. At least, that's how I see it. As for the White male, non-Chicano aspect, I am a scholar interested in past events, especially those that took place in the immediate vicinity. I am also interested in those who use some aspect of postcolonial theory as a framework for their study and thinking. Until now, the color of my skin, my Scotch-Irish ancestry, my "maleness" was never a consideration for me; it (stories of others) is just something I'm interested in. So yes, I am detached.

Okay, I'm stumped. I don't have a clue. For me, the entry point is the action I took, the action I engaged in, not a style of teaching language or feminist theory. These are stationary concepts that are both inclusive and non-inclusive. We can attempt to interpret the experiences of others, but only if we allow ourselves to do so. Naturally, there are those who would object based upon the idea that our having grown up with privilege somehow disqualifies us. Therefore, entry points into the epistemology are necessary, otherwise the research, the work, the findings are all "invalidated". ($1.00 fine?) So the personal engagement through engaging in interpretation itself is not good enough. You suggest that I get through the door by ...what?

Can we meet?

Tuesday afternoon. Office of Dr. Kakali Bhattacharya. The tension within has not abated. I am wound up tight. For me, inner peace is not arrived at through prayer or meditation. For me, inner peace results from letting off steam. I need some answers, but I cannot find them alone. This is the ultimate disappointment – that I have to depend on someone to get me out of a bind. I abhor the fact that I have been defeated by terminology. I am therefore infused with deep cynicism.

DR. BHATTACHARYA: All committee members have agreed to a shorter reading time.

ME: So I have another week.

DR. BHATTACHARYA: You will have to use that time efficiently. Now… *(Takes out hard copy of my draft)*… here is my feedback. First, you describe your research as a "project," then you call it a "study." Stay consistent with your wording. Just call it "the study," nothing else.

ME: The repetition of that word is okay then?

DR. BHATTACHARYA: Yes. And I need two dollars.

ME: Oh?

DR. BHATTACHARYA: There are two places in here where you used the word "validity." This is a highly positivistic term. Two dollars please.

ME: You're kidding.

DR. BHATTACHARYA: I don't joke about my fines.

ME: No, no. I mean about the word "validity." Can you show me?

DR. BHATTACHARYA: Here…and – here too.

ME: Okay. It was the result of a copy-and-paste from an older draft. A perfectly understandable accident for which I'll never forgive myself.

DR. BHATTACHARYA: Beating yourself over the head is a perilous undertaking. I recommend you prevent a life-threatening concussion by using word substitution.

ME: I feel better already.

DR. BHATTACHARYA: Good, because I'm about to attack in other areas. Such as here, where you wrote, "The social awakening that Angie undergoes was duplicated among other Latinas, particularly those who wished to take a more active

163

part than previously allowed in shaping the destiny of the Latino culture, etc." – You may have succeeded in perpetrating the most sweeping generalization since Kipling and "the White man's burden."

ME: Come again?

DR. BHATTACHARYA: How do you know "those who wished to take a more active part" were intent on doing this? What is your source of information? It is too editorialized without evidence.

ME: But the many instances of male Chicano resistance to female membership in the movement was discussed and cited extensively in the literature review.

DR. BHATTACHARYA: Then you will need to cite that information in this section too. And when you discuss Angie's recognition of her own sense of empowerment, I would suggest you question how such a social awakening was represented in the social norms Angie was willing to accommodate and what norms she chose to resist within both Anglo and Latino cultures.

ME *(hesitant)*: In a "generalized" sort of way, she was willing to accommodate and promote the political changes called for by the movement, while resisting the notion of the Latina as Nieto-Gomez's (1973) marginalized "silent Chicana."

DR. BHATTACHARYA: Which would help to connect the dots that represent your previous data. But the image that results from those connected dots will not complete itself unless you face what you are resisting. So let's talk about your entry points.

ME: Entry points. By that, you mean where the dots *don't* connect?

DR. BHATTACHARYA: Partly. But in order to make them connect, you must first make entry into Chicana feminism?

ME:	I already have. For 40 pages.
DR. BHATTACHARYA:	A literature review is not a discussion of a project's implications. Examining the writings of Chicana feminists and analyzing the poetry of Gloria Anzaldúa is not the same as addressing an entry point. I am talking about you, you, the White man, you, the non-Chicano, what is *your* entry point into Chicana feminism as you analyze the themes? You need to analyze *that*. Instead, you stand aloof from the findings, and it makes it seem like your voice is distanced, as if you're God or something. It isn't. You need to put yourself out there. Without discussing explicitly in each of these findings your entry points into Chicana feminism, this study is incomplete. *(Pause)*
ME:	This will be difficult.
DR. BHATTACHARYA:	I know it will be difficult. Now tell me why.
ME:	The ethnodrama was a dramatization of a case study…
DR. BHATTACHARYA:	From whose point of view?
ME:	Angie's. In one version or another, she appears in all scenes. Besides, it's *her* story.
DR. BHATTACHARYA:	No. She may have contributed the raw material, but the dramatization was something that *you* were responsible for. Therefore, it follows that you fulfill the reasonable and necessary obligation of revealing how this method of data-representation took your understanding into the realm of Chicana feminism, a major element of *both* the study and the play.
ME:	And that's the entry point. And once that's done, the dots are connected.
DR. BHATTACHARYA:	First, we will have to see the resulting illustration.
ME:	An ink blot. So inductive analysis becomes self-analysis?

165

DR. BHATTACHARYA: Yes. You must look into yourself when writing this final section – something you don't seem to do in the play. And that could be problematic...So try asking yourself this – where are *you* in this play?

ME: You mean as a character? I deliberately kept my presence out.

DR. BHATTACHARYA: That is not possible. You cannot eliminate your own presence in something you write or anything else you create. It's like a journalist claiming total objectivity when she writes a news story. She can say she just revealed the facts, and therefore it is truth...There is no such thing. And for anyone to claim 100% objectivity in anything they write...it is not possible.

ME: You mean I am there in other ways...through the act of personal expression. But as far as my presence being represented by another character? ...No, I consciously rejected doing that.

DR. BHATTACHARYA: Then, consciously or unconsciously, you were unsuccessful.

ME: How?

DR. BHATTACHARYA: *(pause)*: Let me come back to that later. Here *(handing over draft with comments notated)*, work on what we talked about. I know you can keep this on the right track; but in doing so, you will have to situate yourself transparently in the analysis and discussion.

ME: Okay. *(gets up to leave)*

DR. BHATTACHARYA: Do you still have my cell phone number?

ME: I have it saved on my e-mail.

DR. BHATTACHARYA *(quietly, without looking up)*: One more suggestion: Think about the character named "Johnny." What role does he play in your representation of Angie's life?

ME *(exiting quickly)*: Right.

Dr. Bhattacharya has asked me to consider one of the characters I created for the ethnodrama, and I cannot fathom why. Of all people, why Johnny? The first-grader? The little boy who tells Angie's class how he hated his breakfast so much he gave it to his dog? What could I possibly have in common with *him*? He had two parents at home. I only had a mother. He liked to watch *Whirlybirds* on TV. As far as I was concerned, the show's only draw was a big helicopter. Johnny liked to stand up and reveal his home life to his classmates. I would never dream of doing that. I was too private, withdrawn. In short, Johnny came across as an extraverted know-it-all, whereas I suffered from a severe inferiority complex. I was unlucky.

My cynicism has not faded as I consider this character's unlikely significance. What on earth does Johnny have to do with "entry points" or anything else? I think of the meeting in Dr. Bhattacharya's office. What had she asked? "What role does he play in your representation of Angie's life?" Okay, let's see…he could represent an unpalatable example of Anglo-male pomposity. He certainly projects that. The kind of kid who would feel confident enough to stand up in front of his classmates and turn an answer regarding what he ate for breakfast into a short but moderately interesting vignette of small-town Americana, with a father and a mother and a bratty sister and a dog at the breakfast table each morning, consuming their all-American eggs-and-bacon mini-feast.

A revisit to the scene in which he appears would seem in order. So the next day, I open the computer file containing the ethnodrama and perform a word search, typing in the key term "Johnny." I am surprised to discover that his name is mentioned 10 times throughout the entire play. How could this be? He only had that one speech in the "breakfast" scene. His name should have appeared only once – as speaker of his lines. No, twice, if you count the fact that his first-grade teacher refers to him by name. Where are those other eight times his name is mentioned?

I continue searching through the play for "Johnny." And then I discover that another character, a *different* character with the same name, appeared as a football jock in the play's final scene – at the homemaking dance. This episode was part of the pilot-project for the study. I drafted that scene over a year ago, and I have not looked at it since writing and revising it for Dr. Bhattacharya's advanced-methods class in 2009. When I installed the scene into the current ethnodrama, I did not bother reading through it. I simply copy-and-pasted it from the original pilot-project article – the one I had turned over to Dr. Bhattacharya last fall because I could no longer bear looking at it.

167

This is a mistake, a terrible oversight – two characters with the same name? This will not do...*But*...on the other hand...what if they *are* the same character? Could this be plausible? After all, Johnny and Angie *did* occupy the same grade level...Certainly! All right! Let us assume the first-grader Johnny, the class show-off, has become the high-school Johnny – the half-drunk kid who tries to pick up Angie at the dance, gets rejected, and then attempts to come to her defense when an argument ensues between her and an Anglo homemaking student. This could be the same Johnny, right? Not that this was ever my intention. An intersection, if you could call it that, occurs in this scene. After Johnny attempts to assist Angie, what does she tell him?

"I guess I'm supposed to thank you for sticking up for us, but we can fend for ourselves. It's not your fight anyway."

What was not "your fight?" What "fight" does Angie mean? On the play's surface level, the fight refers to the squabble with another girl, a White girl, one who has access to wealth. (Her father runs the town's bank.) On a deeper level, however, Angie is addressing that line to more than just one person – for who could Johnny represent? White men? Like me? Like the researcher?

Are Johnny and I the same person?

Conceivably, yes; but only if one examines the play in a thematic sense. Certainly, if this is the case, it was unintentional. What is that disclaimer that often appears in association with a copyright and an all-rights-reserved clause? "Any similarities between characters and persons living or dead are purely unintentional." That fits here too. Is this the "entry point" that Dr. Bhattacharya has been referencing...?

...Well, I'll be...She knew it all along! ...But she wanted *me* to make the discovery...

I open the file containing the final chapter of the study and add the following content:

In considering the play's initial scene, Angie explains to the audience the necessity of deceiving her teacher and classmates on the question concerning what she had eaten for breakfast. Instead of telling the class that food had consisted of a taquito, she admits only to having oatmeal in order to avoid the ridicule she might endure if she had told the truth. Before Angie's turn to relate the "oatmeal" version of her breakfast to the class, however, the audience is exposed to the Anglo boy named Johnny and his story of the "runny" eggs he was served for breakfast and how he was caught and punished by his father for attempting to secretly feed the unsavory concoction to the family dog. In reflecting on this scene, I realize the possibility now of having subconsciously posited the boy Johnny as a stand-in for the White male author (me), as he (both myself and the character) would have foreseen little problem in relating the incident of breakfast to his teacher and peers. Johnny/I had been served an Anglicized meal that morning and therefore seeing no need to consider that his/my audience (the class of first-graders) is predominantly Anglo like him/me, there would be no perceived risk of embarrassment or ridicule as the result of such a revelation. Naturally, this is what sets apart Angie (both the participant and the interpretation based on that character) and Johnny (both the character and the researcher). Thus, in composing a scene such as this, with its implication of the ways even children such as Angie can make meaning of the power relations inherent in a matter so apparently "trivial" as a breakfast menu, the author has not only written his version of a significant scene from Angie's school years, but has also succeeded in injecting his own consciousness into the play right alongside the Chicana lead character who represents the author's interpretation of the study's participant…Besides, it should be further noted that this is not the only scene in which Johnny appears.

To provide a transition into the next paragraph, which will explain the significance of Johnny's older, high-school manifestation, I debate whether to mention the accidental oversight of having, without intention, given two different characters – the two Johnny's – the same name. Would any discerning reader not question the veracity of such a "story?" In the end, I decide it matters little. In fact, I assume Dr. Bhattacharya does not even suspect this occurred. On the other hand, she was cunning enough to recognize the representational link between Johnny and myself. So perhaps she does suspect. Nonetheless, I vow *not* to mention the truth; instead, I carry on writing as if the Johnny/me connection had been planted deliberately:

In the play's final scene, the character's manifestation serves as a significant framing device for the entire drama, in that the stratagem enables me, through the actions of Johnny, to maintain the presence of my own consciousness in the presentation of the findings, the overall piece itself. Johnny uses an absurd come-on in order to attract the attention of Angie [who] engages in skillful repartee, making clear that the attempted pick-up will not succeed. Later, Johnny's ex-girlfriend, also an Anglo, barges into the scene, insulting [Angie]. Johnny sends the girl away and then tries to apologize to Angie, but she's not buying it. She tells Johnny, "I guess I'm supposed to thank you for sticking up for us, but we can fend for ourselves. It's not your fight anyway." Angie's snub is intended as more than just a personal rejection of Johnny. Again, functioning as the author/researcher's stand-in, Johnny, in effect, is told by Angie (the author's interpretation of the participant) that she needs no one to "speak for her" – she asserts her own strength in waging her own battles. In other words, to borrow from Alcoff (1991/2009), she needs no one – certainly not Johnny or me – to provide her experiences the "authenticating presence" of a dominant-group member to "confer legitimacy and credibility on the demands of subjugated speakers" (p. 118). The question to address then involves the issue of some researchers and scholars who presume to legitimize the cause of those who are oppressed by the presence of their own dominant positionality.

My own dominant positionality. This is the thought I have left my reader with at the end of the paragraph. Logically, then, this will be the next topic to discuss. I believe I know what the word "dominant" refers to – dominant, as in numbers. So what do I write next? What it feels like to be the member of a numerical majority? I will admit it feels comfortable. Do I experience guilt as a result of my good fortune, granted by birth? Perhaps I should – but I don't. Should I make this admission in writing? No, better not. So what *am* I willing to admit?

Wait just a minute!…Is this how the game is played? Is this the task now at hand – to create a series of admissions – some true, some maybe half-true, all the rest fabrications? A list that others in the academic community would *want* me to write? The sort of prose reflecting only the ideas *they* would want to read? Is this how one is granted the keys to the academy in the form of the highest degree an educational institution can bestow?

Inevitably, I decide to contact Dr. Bhattacharya.

University faculty building, office of Dr. Kakali Bhattacharya, latter part of October 2010.

DR. BHATTACHARYA: Kent, did you read the article by McIntosh?
ME: McIntosh?

DR. BHATTACHARYA:	Peggy McIntosh. I mailed you about it a week ago.
ME:	Are you sure you mentioned it?
DR. BHATTACHARYA:	I am certain I mentioned it…She published an article that includes a list of unearned privileges she enjoys by virtue of being White. I would describe it to you further, but considering your delicate condition, not to mention that of your closing chapter, I think you would benefit by seeing it. I will print a copy.
ME:	Maybe I just overlooked it…What privileges are you talking about?
DR. BHATTACHARYA:	There are approximately 50 – the same types of privileges that you as a White man must unpack in your writing…Retrieve the pages from the printer please.
ME:	Sure, no problem…
DR. BHATTACHARYA:	Hand it to me…Pay attention to her style of expression. Notice the rhetorical technique – the way she begins each entry of the list. "I can" wish for this. Or "I can" avoid that. Or "I can" be sure of this. She is stating that as a White person, she can be guaranteed certain favorable conditions of living and experiencing her terrain. I suggest it would benefit you to emulate this format. You could create a list of privileges for yourself… specifically, a list of examples, similar to these, that would relate your own benefits as a White man, as opposed to your participant, a Latina, who would not. Listen to this. McIntosh (1990): "I can go shopping alone most of the time, pretty well assured that I will not be followed or harassed."
ME:	So?
DR. BHATTACHARYA:	So?! Could Angie do this? Shop alone and not experience harassment?

171

ME:	No, I guess not. For her, it was a bad experience. Shop owners dogging her, making sure she didn't swipe perfume or candy off the shelves.
DR. BHATTACHARYA:	I know. I have read the transcript.
ME:	It became so bad for her family they began buying clothes mail-order.
DR. BHATTACHARYA:	Here is another: "I can choose to ignore developments in minority writing and minority activist programs, or disparage them, or learn from them, but in any case, I can find ways to be more or less protected from negative consequences of any of these choices."
ME:	Angie spearheaded the cultural-affairs degree program that's just now being offered at the college. Why would anyone choose to ignore minority programs? For that matter, why would they object?
DR. BHATTACHARYA:	Who can say? Perhaps learning different cultures and heritages does not fit in with their view of what colleges should teach. Your study, however – your participant – you and she celebrate those choices. But *your* endorsement is the endorsement of a White man. As such, you stand atop the social structure. Unless you unpack your own privileges, you are writing and speaking from the point of view of a person who is, by all evidence or lack thereof, completely unaware of the unearned advantages of which McIntosh speaks.
ME:	Her whole article reads like an extended confessional…
DR. BHATTACHARYA:	It is an example of the kind of testament you will have to make in your study.
ME:	Are there any others on her list that apply?
DR. BHATTACHARYA:	They *all* apply – in one form or another.

ME:	Yes, yes, I see…
DR. BHATTACHARYA:	…Okay, here: "I can go home from most meetings of organizations I belong to feeling somewhat tied in, rather than isolated, out-of-place, outnumbered, unheard, held at a distance or feared."
ME:	Angie and the Homemaking Club…
DR. BHATTACHARYA:	Kent, do you wish to be interpreted as someone who states to his readers *(pitching her voice low)*, "I am the White-man's voice in this conversation and as such, I can lend more credibility than if…?"
ME:	I would never write such drivel. Come on, you know me better than that...
DR. BHATTACHARYA:	Yes, I know you – but the academy does not. This is why you must speak of the unearned advantages you enjoy by right of your White heritage; or else, *you* will not be considered seriously in academia, which has its own privileged hierarchy anyway. But that's another story.

KAKALI'S NARRATIVE

"Uggghhhhh!"

I tilt back my head, looking up to the florescent light on the ceiling. "Kent is everywhere. How could he not be a part of what he has created? Ughhhh."

I am talking to myself, but it looks like I am talking to some invisible being on my ceiling. It was a rough meeting again.

Dorina was walking by when she heard me shouting. I am sure she thinks I am mad. I am. I am certain she could easily diagnose me with some mad head disorder or something. At least I had enough composure to keep it together when Kent was here. Dorina peeks her head in my office and asks, "Are you okay?"

"No. I am not sure if I need to push Kent's dissertation defense to next semester. I don't know if he can do the work that needs to be done." I am exhausted by now.

"What happened?" Dorina comes in and sits down on my couch.

"We didn't even get to talk about his privileges, because he is not able to see that he is in his own play. He thinks somehow his cognitive filtering of Angie's words is making him an objective, detached reporter. Ugggggggghhhhhhh!" I release my frustration vocally.

"What did you tell him?" Dorina asks.

"I told him it's impossible to be detached and gave him a hint to at least start to identify how deeply implicated he is in this work. This is so much privilege, that I don't even know where to start breaking it apart for him." I feel an exhaustion setting in my body. I want to go home and just sleep.

"Do you think he got what you were saying?"

"Oh I don't know. I really don't know. The thing is he is everywhere in his study. Every character is him and not him. He does not get that. He thinks because he has used the participants' words verbatim he is free from having to claim his positionality. This is so much God-like posturing. He creates these characters, scenes, dialogues, actions, but he is above and away from it all. How is that possible?"

Dorina sorts out her thoughts. "Hey even me, who can barely understand qualitative research gets that. It is like a counselor cannot claim that she is not affected by her client. Sure we have coping mechanism but a part of the client always becomes a part of us when we work closely with them."

"Exactly. All the characters that Kent chose, are worked through his cognitive, subjective, aesthetic sensibilities. He is part of all of them and they are part of him. I hope he can come back with some progress. I gotta get out of here. I need to nap and watch some bad TV show or something. Is that show *The Bachelor* on tonight?" I stand up and start to put my laptop in my bag."

"Hell if I know. I have a night class. Get some rest. It will be okay." Dorina gets up and walks out of the office.

Soon afterwards I go home.

KENT'S NARRATIVE

It was a rough meeting, but now I know what I have to add to the chapter. I return to the library and attempt to draft a list of my own privileges, while at the same time adopting a style that is mine, not McIntosh's. She used a tone that was objective, matter-of-fact, without emotion. For her, this strategy proved effective. I, on the other hand, prefer to stress the "hearts and flowers."

I begin slowly, for I am undecided as to whether I should enumerate a list a la McIntosh or go with a typical essay-paragraph approach. I begin to draft. Once I have hammered out the first 3 sentences, I am surprised at how quickly my pace accelerates, as I struggle to keep typing in order to maintain speed with the ideas. Soon the words tumble over one another in an unstoppable torrent. It is an unusual experience. After I revise the thoughts into an edited, coherent paragraph, this is what I am left with:

For my own part, that of a White Anglo-American who has benefitted from privileges not shared by people of color, I have always placed value on personal independence and the choice of solitude (i.e., working in isolation) over communal association. Admittedly, such an option will serve to place a stronger emphasis on my status as researcher, the role of outsider/insider. Accordingly, and in relation to the one whose life I have researched, I can never know the dread or the resentment that she felt while growing up. I will never experience the anxiety of spotting a police-officer who is observing me on the street – or of knowing that the policeman acts as a symbol of repressive authority who serves the dominant culture he represents, protecting that culture from people like me. I can only wonder what it must feel like to be deemed suspect of having committed a wrongdoing, and whether I will be questioned or incarcerated for reasons having less to do with who I am and more to do with *what* I am. And I will never know the angst that accompanies me while walking into a store to browse or possibly consider making a purchase – and being eyed constantly, vigilantly, or even being outright interrogated as to what I am doing there. I will never know what it is like to be made to feel unwelcome by a social group or club because I am "one of those." And I dare not complain when I am confronted by an Anglo because such a reaction may be interpreted as impertinent, "uppity," even threatening. And I can only wonder what it must be like to recall my very first day of school, remembering that I understood only half of what my strict, orderly White teacher was saying to me – a teacher who wasn't like the warm, nurturing women of my culture who also order me about, but do so with love in their hearts. I will never be able to reflect on being enrolled in a school where I observed this White teacher who represented authority, and thought to myself, there is no love here. As Mirande and Enriquez (1997) summarized the reaction of Latino schoolchildren in such situations, where are my role models? (p. 132)

175

Will this be enough? Then, an odd thing happens: My eyes moisten. "Hey, dummy," I tell myself, "Maintain control. You're in a public place." Regaining my composure – it must be emotional exhaustion – I wonder if the "hearts-and-flowers" angle is not taking its toll. Nevertheless, I continue typing:

> Yet I have drawn only half the picture. For I am not only White, I am a man. Thus, I will also never endure the stigma associated with my gender of not possessing the mental ability to grasp mathematical or scientific concepts and theory. I will not know the condescension of being told (whether by a parent or a high-school counselor) that it would be more appropriate to concern myself with the economics of keeping house for a man and the children whom I must bring forth into the world because that is what is expected of me – because that goal, I am further informed, is my preordained mission in life. And since I am not a Latino female (and therefore I do not have those *two* strikes against me), I will never know the need to fit the concept of "sainted mother" or "evil witch" (Blea, 1997, p. 38). In other words, I will not know the implications of fulfilling certain requirements, such as either remaining a virgin at marriage or else disgracing myself. Nor will I know the necessity of bowing to the doctrinaire sentiment of devotion to a husband, body and soul, and to hide alarm if he carouses or occasionally strays by indulging in whiskey or women or both. As a White Anglo male, what do I know of the fear that results when others of my community might possibly accuse me of witchcraft, of using evil "wiles" to entice a mate into a loveless marriage? No, I will never know what it is like to be cursed by those of my family, by members of my own community, not will I ever understand that the only path to redemption will occur only after I have lost my attractiveness and aged beyond beauty. For it is only then would be accorded respect by others in my extended family (Facio, 1996). And these are only a few conditions of a life I have never known and will never know.

I can draft no more. What I have just written consists of thoughts I can never express aloud, either privately or in public discourse. If I ever tried, I would lose control of my emotions. I would soon break down in the middle of speaking. Such is the empowerment of writing – the same power that Angie (see Figure 18) discovered when she began composing English themes her senior year in high school. ("I *do* have a voice…I may not be able to speak it…but I can write it!")

Figure 18. Angie, high school senior picture

My exhaustion has tripled. I am through – for today anyway. Before leaving, I send what I have to Dr. Bhattacharya with a short note:

Correct my path, if it's the wrong one to take.

The next morning, I open her reply. It cites a lyric from the musical version of Shaw's (1912/1930) *Pygmalion*. Somehow it seems appropriate, even if the roles *are* reversed, with me as Eliza.

By George you got it. I am crying in pride. I am beaming. I am humbled. Thank you Kent for putting yourself out there. I know the journey was arduous. I really appreciate the deeper digging. It is now where it needs to be. You are brilliant and awesome.

She continues by informing me that after reading my attachment, she printed a copy and went to the office of a neighboring professor – another White man – and read to him my paragraphs. Curiously, she does not tell me *his* reaction.

But it does not matter. Inwardly, I feel appreciation for the praise. I am relieved to know that now I *am* on the right path. But before my head swells the size of Mount Shasta, I had better finish. So I open the closing chapter's file and read the two paragraphs I processed the day before. Then, I add more:

Instead, as a privileged White male, I know that I can walk the streets of any city or town in America and be reasonably certain that I will not arouse the suspicion of a passing police officer – no matter the ethnicity or gender of the man or woman who represents civil officialdom. This being the case, I can also be assured that I will not experience repression from those sanctioned to keep others in line – people of color. I can walk into any place of business and be accommodated as a person of privilege and not suffer the disgrace of being immediately held suspect as a possible thief. And if my privilege as a White man is challenged, I can respond, I can plea my case, or I can even complain to a higher authority and not be accused of "playing the race card." And in recalling my school years, I can reflect upon the wide array of role models from which I had to choose – so many, so "varied." As a White male, I can further look back on school and remember the encouragement I received from my math and science teachers about the exciting future in the fields of aeronautics and nuclear energy and how such endeavors were right up my alley – mine and those of my White male school chums – because that is the promise the future held for *us*. And like the proverbial cowboy, I knew that come what may, I would eventually marry a pretty White girl, have pretty White children, and settle down in a comfortable suburban neighborhood and in a community where other White couples and other White children would make their homes alongside ours. This was promised. This was ingrained. I was conditioned early in life to receive a White entitlement.

It takes the better part of an hour to get this far; but in the end, the sense of emotional catharsis is overwhelming. My "knapsack" feels much lighter now…And then for the second time in two days, I wonder, "Is this why I feel the need to impersonate a weeping willow?"

It is Friday; there are no classes to teach. Like Sam Peckinpah's (1962) western hero Steve Judd, in *Ride the High Country*, I can now "enter my own house, justified." My study is almost finished. Rough, but the composing is near an end. I will therefore spend all weekend on revision – and enjoy it.

Before departing, I send my Pygmalion/Svengali the following communiqué with attachment:

Sorry to report I got bogged down on chapter 5 – was able to squeeze one page (content in bold type), but then got stuck…

I realize this is a lie. I did not "get stuck." But there is no demon on the planet that can threaten, cajole, or force me to admit to my mentor the truth – that my tear ducts have developed a will of their own.

KAKALI'S NARRATIVE

I am in Kent's dissertation defense. He just finished relaying to us his study and after asking him some questions, we have sent him outside so we can deliberate. Caroline stands up and closes the door. Sitting around the room are the same people who were present at Kent's proposal defense, Bryant, the seasoned professor, Caroline, and Kathleen, the English professor, and me.

Bryant starts the discussion. "Well that was certainly better than what we saw at the proposal. But do you think he has done enough to figure out who he is in relation to his study or his participant?"

Caroline, who is sitting opposite to Bryant, chimes in. "You know I am still uncomfortable with this. I see he has done some work. But I still feel like there could have been more."

Kathleen starts flipping through the pages and reads out loud some sections where Kent has listed the various ways in which his life is different from Angie's. "You're talking about this part, right?" Kathleen asks, looking at Bryant. I choose to stay quiet for the moment, because I want to see where the conversation is going.

Caroline stands up and moves to the front of the room. "Sorry guys, I need to stand up, or else I feel some pain in my abdomen." It wouldn't be until a year later that she would be diagnosed with colon cancer. And it wouldn't be until two years later that she would pass on.

"Yes, that's the part where he actually addresses some of the issues, yeah." Bryant nods his head as he speaks.

"So you don't think this is enough?" Kathleen asks. "I actually quite liked his style of writing and coming from an English background, I thought this was quite confessional. Very few authors put themselves out like that." She looks at Bryant while she says this.

"I get that," Bryant explains. "But this needs to be a social science research, or at the very least educational research. So we need the humanities aesthetics of course, given that he is writing creatively, but some of the content could have been explored deeper."

"Okay, well I only know humanities." Kathleen says. I wonder if that was said with a bit of hurt feelings or if I am reading too much into it.

Caroline then asks, "Kakali, what do you think? What's your take on this?"

I shift in my chair. I think of what Kent might be going through waiting for us outside. I remember during my dissertation defense I came armed with citations so that I could answer all the questions with scholarly references. At one point, one of the committee members asked me what I actually thought and commanded me to not speak with citations. This, I was unprepared to do. I learned that my voice did not matter much unless I spoke with citation. I fumbled through and stated something, I suppose, that I do not remember. However, over the years, I have continued working with my dissertation data, with that one question in mind – what do I really think of this? Where am I in all of this if I could speak from an authentic, invested perspective?

"Yes, I am interested in hearing how you worked with Kent, Kakali." Bryant agrees with Caroline, and I focus on the conversation in the room.

"It was a really difficult process to get him to this point. First he could not figure out the terminology we were using in educational research. Entry point, processing the world, interrogating privileges, were extremely foreign to him. I couldn't tell if someone in his past told him that creative non-fiction needs to be written in such a way where he is presenting facts and somehow he is detached from what he is presenting." I pause and sip my water from a Dasani water bottle.

"Okay, this is making more sense now. So all along he thought he was being a good researcher by keeping himself out of it?" Bryant asks.

"I think I would agree that in creative non-fiction, some people are trained to present only the facts, as in things that can be fact-checked and verified," Kathleen explains. "Maybe Kent thought since this is a research project, he had to bring that kind of understanding."

Caroline continues to pace back and forth in the front of the room, turning towards us, as she moves. "I get that, you know. My beef with some of his prior work was that he was so airy-fairy that I thought he was being esoteric for the sake of being esoteric. I hate elitist writing like that. In Ohio State a lot of qualitative research folks did that. I hated it when…"

"I don't think Kent wrote things in an elitist way though…" Bryant interrupts.

"No, I agree he doesn't write in an elitist way. But I feel like by not fully addressing what we asked him to do, is he saying he is too good for this and taking us for granted?" Caroline asks.

I do not want Kent's committee to think he has tried to disrespect them or dismiss their advice in any way. I hear the protective momma bear in me starting to growl. "So, as I was saying, once I got Kent to really focus on how his and Angie's lives were different growing up and even now, he was able to become a bit more vulnerable than he was before. I was actually proud of him for allowing me to push that much. But I know that it doesn't seem that much to us now. But for him this unpacking was huge, because this is the first time he has ever considered these ideas. And it would take more than this dissertation for him to realize that this will have to be an ongoing work for him." I say.

"Yes, that I would agree." Bryant says. "For me, I would say I am still doing this work."

Caroline sits down. "That's right. That's 100% right. There is always more work to do." She turns towards me and says, "I have to tell you though, Kakali. You have done so much work with him. I cannot believe what you were able to produce. Kudos to you. I struggled in getting him focused. His research topic changed every week when I was working with him. One time he wanted to do something with films, then there was the bus system, remember?"

We laugh. "Yes, I remember. What happened was he started a pilot study with someone who agreed to be interviewed and he carried on, but he never stopped to think the ethics of telling someone else's story from his perspective. Because he thought his perspective is somehow not as entangled in it, as long as he could offer verbatim dialogues."

"So did you have to deal with a lot of resistance?" Bryant asks me. Kathleen has not said much for a while but she seems engaged in the discussion.

"I don't know if I would say resistance. I think it was more like avoidance. As in this is too difficult for me to deal with. Please don't make me do this. Look over here instead, see how nicely I wrote over here about Victor Turner? Isn't that great? It was that kind of a dance. And I would have to bring him back and say, no, YOU look over here," I explain.

Bryan states, "I do agree with Caroline that you have done as much as you could have and Kent has done as much as he could have too. And despite everything this is good work and he is a good writer."

"Yes, I would say he is an excellent writer," Kathleen says. "This was a page turner for me, especially when I was reading the scenes."

"Shall we bring him in?" Caroline asks.

"Yes, let's bring him in," says Bryant. "I think I am comfortable passing this."

"I am too," Kathleen adds.

"Me too." Caroline agrees.

"Okay," I say. "I am going to call him back into the room. He is probably really anxious out there."

Kent was standing in the hallway, with a cup of coffee in his hand. "Kent?" I call for him. He takes his last gulp of coffee, throws the cup in the garbage can next to him and walks towards me. I extend my hand out to shake his. "Congratulations, Dr. Gillen." I figured if I tried to hug him, it would freak him out. Kent shakes my hand. "Let's go inside," I say.

We walk inside the conference room. Bryant, Kathleen, and Caroline shake his hand and call him Dr. Gillen. Kent lets out a small smile. Maybe he is smiling more inside.

KENT'S NARRATIVE

December 2010, toward the end of the semester. So it is over, at least for now. However, Dr. Bhattacharya and I feel that the process of "unpacking" is incomplete. In our final meeting before graduation, she suggests I research the topic of "double-consciousness," a term with which I am unfamiliar. So taking her cue, I enter the college library and embark on a computer search. I learn the term is most often associated with W.E.B. Dubois, writer, journalist, essayist, novelist, etc. Double-consciousness was a condition experienced by Dubois from the very moment he became aware of his own skin-color. He describes the significance of the discovery in the first chapter of his book, *The Souls of Black Folk* (1903/1953):

> It is a peculiar sensation, this double-consciousness, this sense of always looking at one's self through the eyes of others, of measuring one's soul by the tape of a world that looks on in amused contempt and pity. One ever feels his two-ness — an American, a Negro; two souls, two thoughts, two unreconciled strivings; two warring ideals in one dark body, whose dogged strength alone keeps it from being torn asunder. (p. 3)

During the following spring, I prepare a conference presentation on Dubois's interpretation of double-consciousness by focusing almost exclusively on a reflective piece published over a decade ago by Dominic Saucedo (1996), the self-described son of an Irish-American mother and a Mexican-American father, who was born in East Los Angeles. Later, his family moved to rural Oregon, where "there were green trees, but no smog, little crime, and no Mexicans" (p. 92). In time, he began to develop an increasing awareness of faraway Los Angeles as the "place-where-my-people-are-at" (p. 92).

Later while attending a liberal-arts college in Minnesota, he became embittered, aspiring to an existence that ruled out Whites. Instead, he chose to befriend only Asians, Blacks, or other Chicanos (p. 97). Eventually, his bitterness subsided as he discovered that he had inadvertently defined himself in relation to Anglo-Americans: "I have given them too much of my energy, and too much of my time" (Saucedo, 1996, p. 98). Upon further reflection, he concluded Whites have very little concern for ethnic identity and thus "have no concrete idea of why they are outside the sphere of their own personality [and to] be ignorant of one's ethnicity, of one's role in society, and of one's self, is also White privilege" (p. 100). In other words, the denial of one's roots can lead to the denial of one's responsibility as a citizen and member of a heterogeneous community.

Saucedo believed that such denial leads to a condition where Whites are "dissolved into Whiteness" (p. 99). Further, he maintained that to ignore one's own cultural background is to ignore those of others. Thus, he drew implications suggesting that Whites, largely speaking, possess no desire for involvement with others in their community, global or locally. Their concerns are mainly inner-directed, the result of their Eurocentrism, their own cultural "egocentrism."

By contrast, one of Saucedo's contemporaries, Max Benavidez (1997), another Latino native of Los Angeles, wrote that he had "never felt hatred or bitterness toward 'White' or Anglo people" (p. 8). In fact, he describes a brief period when he assumed a White masquerade. Benavidez (1997) described the process as, not a transformation, but a "simulation":

I couldn't change the color of my skin but I could act White, speak White, even pretend to think White. Simulation is to assume a false appearance. This simulation of a plastic Whiteness was a pretense, a false front that I presented to the world, even to myself. I was very good at it. In a sense, it was my first performance art. (p. 9)

To Benavidez, this was his version of "double consciousness." It was also a source of personal self-hatred that, he feels, characterizes the *mestizo* image of self: "Not Native American, yet of the Indian. Not Spanish, yet of Europe, Not even Mexican in the strictest sense of the term. And the U.S.-born Mexican is rarely, if ever, considered 'American'" (p. 1). Benavidez (1997) concluded that the key to resolving the internal crises described above was to discover "who we are, what we are, where we came from, where we are going" (p. 10) – a reflective process he describes as like a constant movement in circles, advancing round and round (as opposed to "straight-line thinking") in an attempt to come to terms with the multiple-cultural paradox that he envisions as the nature of Mexican-American identity.

To Saucedo (1996), however, such inner diplomacy, though acceptable, is also a bit too subtle. He calls on Latinos to actively resist the internal duality that governs their existence "because ultimately those who stand in the middle are torn apart by either side" (p. 100). As for reconciliation with the Anglo culture, he feels such a stance would prove futile, that it

183

would amount to nothing more than "a vain attempt to search for a place in a White society that will continually deny you" (p. 100). But he adds that, "it is even more vain yet to try and escape a culture that has an unyielding grasp on your soul" (p. 100). Thus, perhaps because of Saucedo's refusal to come to terms with a White culture so oblivious to self-examination that it cannot even define itself in words, he has placed overriding value on opting for one heritage (Mexican, his father's side) while rejecting the other (Irish-American, his mother's).

Saucedo and Benavidez sought ways to explore their identities through different methods. In the end, both authors believed the key to such reconciliation was a deeper reflection upon their *mestizo* identity. In the two cases, members of the White culture are not dismissed outright; their significance is merely minimized. They no longer appear to matter. The conclusion drawn by both authors calls for a tighter focusing of their ethnographic gaze inward.

***

As I stated during the "unpacking" section of the study's final chapter, I prefer solitude over community. I am not so certain that this preferred condition of existence is the result of an inherited European trait. But I do admit to a predisposition to remain distant from others, including those of my own ethnicity. So in that sense, how do I fit into Saucedo's assertions concerning Eurocentrism? It is true that I have experienced little desire to investigate my own Scotch-Irish heritage and background. Again, as Saucedo (1996), who is partially of Irish heritage himself, has written, "[i]f one is White one is simply dissolved into Whiteness" (p. 99).

Building bridges across cultures is, of course, possible. But is an application of the ideal probable? Dr. Bhattacharya (2013) suggests the foundations of such structures can be laid through the de-mystification of colonizing epistemologies, particularly in higher education, that (intentionally or not) perpetuate condescending images of the exotic Other. To this end, I have assigned Saucedo's article to students in my English classes, a majority of whom are Hispanic. With three exceptions thus far, their reactions have been sharply negative. During class discussions, many attempt to rebut each of Saucedo's points. Overwhelmingly, they register outrage that a student, even *if* Latino, would dare to isolate himself from his White classmates. They consider such behavior racist. I attempt to make certain I understand their objections: "So your argument is that Saucedo is a bigot because he deliberately separated himself from the White community, and therefore this makes him automatically guilty of racism?" In near-solidarity, the students cry, "Yes!"

"Well, I disagree!" But my rejection is accompanied with a smile, and we all laugh before resuming.

Still, I am engaged in discourse with a class of students, some of whom presumably have been made witnesses to stories narrated by their elders of injustices perpetrated upon them by a White society. Yet these same students reject the narrative of Saucedo and his bitter remembrances of being told repeatedly by the White adults of his Oregonian community that he was "special," not like "those other Mexicans" (p. 97). How do such experiences influence one's perception of the dominant culture? Would this not cause *any* person, not just Saucedo, to seek isolation from those who act as agents of such oppression?

Perhaps Saucedo's term, "dissolved into Whiteness," may one day extend to more than just the dominant segment of society – White America – refusing to define its own past. For us, such confrontation with our own history requires facing the injustices performed in the name of *our* culture. Will there come a time when *all* racial segments of the nation will unsuspectingly extend Saucedo's concept of "Whiteness" beyond our various cosmetic appearances and advance its significance into other areas – such as matters of deciding what traditions to celebrate from one's cultural past as opposed to decisions regarding what to discard regarding one's own heritage (the "get-over-it-and-move-on" mentality) that we *all* become dissoluble because of a new inability to distinguish between the past ("where we came from"), the present ("what are we, who are we") and future ("where we are going")? When I consider the possibility of this new homogenization – this "bleaching" of the psyche of the collective American – I question whether this is the nature of the oppression Arundhati Roy (2003) had in mind when she urged readers to assist her in calling out and exposing a structural entity she has labeled "the Empire" of today's global politics? And if that Empire prevails, will there still be some of us remaining who will reflect on how such dissolution occurred within the cultures and souls of people of *all* colors?

I realize all that I have described above seems unlikely. As Hannerz (1990) observed in relation to world cultures, "No total homogenization of systems of meaning and expression has occurred, nor does it appear likely that there will be one any time soon" (p. 237). But this was written over 20 years ago. And when considering my students' hostile reactions to Saucedo, I think of Ramon Saldivar's (1999) English translation of the words to an old song by the popular Latino band, Los Tigres del Norte:

My children don't speak to me.
They've learned another language
and forgotten their Spanish.
They think like Americans;
they deny that they are Mexican
even though they share my color.

Enrique Franco (1983)

KAKALI'S NARRATIVE

A year later. Kent and I are again at the International Congress of Qualitative Inquiry conference at the University of Illinois, Urbana campus. Kent is presenting something from his dissertation. One of my mentors from my doctoral studies at the University of Georgia, Jude Preissle, is in the audience. She is a well-known, respected educational anthropologist. About three years later, Jude would win the Lifetime Achievement Award in Qualitative Research at this conference.

Kent begins to present. He talks about Angie. He talks about him. He parallels their lives. He demonstrates how well rooted Angie is to her culture. He speaks of his European roots. He has Irish heritage. He speaks of how different his connection is to Ireland than Angie's connection to Mexico. He reminds us that growing up, when Kent's mother was a teacher, Angie's mother was cleaning the houses of her peers. He brings up DuBois, Saucedo. He uses Saucedo's notion of "fading into Whiteness" and eventually his picture on the screen blurs into the plain white backgrounds of the screen (See Figure 19).

Figure 19. Kent, dissolving into Whiteness

I am spellbound. Kent has done some deep excavating work. During the question answer portion of the talk, Jude asks Kent how he got to this point and what was his process. Kent, being the deep thinker that he is, starts to think on the spot, gets lost in his thought, and does not offer an answer. I respond briefly. "I cannot speak of Kent's individual process, but as his dissertation chair, I would say it was challenging and perhaps with a lot of tears and soul searching." The talk ends.

Kent walks towards me. I introduce him to Jude Preissle. All of us walk out together. As we are walking on the campus quad, Jude asks again, "Kent, I would be very interested to know how you got to this point. This is not an easy point to get to." I can tell Kent has not stopped thinking about the question, when it was first asked. He nods his head and barely mutters a "Yes." Later, I tell Jude that Kent's lack of response is not his lack of ability to answer. Rather he is deeply lost in thought. Jude gives a nod of understanding.

This book is Kent's thoughtful response to that question – how he got to that point of understanding.

KAKALI'S AND KENT'S NARRATIVES: COMING TOGETHER

Kent and Kakali are at a summer writing retreat, years afterward. This retreat is part of a summer writing class that Kakali teaches. Kent, even after his graduation, has chosen to visit the retreat to work on the proposals for this book and for a conference. The retreat is at a huge rented apartment by the Gulf of Mexico. We have direct view and access to the blue/green water and the almost golden sandy beach. We are seated outside on the back-porch deck. Inside, there are a dozen other occupants, all current graduate doctoral students, slaving away at their writing.

Kent is drinking coffee, while Kakali is pulling up some documents on her laptop. Kakali looks up at Kent and asks, "How many cups of coffee did you have today?"

"I am a reformed addict now. I don't drink as much coffee."

"Interesting that you call yourself reformed and addict still." Kakali smiles.

"Yeah, not ready to fully quit, so not completely cured, but still making an effort. So are we really doing this book?" Kent asks.

"Yes, we are. I think we should," Kakali says, adding, "We could write from your perspective and mine and show how we experienced this process."

"That could be fun. I am dying to do some more writing. I miss my writing days as a doc student," Kent says. If the doctoral students inside the house heard that Kent is missing the pressure of writing, they would gladly trade places with him.

"Okay, let me ask you a question I kept asking you through your doc program. Do you know what your entry point is now to your study?" I ask.

"Nope." Kent responds immediately. "I don't have an entry point. I couldn't. All I could do is understand my own Whiteness as a result of engaging with Angie's story."

A smile spreads across my face.

CHAPTER 6

PEDAGOGICAL PRACTICES

We thank our readers for thinking of using our book in their pedagogical practices. In this chapter we share some pedagogical practices that could be helpful in teaching, race, ethnicity, multiculturalism, power, qualitative methods, and arts-based research. While we offer some exercises, we leave it to our readers to customize them as they need in their learning environments. We think this book and the exercises are relevant to various undergraduate and graduate level classes. A note of caution from our experiences of using some of them in our pedagogical spaces. Sometimes these exercises work brilliantly and the classroom becomes a space of transformative learning and illuminating discussion. At other times, these very same exercises could cause conflict within and outside the classroom. Thus, before proceeding with any of these exercises, there should be some guidelines established at the start of the class. Below we offer our suggested guidelines.

SUGGESTED GUIDELINES FROM OUR PEDAGOGICAL PRACTICES

1. State from the beginning of the class that the classroom is a safe environment. Set up rules for establishing safe environment. Our rules have been the following:
   a. Our classroom is like Las Vegas. Whatever happens there, stays there. We do not gossip about anything beyond the classroom.
   b. We do not denigrate any other perspective, even if it is remarkably different from ours. We listen, dialogue, sit with the differing idea, express discomfort, and engage in conversation with an open heart.
   c. We do not negate anyone else's experience to legitimize our own, especially if it is something about which we have been unaware.
   d. We bear witness and listen. Class participation should not always mean class domination. We offer our silence to make space for multiple voices in the learning environment and to become an active listener.
   e. We listen with an open heart and mind.

   f. We accept that there are multiple ways in which we make sense of the world and instead of opposing each other's ways, we focus on understanding and building bridges.

   g. We forgive each other if and when we mess up. We are trying. This is hard work. We are willing to fail and keep trying.

   h. We embrace vulnerability as a way to have honest conversation. We do not blame anyone individually.

   i. We do not expect any one person to speak for their entire race, gender, sexual orientation, ability, etc. We see each other as individuals with their own way of making sense in the world.

   j. We understand even with our differences we have a shared humanity that connects us all. Our struggles and our liberation are interconnected. One piece moved, affects all the other pieces.

2. Build capacity for resistance. Regardless of the ground rules setting the tone in the beginning, there are people who would resist discussing difficult topics. We accept that we cannot force people to shift their perspectives. We also accept and acknowledge that sometimes this work is hard to do as an educator. So it is important that we focus on self-care and build capacities for ourselves, so that when resistances arise, we would not be unsettled or unbalanced but could address conflict with equanimity.

3. Consider what might be your limit as an educator beyond which you cannot move to meet the student where the student is situated in his/her/hir thinking. In other words, do you have the capacity to meet a student, if the student states that Black folks deserve to be called the n-word? This is an extension of building capacity, but it is also an invitation for deep introspection. Do we have an obligation to meet the student wherever the student is situated if we find that position to be incredibly unacceptable to our values, beliefs, and ethics? There is no right or wrong answer to this, but discussions about race, class, power, and other social axes of differences require this kind of preparatory and ongoing reflection.

4. Create clear guidelines for assessment. This way you can communicate transparently with the students how the students' work will be assessed. This also is a self-check mechanism to ensure that you are evaluating every student across the same standard of expectation and no one is unusually favored or punished based on their dis/agreements with you.

5. Forgive yourself and the students because there would be moments when some of you will mess up. There will be nights where you would stay up and think of how you could have done something better. You can. Just not by reversing time, but by starting fresh the next time you have to teach.

6. Don't judge yourself or the students harshly if you do not see or realize what you think ought to happen by the end of the class. Perhaps they were not ready to accept your invitation to take on the journey ahead. Perhaps you planted a seed and they will sort things out, much later, after the class is over. Or perhaps the spaces that you opened up were not spaces that they felt they could enter. Critical reflection on one's teaching is important, but if we could judge ourselves less harshly when we did not reach all the students, and understand that maybe this bridge-building work is not something everyone buys into, then we could respect our students' agency to take on a path different than what we had hoped.

PEDAGOGICAL PRACTICES

We offer the following practices for consideration when teaching undergraduate and/or graduate level classes.

Privilege Relay

This exercise is appropriate for undergraduate and graduate students as the discussion after the activity could be used to connect to the class material.

- Divide students into two groups by asking them to count to 2, so that one group is group 1 and the other group 2.
- Members of group 1 stand on the side while you ask members of group 2 to help you set up the activity.
- Select one member from group 2 to help you with creating two parallel lines on the floor using a long string of rope. If people from Group 1 try to volunteer, treat them nicely, and tell them that they could relax, Group 2 is on the job. If members of Group 2 start being chatty, tell them that they need to be quiet to help you focus. If members of Group 1 are chatting, allow them to do so.
- Place two parallel lines of rope on the floor, except one line is 3/4 length of the other line.
- Now ask members of group 1 and 2 to line up for a relay at one of the rope. Make sure that group 1 gets the shorter rope and group 2 gets the longer rope.
- Take a tablespoon and pour a heap of peppercorn in it and hand it to the first member of group 2 who would lead the relay.
- Take a ladle and pour some peppercorn (less than what you had for group 2) and hand it to the first member of group 2 who would lead the relay.

- Then drop some chairs and tables on group 2's rope so that if a member from that group were to walk the full length of the rope, she would have to cross over chairs and tables to get to the other side.
- Now announce the rules of the game. This is a relay. Each member has to get to the other side of the rope, and then turn around and come back to the point from where they started and pass on their spoon or ladle to the next member without dropping any peppercorn on the ground. If they drop any peppercorn, they would have to start again. Group 1 is allowed to communicate and cheer each other on. Group 2 members are not allowed to talk, strategize, or communicate with each other. Members of group 2 will have to figure out how they will go over chairs and desk to get to the other end and come back. Members of group 1 will have no such issues, as their path is clear. When you say go, they should both start the relay.
- Say "Go." As the relay starts pay close attention to what group 2 members are doing. If they violate any rules of the game, tell them to start over again.
- It would become clear that by the time one member or two members of group 2 finish their turn, the entire team of group 1 would have finished their relay.
- Announce group 1 to be the winner. Ask everyone to clap and cheer for group 1.
- Announce that you will do a rematch. You want group 2 to improve themselves. So you take out a few chairs and tables and say that you are feeling generous so you made things a bit easier for group 2. Be okay with the looks that you will get from members of group 2. Try to keep a straight face. ☺
- Do the relay one more time. Group 1 will win this time too. Reproach members of group 2 for a poor-spirited showing if you want to amplify the intensity.
- End the activity and facilitate an open and organic discussion
- Discussion prompts
- What happened? How was the activity for you?
- Members of group 1 – what was it like to be on group 1? What was it like to see group 2 members having more obstacles?
- Members of group 1 – Should group 2 members feel that you were oppressing them?
- Members of group 2 – Why didn't you just take the chairs and tables off the path (if they indeed kept them there?)

- Usually, a deep, rich discussion emerges from the exchange. Students have a strong emotional charge. Group 2 members start talking about feeling dejected, and insulted even when you take off some chairs and desks, because it still does not make things equal. Sometimes Group 1 members choose to help out Group 2 members by going slow, by taking some of their chairs and desks and putting them on their path. One time, the group 2 members enacted civil disobedience and refused to participate in the activity. Each time this activity has been done, the students' perspectives and reactions drove the debriefing.
- If time permits, repeat the relay again with the same grouping. See how they behave. Debrief afterwards with similar questions.
- Perhaps end with a discussion or reflective writing about what might be one's responsibilities if they witness social inequities.

The Story of Self and Other

Based on and changed substantially from "The Case of Maria Elena." (Shanks, 1996).

This activity is one that requires printing what is written below as a handout and allowing students ample time for writing and reflecting. This is most appropriate for students who want to learn to write compelling stories, creative writing students, students who need to understand and empathize with perspectives that are different from their own, or graduate students pursuing qualitative research who might need to develop skills for narrative storytelling.

Activity. Let's suppose that you are a—*(you supply the gender and ethnicity)*—homeowner in South Texas, many times removed from your European ancestors who came to these shores generations ago to carve out a more prosperous life. You represent their ultimate dream. You are rich – so rich you can afford a housekeeper. And these days, that's saying something!

Your housekeeper's name is—*(you supply a name and ethnicity)*—and she has kept your house more than adequately. In fact, she is remarkably efficient. You pay her—*(you supply a realistic salary)*. You also find her likeable, considering her familiarity with the English language and idiom has improved over time, you have interesting conversations in which you learn of her experiences, both here and in her former country of residence. One day, she tells you how she came to be in Texas.

She immigrated to the United States from another country several years ago from—*(you name the country)*—with her child—*(you supply the name)*—

193

who is now 7. They entered the country on a visa, but it has long since expired. She now uses a Social Security number she purchased on the black market.

She has a husband. He had come to the United States first, entering the country illegally by—(*you supply the method*). When he saved enough money from day labor, he sent for the woman who is now your housekeeper. Her husband currently works washing dishes and cleaning tables for a restaurant whose owner—(*you supply the ethnicity and gender of this character*)—is so cheap he can barely afford to pay his staff a salary. In fact, he withholds half his wages in exchange for not blowing the whistle on him to the INS.

Writing prompt.   Now remain in the role of the story's "you". Think from her or his or her point of view. Thus far, here is what you, the rich homeowner, has learned about yourself:

I.   In relation to your housekeeper, you enjoy the *privileges* of … what? Make a list.
II. Then, write a story from scratch surrounding these events and using the first-person point-of-view. Create a series of scenes that center upon any situations or themes associated with race and culture you wish to explore. Use as many of the characters in the above situation as you like, and create more if it is necessary. Set scenes anywhere you wish. (No, it doesn't have to be in South Texas. If you are not from that area, you could set the story in your own place of origin or home area.)
III. Most important: Create a central conflict on which to base your story. You may state this to your readers at the outset, or you may wish to free-write scenes first in an effort to discover that conflict as you go along.
IV. As you expand the scenes into a coherent narrative, you may discover yourself concentrating on one or more of these thematic possibilities:
   a. Legal
   b. Ethical
   c. Moral
   d. Philosophical
V.   When you conclude your story, try for an open-ended summation that leaves in doubt any definite resolutions of either individual characters or situations.
VI. (Offer this instruction in a follow-up class meeting) Write the whole story (steps I–V) from the housekeeper's perspective.
VII. As a class then discuss the experience of perspective taking. What changed when the story was written from the perspective of the

housekeeper? What was present in the second story that was absent in the first? How do students understand personal plight and social system of oppression?

Reading Theatre

This activity could be conducted in undergraduate and graduate classes focusing on a variety of subject matters such as race, multicultural understanding, power, qualitative research, ethnodrama, arts-based research, etc. The discussion following the activity would be the space for connecting to the course and class' learning objectives.

- Get people to select a line or a phrase, or a few sentences from anywhere within the book, or from the day's assigned reading
- Tell them that you are expecting a popcorn-like read aloud method, meaning that people will read aloud the part that they highlighted when they feel inspired. Even if two people start together, tell them, that it would be okay. One would automatically make room for the other to read the chosen part and take the next turn.
- Once everyone completes the reading, initiate a debriefing discussion. What stood out for people and why? What were they surprised by? What resonated well? What is disturbing, unsettling, challenging? What has a strong emotional charge? What other readings from the class connect to this reading? Conclude the discussion with what might be one idea with which the students are walking away from the class? It does not have to be something they agree or like, it could be something that they need to think about more, or something they disagree, or something that might have challenged their perspectives, or anything else.

Perform It!

This activity is appropriate for undergraduate and graduate students. The conducting of the discussion after the activity will assist in connecting to the course material and learning objectives.

- Divide students into groups of 3–4 people.
- Ask them to choose a scene or narrative from the book, or that day's readings.
- Then ask them to perform the scene.

- The students can perform exactly as the scene is written, or they can add or subtract information from the scene to their liking. Perhaps they want to add another character. Perhaps they want to imagine an exchange that informed the scene. Allow students to experiment.
- Give them about 20 minutes to prepare for a 5-minute scene. Tell them to be mindful about how they place their body in space, how it feels to have certain words mouthed by them, feeling certain emotions in their bodies. Ask them to perform a scene that engages as many senses as possible.
- After each performance allow for debriefing and processing time. This is where the prompts for discussion could tie into the course objectives. Some suggested questions could include:
- What was it like to take on the character that you took on?
  o What was it like to perform the scene? To mouth the words? To put you body in relation to your team members' bodies?
  o What emotions did you feel?
  o How connected did you feel with the character you played?
  o How dis/connected did you feel with the other characters that your peers played?
  o What was your process of creating this scene? What decision-making paths did you take?
  o How do you understand the readings thus far in class as a result of this performance? Where are you making connections, if at all?
- Once all the groups have performed, conduct a big group discussion. To help students' buy in, consider focusing on the following topics in the big group discussion.
  o Relevance of enacting a play (multisensory, perspective taking, empathy building, embodied experience, learning by doing, by creating, creativity as inquiry, body as a site of stories, bodies in space)
  o Connection between the topics discussed after each performance to the assigned readings thus far in the class
  o Connection between the topics discussed beyond the scope of the class, as a contribution to the field, such as social justice agendas, policies, law, morality, ethics, etc.
  o Possibility of integrating some of the aspects of the plays and discussion in future class assignment.
- End the discussion by offering a closure. What would students like to offer as a final thought? What are they walking away with? What do they need to think about more? What are they struggling with? What resonated well

or reinforced something they knew? What brought on a more crystallized or clarified understanding?

Creating Found Poems

This activity is appropriate for undergraduate and graduate students. The discussion at the end could be used to connect with course and class learning objectives.

- Ask students to select lines from the book or from the days reading that are meaningful to them
- Then ask them to organize the lines in a way that could be considered a found poem
- Tell them that they do not need to rhyme
- Tell them that they can have some aesthetic license to alter some words here and there for poetic flow
- Ask for volunteers who might be interested in reading out their poems
- As each student reads out their poem, discuss with them their process of creation, use of discernment, and how they related to the poem. Then ask the class to react and relate to the poem.
- After everyone has read the poems, close the circle by conducting a big group discussion about the relevance of this activity.
  - What were the discoveries in writing the poem? In listening to other people's poems?
  - What were the surprises in writing and performing the poem? In listening to other people's poems?
  - What sits well?
  - What does not sit well?
  - How does this reading/activity connect to other class readings, class objectives, course objectives, field's objectives?
  - What is the final take-away thought from this activity?

Tracing Roots

This activity can be conducted with both undergraduate and graduate students. The end-of-the-activity discussion could be used to connect the reflections from the activity to class and course's learning objectives.

- Ask students to do a 5-minute presentation about their ancestral roots where they focus on how their ancestral roots shape how they move about

197

in their world (as in fading into whiteness, becoming aware of otherness, or something else)
• Conduct a discussion after each presentation to explore the points made in the presentation and connect them to the class and course's learning objectives.

Parallel Narratives

This activity could be conducted with undergraduate and graduate students. This activity could only be done after the students have read chapter 5. The discussion at the end of the activity could be used to connect with class and course objectives.

Instruction for students.

• Think of a friend/colleague who is minoritized in some way.
• Just as Kent did when comparing his experiences with Angie in chapter 5, what would you imagine your friend/colleague's experience is like everyday compared to yours?
• You can also use the Peggy McIntosh article Unpacking Invisible Knapsack to help you think through the activity.

Discussion suggestions for instructors.

• This activity could be done in class, or could be a take-home assignment.
• Once the activity is completed, several pedagogical strategies could be used to elicit discussion.
• Students could read out a statement or two of their parallel narratives followed by a discussion.
• The class can do a reading theater activity, followed by a discussion
• Discussions focusing on the following questions could also be posed to the students:
   o How do you understand privileges now as a result of doing this activity?
   o What is your understanding of personal plight versus systemic inequity?
   o Does discussing and identifying privileges mean that you are the bad guy and to be blamed if you occupy a dominant group? Why or why not?
   o How would you engage in discussion with others who occupy the same dominant group as you do, who might not understand privileges the way you do?

o What do you consider to be your social/ethical responsibility as a person who enjoys certain privileges that your friend/colleague does not?
o Are there other issues that came up when conducting this activity that need to be discussed?

Thank you for journeying with us thus far to the end of the book. We hope what we have offered both within the first five chapters and in this pedagogical practices chapter have opened up possibilities for you. This has been a passion project for both of us and we are honored to have been able to share our journey with you.

REFERENCES

Alcoff, L. M. (1991/2009). The problem of speaking for others. In A. Y. Jackson & L. A. Mazzei (Eds.), *Voice in qualitative inquiry: Challenging conventional, interpretive, and critical conceptions in qualitative research* (pp. 117–135). Abingdon, UK: Routledge.

Anaya, R. (1972). *Bless me, Ultima*. Redwood City, CA: Quinto Sol.

Anzaldúa, G. (1987). *Borderlands: La frontera – the new Mestiza*. San Francisco, CA: Aunt Lute Books.

Anzaldúa, G. (1990). *Making face, making soul/Haciendo caras: Creative and critical perspectives by feminists of color*. San Francisco, CA: Aunt Lute Books.

Anzaldúa, G. (2009). Creativity and switching modes of consciousness. In A. Keating (Ed.), *The Gloria Anzaldúa reader* (pp. 103–110). Durham, NC: Duke University Press.

Anzaldúa, G. E. (2009). Speaking across the divide. In A. Keating (Ed.), *The Gloria Anzaldúa reader* (pp. 282–294). Durham, NC: Duke University.

Anzaldúa, G. E. (2015). Flights of the imagination: Rereading/rewriitng realities. In A. Keating (Ed.), *Light in the dark Luz en lo oscuro: Rewriting identity, spirituality, reality* (pp. 23–46). Durham, NC: Duke University Press.

Benavidez, M. (1997). Subterranean homesick blues. In C. A. Noriega & W. Belcher (Eds.), *I am Aztlan: The personal essay in Chicano studies* (pp. 1–10). Los Angeles, CA: UCLA Chicano Research Studies Center Press.

Berg, C. R. (1992). *Cinema of solitude: A critical study of Mexican film, 1967–1983* (pp. 56–71). Austin, TX: University of Texas Press.

Bhattacharya, K. (2009). Negotiating shuttling between transnational experiences: A de/colonizing performance ethnography. *Qualitative Inquiry, 15*(6), 1061–1083.

Bhattacharya, K. (2013). Border crossing: Bridging empirical practices with de/colonizing epistemologies. In N. K. Denzin & M. Giardina (Eds.), *Global dimensions of qualitative inquiry* (pp. 115–134). Walnut Creek, CA: Left Coast Press, Inc.

Bhattacharya, K., & Varbelow, S. (2014). Cultural brokers and aliens: Marking and blurring interlocking spaces of difference. *Qualitative Inquiry, 20*(10), 1157–1168.

Blea, I. I. (1997). *U. S. Chicanas and Latinas within a global context: Women of color at the Fourth World Women's Conference*, Praeger, Westport, CT.

Buzbee, B. B. (1942, January 11). 50,000 pupils scattered in 114 public school districts start study of Spanish February 1. *Corpus Christi Caller*, p. 4.

Charmaz, K. (2006). *Constructing grounded theory: A practical guide through qualitative analysis*. London, UK: Sage.

Conquergood, D. (1985). Performing as a moral act: Ethical dimensions of the ethnography of performance. In Y. S. Lincoln & N. K. Denzin (Eds.), *Turning points in qualitative research: Tying knots in a handkerchief* (pp. 397–414). Walnut Creek, CA: AltaMira.

Denzin, N. K. (2003). *Performance ethnography: Critical pedagogy and the politics of culture*. Thousand Oaks, CA: Sage.

Denzin, N. K., & Lincoln, Y. S. (2008). *Collecting and interpreting qualitative materials* (Vol. 3). Thousand Oaks, CA: Sage Publications.

DuBois, W. E. B. (1903/1953). *The souls of Black folk*. New York, NY: Blue Heron Press.

Elam, H. J. (1997). *The social protest theater of Luis Valdez & Amiri Baraka*. Ann Arbor, MI: The University of Michigan Press.

REFERENCES

Facio, E. (1996). *Understanding older Chicanas*. Thousand Oaks, CA: Sage Publications.

Fish, S. (1993). Reverse racism or how the pot got to call the kettle Black. *Atlantic Monthly, 272*(5), 14–21.

Franco, E. (1983). La jaula de oro. [Los Tigres del Norte.] On *Jaula de oro* [Audio CD]. Woodland Hills, CA: Fonavisa.

Franco, J. (1988). Beyond ethnocentrism: Gender, power, and the third-world intelligentsia. In C. Nelson & L. Grossberg (Eds.), *Marxism and the interpretation of culture* (pp. 503–515). Champaign, IL: University of Illinois Press.

Gillen, N. K., & Bhattacharya, K. (2013). Never a yellow bird, always a blue bird: Ethnodrama of a Latina learner's educational experiences in 1950–60s South Texas. *The Qualitative Report, 18* (Art. 28), 1–18.

Goffman, E. (1959). *The presentation of self in everyday life*. New York, NY: Anchor Books.

Goodwin, B. (1968, February 2). Only one in the nation: Schools here to try bilingual experiment. *Corpus Christi Caller*, p. 1A, p. 16A.

Haining, P. (Ed.). (1994). *The television crimebusters omnibus* (p. 94). London: Orion.

Hannerz, U. (1990). Cosmopolitans and locals in world culture. *Theory, Culture, & Society, 7*, 237–251.

Harrison, F. V. (1997). Anthropology as an agent of transformation: Introductory comments and queries. In F. V. Harrison (Ed.), *Decolonizing anthropology: Moving further toward an anthropology for liberation* (pp. 1–16). Arlington, VA: American Anthropoligical Association.

Hart, M. (1959). *Act one: An autobiography*. New York, NY: Signet/Random House.

Johnson, N. (Producer), & Hathaway, H. (Director). (1951). *The desert fox* [Motion picture]. USA: 20th Century Fox. (DVD, 2003)

Kael, P. (1980). *When the lights go down* (p. 509). New York, NY: Holt, Rinehart and Winston.

Kochman, T. (2011). Meltdown: White men in the melting pot discussion. *Diversity Factor, 19*(2), 1–7.

Leavy, P. (2009). *Method meets art: Arts-based research practice*. New York, NY: Guilford Press.

Lorde, A. (1984). The master's tools will never dismantle the master's house. In *Sister outsider: Essays and speeches by Audrey Lorde* (pp. 110–113). Freedom, CA: The Crossing Press Feminist Series.

Lyons, R. E. (Producer), & Peckinpah, S. (Director). (1962). *Ride the high country* [Motion picture]. USA: Metro-Goldwyn-Mayer.

Macdonald, D. (1969). *Dwight Macdonald on movies*. Englewood Cliffs, NJ: Prentice Hall.

Maso, I. (2003). Necessary subjectivity: Exploiting researchers' motives, passions, and prejudices in pursuit of answering 'true' questions. In L. Finlay & B. Gough (Eds.), *Reflexivity: A practical guide for researchers in health and social sciences* (pp. 39–51). Oxford, UK: Blackwell.

McIntosh, P. (1990). White privilege: Unpacking the invisible knapsack. *Independent School, 49*(2), 31–36.

Minh-ha, T. T. (1989). *Woman, native, other: Writing postcoloniality and feminism*. Bloomington, IN: Indiana University Press.

Mirande, A., & Enriquez, E. (1979). *La Chicana: The Mexican American woman*. Chicago, IL: University of Chicago Press.

Mitchell, M. (1936/1972). *Gone with the wind*. New York, NY: Scribner.

Nieto-Gomez, A. (1973). The Chicana: Perspectives for education. *Encuentro Feminil, 1,* 34–61.

Osborne, J. (2000, August 31). Nueces Hispanic population is 59%: Census report also indicates more Asians, Blacks. *Corpus Christi Caller-Times,* p. 1A.

Peterson, D., & Hamrick, F. A. (2009). White, male, and "minority": Racial consciousness among White male graduates attending a historically Black university. *Journal of Higher Education, 80*(1), 34–58.

Phillips, A. (1995). *The politics of presence.* Oxford, UK: Oxford University Press.

Phillips, D. C. (1994). Telling it straight: Issues in assessing narrative research. *Educational Psychologist, 29*(1), 13–21.

Roy, A. (2003). *War talk.* Cambridge, MA: South End Press.

Saldaña, J. (2003). Dramatizing data: A primer. *Qualitative Inquiry, 9*(2), 218–236.

Saldivar, R. (1994). Transnational migrations and border identities: Immigration and postmodern culture. *South Atlantic Quarterly, 98*(1/2), 217–230.

Saucedo, D. (1996). Chicanismo, DuBois, and double consciousness. *Latin Studies Journal, 7*(3), 90–101.

Shanks, T. (1996, Feb. 1). The case of Maria Elena. *Markkula Center for Applied Ethics, Santa Clara University.* Retrieved from: https://www.scu.edu/ethics/focus-areas/more/resources/the-case-of-maria-elena/

Shaw, G. B. (1912/1930). *Androcles and the lion, Overruled, Pygmalion.* New York, NY: Dodd, Mead, and Company.

Shockley, J. S. (1974). *Chicano revolt in a Texas town.* Notre Dame, IN: University of Notre Dame Press.

Smith, L. (1999). *Decolonizing methodology: Research and indigenous people.* London, UK: Zed Books.

Spivak, G. (1990). Questions of multiculturalism. In S. Harasayam (Ed.), *The post-colonial critic: Interviews, strategies, dialogues.* New York, NY: Routledge.

Turner, V. (1982). *From ritual to theatre: The human seriousness of play.* New York, NY: PAJ Publications.

Wildman, S., & David, A. D. (1995). Language and silence: Making systems of privilege visible. *Santa Clara Law Review, 35,* 881–906.

Yamada, M. (2002). Invisibility is an unnatural disaster: Reflections of an Asian American woman. In *This bridge called my back: Writings by radical woman of color* (pp. 35–40). Berkeley, CA: Third Woman Press.

Yamato, G. (1990). Something about the subject makes it hard to name. In G. Anzaldúa (Ed.), *Making face, making soul (haciendo caras): Creative and critical perspectives by feminists of color* (pp. 20–24). San Francisco, CA: Aunt Lute Books.

Young, D. (1950). *Rommel, the desert fox.* New York, NY: Harper & Brothers.

ABOUT THE AUTHORS

Kakali Bhattacharya is a qualitative methodologist and an associate professor at the Kansas State University in Manhattan, Kansas. Manhattan, Kansas has unfolded as one of the most scenic places she has ever lived with rolling hills, hiking trails, and lush greenery. Born in India, Kakali migrated to Canada when she was about 14 years old. She moved to the U.S. in the late 1990s to pursue her graduate degrees and obtained a doctoral degree from the University of Georgia in Athens, Georgia.

Kakali's research interests include exploring de/colonizing epistemologies and methodologies, transnational issues of race, class, and gender in higher education, and technology-integrated social and educational learning environments. She has become aware of how deeply important contemplative approaches have become in her personal and professional lives. Thus, Kakali integrates contemplative practices in her teaching, scholarship, and in everything else she does.

Within qualitative research, Kakali has been employing various interpretive, critical, and deconstructive methodological approaches her work, but her true love is in arts-based approaches to research as she values creativity as inquiry. Drawn to various genres of creativity, Kakali's work has been published widely in journals like Qualitative Inquiry, International Journal of Qualitative Studies in Education, Cultural Studies ←→ Critical Methodologies, and International Review of Qualitative Research. At the thrust of Kakali's work is a desire to meet her shadow and dialogue with her shadowy fragmented parts. This produces healing, which then transforms how she teaches, writes, and works with her students, and those who engage in oppositional discourses.

Norman K. Gillen was born in Corpus Christi, Texas, but spent most of his early school years in small towns located in the northern part of the state. Returning to his city of birth, he graduated from W. B. Ray High School and then embarked upon an on-again, off-again collegiate career as a sort of journeyman-student on various campuses, working at several clerical jobs in between. Eventually he received a Bachelor's Degree in Communications at a two-year, senior-level college, and then obtained employment managing his family's real-estate holdings, with an additional job in audio/video retail sales and service. After his mother's death, he sold his share of the family's business and returned to school, receiving a Master's Degree in English and ultimately a Doctor of Education in 2010. As an adjunct instructor, he has taught classes in English and Industrial Communications at Del Mar College since 1999.